"Both Mann and Kretchmar-Hendricks have opened a rare window into the complex challenges of foster care. This fine book helps the reader recognize the cost we pay in separating children from their primary caregivers and how this can become an eventual obstacle to reunification. With a high degree of reverence for this complexity, it challenges society: if we want to help the child, we must help the family."

—*Father Gregory J. Boyle, Founder of Homeboy Industries and Author of*
Tattoos on the Heart: The Power of Boundless Compassion

"This book is a gem! Using the highly evocative stories of parents and their children who have experienced maltreatment, the authors present a relationship-based system of foster care grounded in attachment research. This book is essential for professionals working in the child welfare system, juvenile and family courts, social work, psychology, psychiatry, and pediatrics."

—*Julie A. Larrieu, Ph.D., Professor of Psychiatry and Behavioral
Sciences, Tulane University School of Medicine*

"*Creating Compassionate Foster Care* is an important book and a great read. I recommend it for those who are passionate about improving the way we work with children in care and want to assist their parents and families. It achieves a thoughtful balance between the power of the narrative about the plight that many people captured within child protection systems experience, and the knowledge derived from research and theory of the efficacy of our collective attempts to prevent child maltreatment and address its impacts. Its relational practice orientation provides a welcome, compassionate and practical guide for those who work in this area or just wish to better understand how we can change things for the better. Authors Mann and Kretchmar-Hendricks have excelled with a timely and valuable book that offers insight, judicious examination, compassion, hope and authentic guidance in what is an emotionally charged and challenging area—well done!"

—*Bob Lonne, B.Soc Wk, Ph.D., Professor of Social Work &
Discipline Leader, University of New England, Past President
of Australian Association of Social Workers*

"*Creating Compassionate Foster Care* offers the reader a profound window into the minds of children placed in foster care. If everyone in the foster care system, from policy makers to parents, embraced the relational knowledge in this book, I believe it would revolutionize the entire approach to helping some of our most vulnerable children and families. This book inspires hope and offers a clear path for the healing that is so urgently needed."

—*Bert Powell, co-creator of* The Circle of Security

"Janet Mann's and Molly Kretchmar-Hendricks' *Creating Compassionate Foster Care: Lessons in Hope from Children and Families in Crisis*, contains powerful stories of troubled parents' struggles to become nurturing for their infants and toddlers. It is rare for a book about abused and neglected children and their parents written from an explicitly theoretical perspective to convey the destructive power of dysfunctional beliefs and attitudes resulting from early experiences to undermine the capacity for the care of children, and even rarer for an account of healing processes that describes maltreating parents with compassion but without excusing or minimizing their parenting deficiencies.

Creating Compassionate Foster Care makes the therapeutic challenges of helping abusive and neglectful parents real and compelling. It is also an unusual example of a well thought-out day treatment model based on attachment theory combined with a hard won compassion. Janet Mann and Molly Kretchmar- Hendricks have also explained how foster care systems oriented around the needs of infants for safety and responsive caregiving would be different from current practices. Their book is both a meditation on changing 'internal working models' that lead to child abuse and neglect and the outline of an agenda for reinventing foster care for infants and toddlers."

—Dee Wilson, *former child welfare administrator and author of* The Sounding Board, Child Welfare Commentaries.

"Vulnerability, by its nature, implies that one's heart will be broken. But not only that. Vulnerability also opens new possibilities that simply could never have happened without its risk. The stories within these pages offer every reader hope and something of a roadmap as to how vulnerability, mixed with commitment and solid science, can create opportunities for children and families that are often considered beyond hope. How wonderful that these authors have found a way to offer the steps (clarity, compassion, and commitment) necessary for future generations to build upon what began at the Children's Ark. For any parent or professional working with children-at-risk, this book is essential reading."

—Kent Hoffman, *Circle of Security International*

"This gem of a volume is wise, sensitive, honest and informative. For those who work with children and families who are struggling, it is a refreshing reminder of the value of embracing all involved. Read this book!"

—Charles H. Zeanah, Jr., M.D., *Vice Chair, Child and Adolescent Psychiatry, Professor of Psychiatry and Pediatrics, Tulane University, USA*

CREATING COMPASSIONATE FOSTER CARE

of related interest

Adopting
Real Life Stories
Ann Morris
Foreword by Hugh Thornbery CBE
ISBN 978 1 84905 660 1
eISBN 978 1 78450 1556

Creating Stable Foster Placements
Learning from Foster Children and the Families Who Care For Them
Andy Pithouse and Alyson Rees
ISBN 978 1 84905 481 2
eISBN 978 0 85700 856 7

Assessing Adoptive Parents, Foster Carers
and Kinship Carers, Second Edition
Improving Analysis and Understanding of Parenting Capacity
Edited by Joanne Alper and David Howe
ISBN 978 1 78592 177 3
eISBN 978 1 78450 456 4

Attachment, Trauma, and Healing
Understanding and Treating Attachment Disorder
in Children, Families and Adults
Terry M. Levy and Michael Orlans
ISBN 978 1 84905 888 9
eISBN 978 0 85700 597 7

Child-Centred Foster Care
A Rights-Based Model for Practice
Annabel Goodyer
ISBN 978 1 84905 174 3
eISBN 978 0 85700 402 4

Understanding and Working with Parents of
Children in Long-Term Foster Care
Gillian Schofield and Emma Ward
ISBN 978 1 84905 026 5
eISBN 978 0 85700 489 5

CREATING
COMPASSIONATE
FOSTER
CARE

Lessons of
Hope from
Children and
Families in Crisis

Janet C. Mann and Dr. Molly D. Kretchmar-Hendricks

Foreword by Glen Cooper, M.A.

Jessica Kingsley *Publishers*
London and Philadelphia

The photographs on pages 28–29 are credit of Brett Hendricks.

Please see page 8 for details of permissions granted.

First published in 2017
by Jessica Kingsley Publishers
73 Collier Street
London N1 9BE, UK
and
400 Market Street, Suite 400
Philadelphia, PA 19106, USA

www.jkp.com

Library of Congress Cataloging in Publication Data
A CIP catalog record for this book is available from the Library of Congress

British Library Cataloguing in Publication Data
A CIP catalogue record for this book is available from the British Library

ISBN 978 1 78592 727 0
eISBN 978 1 78450 381 9

Printed and bound in Great Britain

MIX
Paper from
responsible sources
FSC® C013056

*This book is dedicated to the children and families of
The Children's Ark whose courage, strength,
and wisdom forever changed our lives.*

COPYRIGHT ACKNOWLEDGMENTS

CONTENTS

Foreword by Glen Cooper, M.A.   13

Acknowledgments   17

Preface   21

Part 1   **Lessons Learned from Children and Families**

Chapter 1   **Rickie**   **33**
The inspiration of Rickie and his family   33
Research and theory: An overview of attachment theory   40

Chapter 2   **Rachel**   **46**
A disorganized toddler   46
     Principle 1: "I am here. You are worth it"   48
     Principle 2: Behavior as need   50
     Principle 3: Cues and miscues   51
     Principle 4: "Being with"   53
     Principle 5: Repair   55
     Principle 6: State of mind[9]   57
Research and theory: Disorganized attachment and foster care   59

Chapter 3   **Barbara and Nathan**   **63**
Repeating the pain of the past   63
Research and theory: The Circle of Security intervention   66
Nathan's transition   69
Research and theory: Transitions that support children   72
Nathan: Follow-up   73

Chapter 4	**Hannah and Ashley**	**74**
	A story of two girls: Part 1	74
	Research and theory: Trauma, attachment, and the developing brain	78
	A story of two girls: Part 2	82
	Research and theory: From foster care to adoption	86
	A story of two girls: Part 3	88
Chapter 5	**Lucy**	**90**
	Lucy's history	90
	Our ongoing relationship	97
	Lucy's future	99
	Research and theory: Children with special needs in foster care	102
Chapter 6	**Desirae and Her Children**	**106**
	Discouraging reunification	106
	The lessons	110
	Lesson 1: Safe parenting is not an information issue, but rather an emotional integration issue	110
	Lesson 2: Being engaged in a caring, long-term relationship within the safety of a holding environment optimizes growth and change	111
	Lesson 3: Meeting the needs of children and families at risk requires an ability to hold with compassion the ambiguity of good people doing bad things	112
	Lesson 4: Real change takes time	114
	The implications	114
	Research and theory: The intergenerational transmission of caregiving	116
Part 2	**Ideas for More Compassionate (and More Effective) Foster Care**	
	Introduction to Part 2	122

Chapter 7	Through the Eyes of the Child	127
	Considering the child's experience	127
	Validating the child's experience	129
	Creating child-centered environments and interventions	130
	When to stop intervening	134
	Knowing when not to start	137
	When children lose their parents	139
	Research and theory: Reimagining foster care for infants and young children	*142*
Chapter 8	Insights into Intervention	146
	Keeping the child's experience at the center	147
	Recognizing that parents were once children too	148
	Continuity and reliability of relationship	152
	Being who we are	152
	The process takes time	154
	Telling the truth	156
	Underlying theoretical foundation	158
	Focus on reflective functioning	165
	Research and theory: Attachment-based intervention with at-risk families	*173*
Chapter 9	The Meaning and Measure of Change	178
	Prerequisites to change: Resilience	178
	Tenacity	180
	Capacity for relationship, reflective functioning, and empathy	181
	Hope	181
	Prerequisite to change: Surrender	185
	"The Shift"	185
	Understanding change	189
	Success	193
	Success: The children	194
	Success: The parents	195
	Research and theory: The seeds of change	*197*

Chapter 10   Final Reflections   **202**

              Putting children first   202

              Parents' need for ongoing support   204

              Support for foster families   205

              Systemic change   206

              Research and theory: from science to practice and policy   *210*

                    Recognizing the costs of separation   *211*

                    Creating secure and stable placements   *214*

                    Building community   *216*

                    A wider view of reform   *218*

                    Being in relationship   *219*

Notes   **223**

References   **234**

Further Reading   **245**

Subject Index   **247**

Author Index   **252**

FOREWORD

Janet and Paul Mann examined the mixed results of their efforts in traditional foster care and asked the question, "What if?" What if we made biological parents part of the solution rather than treating them as the problem? What if we offered parents the same level of care that we give to their children? What if we created a community of professionals to provide a wide range of services for families? What if we opened our homes and hearts to both children and their parents so that they can heal together? By doing just that, they began an odyssey that sets a new standard for best practices in foster care.

This book tells the truth about the demands, anguishes, and successes of caring for deeply troubled families. With engaging stories to illustrate the underlying theory, it will touch your heart and expand your thinking as you explore the complexity and humanity of the lives of foster children, their parents, and those who serve them.

The authors bring decades of theory and practice to life. Janet Mann reflects on what she has learned from her extensive involvement with foster children and their families, while Molly Kretchmar-Hendricks, an academician and gifted teacher, outlines the clear research-based, theoretical framework that underlies the practice. Both the theory and the lived experience are compelling in their own right but the combination provides a much needed primer for creating a more effective and compassionate foster care system. In addition, it provides theory and clinical insights, which reach far beyond the realm of foster care to illuminate the fundamentals of responding to the needs of vulnerable families and children.

My involvement in this story began by reading an article in our local paper featuring an innovative foster care program, The Children's Ark. As a family therapist with years of experience as a foster parent, working with foster families, and consulting with a variety of foster care programs, I tend to be a bit skeptical of new and improved approaches. The Children's Ark was different. Acting on the wisdom that we need to treat families rather than individual children, they were proposing the radical idea that it is imperative that we take parents into care along with their children.

I was impressed that, based on the article, Janet and Paul Mann seemed to have their rescue fantasies in check, and they did not have a psychological, religious, political, or social agenda that they wanted to foist on foster children and their families. In addition, they spoke with knowledge and maturity about providing a comprehensive approach, which convinced me that they could turn words into action.

After reading the article, my thought was that I would love to take part in this exciting and worthwhile project. Then, out of the blue, I received a message from Janet Mann saying that she had heard about my interest in the clinical application of attachment theory for the foster care system and wanted to talk to me about The Children's Ark. I was delighted with the opportunity to spend the next 15 years engaged in such rewarding work. What I have learned since is that Janet's determination is an unstoppable force and even if I had wanted to decline, she would not have taken no for an answer.

The timing was perfect. My colleagues, Kent Hoffman and Bert Powell, and I were looking for more opportunities to pilot the attachment-based early intervention program, Circle of Security (COS), which we were developing. Janet and Paul were eager to incorporate this approach. The Children's Ark became one of the crucibles for the unfolding intervention and, in turn, COS became the organizing principle for The Children's Ark. This symbiotic relationship proved central to the development of both programs. To add to our good fortune, we met Molly Kretchmar-Hendricks, who has expertise in attachment theory and research. It was an unexpected gift to find someone with her extensive background and depth of knowledge residing in Spokane, and she became a tremendous asset both personally and professionally.

I was a consultant at and advocate for The Children's Ark, but my central and most rewarding role was leading weekly COS parent groups. The opportunity to use ongoing videotape reviews with families was as much a gift to me, both personally and professionally, as it was for the parents. As always, when working with families who are struggling, I felt a tremendous sense of gratitude and humility in witnessing parents overcome profound obstacles which, if I were in their shoes, would have overwhelmed and stymied me.

The Children's Ark's level of involvement with families was new to me. The intimacy of long-term, day-to-day, 24-hour collaboration between staff and parents for the benefit of the children brought a richness that deepened everyone's experience. To be clear, boundaries and roles were rigorously maintained, but the staff's willingness to pour their hearts into these families was not lost on the parents, and in return the parents' willingness to invite us into the pain and joys of their lives was an opportunity we fully embraced.

Bert, Kent, and I made good use of our learning at The Children's Ark to augment the broader applications of COS, which has flourished and grown over the years. We carry lessons from our time at The Children's Ark with us as we travel throughout the United States and around the world to train professionals in the use of COS early intervention for families with young children. In my 40 years of clinical work with families and my travels in the US, Europe, Asia, Africa, and Australia, I have been introduced to many foster care programs. The Children's Ark continues to be the best example of an intensive foster care approach that I have ever encountered.

There is no easy recipe for fixing the multitude of problems in our child welfare system. However, The Children's Ark is a compelling, multifaceted, example of how lasting change can be achieved through clinical sophistication, a working understanding of relationship needs, and a profound and enduring commitment to each family. It clarifies that, even if we develop the political and economic motivation to adequately fund child welfare programs, working with profoundly traumatized families will always depend on courageous individuals willing to bear the many heartbreaks of this demanding work.

Glen Cooper, M.A.
Circle of Security International
Spokane, WA

ACKNOWLEDGMENTS

Together, we thank our readers: Stanley Rutherford, Paul Mann, Sandra Powell, Glen Cooper, Ric Clarke, Courtney Moore, Brett Hendricks, Laurie Rydell, and Vicki Willis, whose comments and ideas made this book better. We are also grateful for the research and technical support provided by Derek Caperton, Brett Hendricks, and Emma Hendricks.

We want to acknowledge Zero to Three for supporting earlier publications of some of the case material contained in this book. It was their late editor, Emily Fenichel, who initially planted the seed for a book, and we are grateful for her inspiration. We also appreciate their generous commitment to this project by allowing us to republish material that originally appeared in the *Zero to Three* journal (Mann and Kretchmar 2006; Mann, Kretchmar, and Worsham 2008, 2011).

Finally, our thanks to Stephen Jones and Jessica Kingsley Publishers for believing in this project and for helping us to move it from conception to realization.

Janet's acknowledgments

I first want to acknowledge and thank Molly Kretchmar-Hendricks, without whom this book would not have been possible. Molly's wisdom, competence, confidence, and calming influence have seen me through this process. It was Molly who first envisioned the idea of getting The Children's Ark experience down on paper, and it was Molly who guided us through to the finished product.

I next want to acknowledge Sandra Powell, who lives in every page of this book as much as do I. Sandra was on board with The Children's Ark from the very beginning, from advisory member to therapist to clinical director. She shaped and directed every aspect of the program and taught and encouraged me every step of the way. She was and remains my secure base.

I will forever be grateful to every child and family who came through the doors of The Children's Ark. They were, each and every one, a gift to me. They taught me much, and my life was forever changed and enriched by their presence in it. I am grateful also for the Ark staff, who not only embraced and nurtured our families but also were willing to do their own work and to walk into their own pain in order to better and more genuinely serve those at risk. I especially want to acknowledge Emma Sumler, our "baby whisperer," who has been a wise and loyal friend for decades.

Time spent in relationship with Ezra Bayda and Robert Baxley over the years changed the way I experience and am in the world. Their influence is therefore profoundly embedded in this book.

I want to extend a special acknowledgment to my colleagues, Glen Cooper, Kent Hoffman, and Bert Powell, who joined Sandra in patiently and tirelessly teaching, supervising, encouraging, coaxing, and supporting me through every day of life at The Children's Ark. Thanks to their time, wisdom, commitment, and generosity, the philosophy and language of their intervention protocol, The Circle of Security (COS), laid the foundation for The Children's Ark program and is woven into the very fabric of this book. Although we cite the COS ideas and terminology throughout, individual references cannot possibly capture the impact that my training and experiences with these four individuals and the COS intervention had on both my life and this book. I will forever hold them with gratitude and in high esteem. They are my heroes.

Finally, I want to acknowledge my children John, Genevieve, and Elizabeth, who are my inspiration. Unfortunately, they did not grow up enjoying the benefits of what I now know but are, nonetheless, simply amazing human beings. And to my husband,

Paul, thank you for always loving and supporting me, not only through every day at The Children's Ark and the completion of this book but also through almost 50 years of marriage.

Molly's acknowledgments

I would like to acknowledge Deborah Jacobvitz, my dissertation advisor, who inspired my initial study of attachment theory; Alan Sroufe, one of my intellectual heroes; and Glen Cooper, Kent Hoffman, Bert Powell, and Bob Marvin, my Circle of Security colleagues, whose application of attachment theory has deeply impacted my thinking.

Thank you to my colleague, Nancy Worsham, who invited me to participate with her on an evaluation project of an innovative approach to foster care—what would turn out to be The Children's Ark. As the principal investigator, Nancy led our work over a multi-year period and committed hundreds of hours to our research, some of which is reflected in this book.

Without Nancy's initial invitation, my research would not have moved in the direction of foster care, and I would have missed the opportunity to work with Janet Mann, whose wisdom, insight, and example have made me a better person and parent.

Finally, I am so blessed by my children Emma and Ian, and by the patient understanding and support of my husband, Brett. I could not have done this without you, and I love you very much.

PREFACE

Too often children pay the price for the adversarial processes created when legal systems, child protection services, and parental rights collide. Children in foster care are at the mercy of judicial systems that are not always well informed; caseworkers who are overwhelmed and under-supported; and parents (both birth and foster) who often cannot see beyond their own needs, fear, and pain to recognize what is in their children's best interests.

In response to these challenges, Janet and Paul Mann, of Spokane, Washington, dedicated more than 20 years of their lives to foster care, keeping the well-being of the children entrusted to them at the center of their work. Recognizing that separation from parents often became the biggest obstacle to reunification, the Manns founded The Children's Ark, a program that offered parents the opportunity to reside, under supervision, with their children. This innovative approach to foster care focused on the children's best interests but also addressed, with compassion, the needs of their parents while working to educate the professionals who were responsible for custodial decisions. Informed by attachment theory and the Circle of Security intervention,[1] and with its guiding principle "being in relationship," The Children's Ark left an indelible imprint on our child welfare community.

This book is about the insights gained from the children and families with whom the Manns worked over their many years of service, including the 15 years during which The Children's Ark was in operation. Some families regained custody after engaging in difficult and often painful work; some chose voluntarily to relinquish their parental rights, coming to understand and honor what was in their children's best interests; and some—though fewer than in traditional foster care—continued to fight the system. All of the children and families served offered lessons about how we might envision a better way forward; about how we might reimagine foster care in ways that are both more compassionate and more effective.

The book is structured in two parts. Part 1 focuses on the case accounts of some of the children and families served by the Manns—stories of hope, courage, and wisdom—in the context of current research and theory. Part 2 offers reflection: what Janet and the Ark staff learned about what children and families in crisis really need; how they came to identify positive change; and ideas about how we can redesign our approaches to foster care, not only to respond with more compassion but also to lead to better outcomes. Woven throughout the book are the accounts and experiences of Janet Mann, who—in addition to being co-founder of The Children's Ark—was its director. As such, Janet is the primary voice in this book, and most of the accounts and examples are written by her and told from her perspective. Molly Kretchmar-Hendricks, a professor of developmental psychology with expertise in attachment theory, supports and extends Janet's insights in the "Research and theory" sections included in each chapter (for greater readability, in-text citations are kept to a minimum. Instead, we direct readers to our references and, in some cases, to additional research and theory by including notes for each chapter).

Our primary hope is that the ideas shared in this book will fundamentally alter how we approach our complex work with families and young children in crisis. Although some of the changes we envision will take a fair amount of collective effort, we also believe that there are changes each of us can make in our daily work with vulnerable families to enhance what we are already doing.

Janet's preface

After having invested six years of our lives in traditional foster care and having cared for and transitioned to permanent homes over 40 abused and neglected infants and toddlers, it became clear to my husband, Paul, and me that to make a transformational difference in the lives of at-risk children and their families and to increase the probability of their successful reunification, interventions needed to include the infants' significant caregivers.

Experience convinced us of two critical truths about the needs of families whose children had been placed into foster care. The first truth was the realization that, although we never disputed the need to remove the children placed in our care from their homes for their own protection, the separation from primary caregivers often became the greatest obstacle to eventual reunification.

During those early years, I heard a young mother who had lost all three of her children to foster care speak at a conference. "Rosie" talked about how her life spiraled out of control when she was left by her children's father, and she plummeted into poverty and substance abuse. Her two older children were placed with their grandmother, Rosie's mother, while the baby was placed with a nearby foster family. Over time Rosie sought treatment for her chemical dependency, completed her education, secured a job, and got her own apartment. Throughout this process, she had easy access to her older children, was very much a part of their lives, and for some of the time was actually living in the same household with them. Although the foster family caring for Rosie's baby was nearby and open to contact, Rosie reported feeling like a visitor in their home rather than her baby's mother and as a result visited less and less frequently. Ultimately Rosie's children were returned to her care. Fighting back tears she explained to all of us how she just couldn't connect with the baby. None of them had a relationship with him, and Rosie could see early on that adding him into the mix, when the rest of them had really experienced this trauma together, threatened to tip the delicate balance and confound the fragile repair work already underway. In addition, the baby grieved deeply for the only parents he knew, his foster family. Rosie finally made the heartbreaking decision, for the sake of them all, to relinquish her parental rights to her youngest child so that the foster family could adopt him. Although Rosie courageously acted in what she believed to be everybody's best interest, this was a heart-wrenching ending to a "success story," and one I am sure nobody intended. But it is a reality that plagues systems designed to protect children, especially children in the first few years of their lives. If that very early reciprocal bond is not established and maintained between parent and child, something critical is forever compromised.

The second truth that became apparent was that if you really want to help the child, you must help the family. Struggles within families that lead to the abuse and neglect of children are relational in nature; the "problem" rarely resides in isolation within a single family member. If the problem is relational, so must be the solution.

These beliefs became the inspiration for our creation of The Children's Ark, an intervention designed to embrace and transform families at risk. Our vision was to keep parents and children together during the evaluation and treatment process while assuring the child's safety and to focus treatment on the relationships among them. Built on a foundation of attachment theory and grounded in the principles and language of The Circle of Security, now an internationally acclaimed intervention, The Children's Ark served children and families in the Spokane, Washington area from 1994 until 2010.

Housed in a large historic home in an old, eclectic neighborhood, The Children's Ark began as a foster home in which the mothers of the infants in care were also invited to live. Over time, as the program became robust enough, we transitioned to day treatment. Without the residential component, we were able to serve not just mothers but also couples, single fathers, and families with multiple children.

Underlying our thinking always was the belief that children's development and behavior cannot be understood outside the context of their relationships with their early caregivers; that children's sense of self, expectations of others, and understanding of how the world will respond to them develops out of those interactive experiences during the first few years of life. We further believed that until parents recognized and began to soften the destructive defensive strategies and emotional barriers created during their own childhoods, they would not be able to recognize and meet their children's needs responsively and directly. It therefore became our mission not only to protect children at risk and to promote their development, health, welfare, and competency in relationship, but also to increase the experiential knowledge, understanding, sensitivity, and security of their parents.

This book is based on our more than 20 years' experience in foster care. It includes accounts of some of the children and families who came into our lives as a result and the lessons they taught us. They are true stories about real people. Although my memories of the people and events were bolstered by files, journals, reports, and conversations with other Ark staff and participating families, they are my memories and so are, of course, imperfect. I made every effort to remain accurate. However, there are moments I am sure where time is telescoped, details forgotten or highlighted, or even minor facts remembered erroneously. In a number of cases I intentionally changed personal characteristics to further conceal and protect participants' identities, and in at least one account I merged the details of two cases. For the most part, however, the cases contained in this book are truth as perceived and remembered through my particular lens. I will forever be grateful to these families for allowing me to tell their stories, for the wisdom thus shared, and for enriching my life by their presence in it.[2]

It is important to note that most of our foster care experience was with children aged two years and younger. On occasion children turned three years old while in our care, and we involved older siblings on a limited basis, but primarily we served infants and toddlers. Thus, as a reflection of our experience, the children described in this book represent the youngest children in foster care. I believe that children in care under the age of five represent a unique and particularly vulnerable population. They are physically and emotionally laying the foundation for how they will operate for the rest of their lives. Trauma suffered during these early years does not just impact the brain but becomes a building block in its very formation.[3] And what children learn in these early years about relationships and how they work dictates and drives future patterns of behavior, relationship dynamics, and defensive strategies.[4] It is crucial, therefore, that decisions involving these children be made with particular attention to their emotional and developmental needs and vulnerabilities. Although our focus is on the youngest children in foster care, I believe that there is much here that applies to all children: young or older, at risk or not.

One Day

One day a little girl came in
She was scared and unsure
Everything she had known was true
Wasn't true anymore

The rules she learned did not apply
And people were misread
She learned things were not the same
There was no need for dread

Taking a leap of faith she left
The world as she once knew it
Trusted strangers to lead the way
And hoped not to blow it

This chance she had was truly rare
To build friendships that couldn't compare
To the ones she knew all her life
That were filled with so much pain and strife

She knew she had to leave them all
And take the chance that she might fall
Each day there was work to be done
That meant crying with everyone

It took much thinking
And so much doing
It felt really bad
And so unnerving

Soon she wasn't so scared
It wasn't as hard
And as each day passed
Both were less on guard

The more time had passed
It became really clear
This feeling is how
It's supposed to feel

There's always stuff to look at
And pieces that need to be changed
The best reason to do it
Shows in the relationships she made

Without the love and support
Of those special people
Nothing would have come of this
Their lives would not be equal

Airin Hazelwood (Ark mom)

Housed in a large historic home in an old, eclectic neighborhood, The Children's
Ark began as a foster home in which the mothers of the infants in care were also
invited to live.

Very important to the philosophy of The Children's Ark was to create a place
that had the warmth of home, rather than the impersonal feel of an institution.

A view of the inviting entry and porch from the walkway.

The babies' napping room—each crib is personalized for a particular child with familiar objects.

Part 1

LESSONS LEARNED FROM CHILDREN AND FAMILIES

*We are wounded in relationship, and
we need to heal in relationship.*

Brach 2003, p.285

Chapter 1

RICKIE

The inspiration of Rickie and his family

Paul and I were used to, on occasion, opening up the newspaper and reading a small notation in the arrest column about a member of one of our families; but the day I opened the paper and read that one of our former foster babies had, at 19 years old, murdered his girlfriend and unborn son, my heart broke. The newspaper article went on to describe how the life of the darling baby boy I remembered became a series of missed opportunities and failed interventions ending in murder.

Rickie represented a turning point for us in our lives as foster care providers; it was our experience with his family that ultimately inspired us to create a residential approach to foster care, which we called The Children's Ark (see the Preface for description). Rickie and his family are representative of many families that find their way into the foster care system: families struggling to survive, families in pain, families in need. Like others in danger of losing custody of their children, this family did its share of resisting and defensive acting out. For the most part, however, they sought and cooperated with the help offered them. Given the tragic outcome, questions persist. What happened? Was the system's response to this family appropriate and helpful and the bad outcome somehow inevitable; or were the system's interventions ineffectual—even punitive at times—perhaps contributing to the bad outcome? Did the system recognize this family as a group of individuals with unique strengths, struggles, and relational issues and provide them with specific interventions, or were they plugged into one-size-fits-all solutions? Did the system truly understand what children like Rickie need to survive and thrive? Rickie's story is packed full of "what ifs," beginning with his experience with us.

Rickie came to us as an infant, just six months old. He was discharged to us from the hospital, suffering from bruises to the chest and an old leg fracture. His father had admitted to the abuse. I don't think I had ever seen a baby as depressed looking as Rickie, with sad, slightly fear-filled eyes, and fingers stuffed soothingly into his mouth. He seemed quite content just to sit quietly on my lap. Coaxing a smile out of him was almost impossible and convincing him to move about and explore even harder. He seemed satisfied just watching the world unfold around him, perhaps convinced that there was safety in invisibility.

Rickie was behind developmentally. He had very poor muscle tone. He was sometimes stiff, arching away and resisting cuddling; at other times he was limp, weak, and lifeless. He was not sitting up, turning over, or attempting to crawl in any way. When put on his tummy he did not lift up to look around. When propped in a sitting position, he could not control his leaning. He lacked the strength, eye/hand coordination, and alertness one would expect from a six-month-old; in fact, his movement patterns and cry resembled more those of a newborn.

Many of Rickie's responses suggested fear. He startled at loud or sudden noises. He screamed and arched backward in the bathtub. And when upset, tired, or scared he avoided eye contact altogether, looking instead upward with a glazed-over, frozen stare.

Rickie's dad was young and immature. Overwhelmed by his situation, a wife and baby and too little income, he was forced to depend upon and align with his overbearing and aggressive mother. Rickie's mother was quiet and timid, living in the shadow of her powerful mother-in-law and sometimes volatile husband. When their son was taken into care, both parents turned their fear to anger and targeted the least threatening, most available enemy—me, their son's foster mother.

When Rickie was taken for supervised visits with his parents, they constantly complained about how he looked, what he was wearing, what was missing from his diaper bag, and so forth, and often sent cryptic, critical notes back with him. One day while I was out running errands my sitter received a phone call from Rickie's social worker indicating that Rickie's parents had filed a formal complaint accusing us of abusing him. Rickie had gone on a visit that morning, and his social worker had transported him. The social worker assured my sitter that she knew the complaint was groundless, but that once a formal complaint was made they needed to follow through with the appropriate procedure. She was told that an investigator and a photographer were on their way to the house. I hurried home.

Over the next hour, we awoke Rickie from his nap so that his entire body could be photographed, and we answered a myriad of questions. Although ultimately the complaint was deemed unfounded, the experience was distressing and humiliating. So the day that another of our foster babies rolled over while sitting in an infant seat and landed on Rickie, causing an angry red scratch across his forehead just before a visit, I knew we were in trouble. I even considered—briefly—saying that he was sick and not sending him to the visit, but honesty prevailed. I buckled him into the volunteer driver's car with a kiss and an apology and held my breath.

Shortly I received a call from the social worker indicating that once again Rickie's parents had moved to accuse us, though this time rather than filing an official complaint they merely phoned Child Protective Services (CPS) to report us. "I am so sorry," the social worker said to me, "How about if I move Rickie to another foster home? You don't need this." "No," I said, "I want to meet his parents."

We arranged, shortly thereafter, to have me collect Rickie from a visit so that I could introduce myself to his parents. Coincidentally, I had just picked up pictures of him that day, which were still in my purse. As I entered the visitation room, Rickie responded to my presence with enthusiasm, turning to me and reaching out. I greeted him and picked him up, and, as he settled into my arms, introduced myself to his parents and commented on what a wonderful little boy he was.

I believe that replacing the feared unknown with a friendly face, together with the obvious affection I held for their son—and he for me—soothed and softened Rickie's parents toward me that afternoon. They were able to override the idea of who I was and open to the reality of me. The adorable pictures, which I gave them to keep, of course didn't hurt. From that day forward I became more of a trusted grandmother figure, especially to Rickie's mom, and less of a threat to their right to parent.

I began transporting Rickie to visits, and his mom and I began to feel like a team. She clearly loved her son and wanted to learn how to give him what he needed. She showed a willingness to consider new ideas and empathized deeply with her son's experience. She looked to me for guidance, though remaining shy and timid. Ultimately, she even initiated calling me on occasion. One day I said to my husband, "If I had both Rickie and his mother I think I could really make a difference in their lives." She needed to get out of her environment, which constantly undermined her authority as Rickie's mother and eroded any confidence in her own ability to parent.

This, I think, was the tiny seedling from which The Children's Ark grew. Unfortunately, in that moment none of us was ready to take the leap. Our minds were just beginning to fantasize solutions, and Laura, Rickie's mother, could not yet imagine escaping her particular hellish circumstances. So we each continued to stumble down our own familiar road, though fortunately no longer fighting each other. I can't help but wonder what might have been different if we had been ready and able to take them both at that time.

Sometime around his first birthday, after six months in our care, Rickie was returned to his mother, but only after she had left the family home and her husband and moved into a supervised transitional living center. At least twice I was called upon to provide respite care for Rickie in those early weeks, a good-news indicator of Laura's trust in me. However, within weeks of Rickie's return to Laura, a child protection team consultation was scheduled to consider whether or not he was safe in his mother's care. According to reports, already he had fallen off the bed and out of the highchair, and had sustained a significant bump on his head when Laura tripped with him in her arms and his head hit a picnic table. Even though it was clear that Laura aspired to meet her son's needs and keep him safe, it seemed as if she was unable to generalize specific knowledge from previous experience. Once he had fallen off the bed, she was careful not to leave him unattended on the bed again, for instance, but she did not apply that same principle to leaving him unattended in the highchair. Apparently, the balance never tipped far enough into the perception of real danger, however, for the courts to feel justified in removing Rickie again from his mother. Ultimately, Rickie and his mother reunited with Rickie's father and returned to the family home. The family struggled on.

In fairly rapid succession, three girls were born. Life became even more challenging. Although we stayed in touch, and I visited occasionally, I no longer had real access to the details of their lives. What I did notice during my interactions with Rickie's family over time was that Laura continued to attune to Rickie's experience, but her efforts on his behalf were overridden and often ridiculed. I witnessed her attempts to come to his defense more than once, only to watch her be dismissed and ultimately to collapse into overwhelming defeat. Thus, Rickie was left at the mercy of a devaluing, aggressive, and punitive father who was supported and encouraged by like-thinking relatives, all of whom seemed to assess Rickie as somehow "evil." And even though Child Protective Services was still involved in their lives, this family never received the kind of comprehensive treatment that might have really made a difference.

My last visit with Laura occurred when Rickie was 12 years old.[1] I didn't see him that day because he was already residing in a group home. Laura was by this time out of the marriage to Rickie's father and raising the girls alone. She has since remarried and has had one more child.

Over the first 19 years of his life, Rickie experienced many out-of-home placements: from foster homes to group homes to psychiatric wards. He was diagnosed with various developmental disabilities and mental illnesses and, as we knew, had come to the attention of Child Protective Services as an infant. Providers from every sector of the social service world had been a part of this family's life from the very beginning. Sorting out causation for Rickie's course is a complicated, potentially controversial, and probably impossible task, but I believe that there are some lessons to be learned from this family's experience.

Struggles in families always have a significant relational element. Every member of a family is a unique individual who brings to each relationship their own way of being in the world, a way of being that may include specific deficits, disabilities, and disturbances. As individuals come together in relationships, however, it is largely the relational dynamics that impact interactions and ultimate outcomes. The family as a whole, then, the relationships, must be the focus of intervention, with additional individual treatment for particular conditions when warranted.[2]

There is a way in which very early in this family's course, Rickie was identified as "the problem," and although attempts were made, never was it effective to remove him, "fix" him, and return him to an otherwise unchanged environment. The environment was always bigger than Rickie. I of course can't help but wonder how history may have been changed if, instead of simply removing him as an infant for a period of six months or so, attention had been focused on the whole family, on the relational dynamics. What if, for instance, the focus had been on building the bond between mother and child, allowing their connection to grow in a healthy, supportive environment, encouraging and empowering Laura to access her innate wisdom as a mother? And what if Rickie's father also had had to participate in learning about his son's real needs, or had been given the opportunity to express his inability or unwillingness to do so? What if there were opportunities for this family to come together in everyone's (especially Rickie's) best interests, and real consequences for not putting Rickie's needs first?

I also find myself wondering what might have been different if the individual struggles and disabilities of each family member had been explored, identified, and worked with in an attempt to minimize the negative impact, resolve the resolvable, and maximize the strengths. It was clear, for example, that Laura suffered from depression. I don't know what attempts were made to treat her over the years, but I am quite confident that the impact of Laura's depression on the rest of the family—particularly her son—was never considered or addressed directly. We now know that the babies of depressed mothers also tend to be depressed; their development—mental, emotional, and physical—can't help but be affected by the lack of reciprocal responding.[3] What if Laura's depression had been recognized as not only a costly struggle for her but also a contributing factor in Rickie's presentation?

How might Laura's future have looked if she had really had the time and resources to explore how she operates in the world and why: to explore what she expected in relationship with others, how she defended herself, and her own sense of worthiness while she only had one child and before her life had spun further out of control? What if instead of telling her that she had to leave her husband to get her son back, knowing that it was a temporary and artificial demand, she was really supported to face the costs to herself and her son of continuing to live out of fear and pain in an abusive family environment?

None of this was possible in the system as it existed. Though the individual social workers and service providers were caring and well intentioned, the system itself was not set up to accommodate what this child and family needed: individualized, relationship-based, and continuous intervention. This family needed people and an environment to challenge yet support them and hold them long enough for them to gain the confidence for real change. Although I determined that Rickie had been in my care too long for it ever to work to also bring Laura into our home, we did begin to think seriously about creating just such an environment as a result of our early experiences with Rickie and Laura. By 1993 we had decided to take the plunge, and in early 1994 we opened the doors of The Children's Ark.

Although too late for Rickie and his family, The Children's Ark became, I believe, an intervention that developed over time a way of embracing and transforming families at risk. A solid understanding of attachment theory, deepened by the development and use of the Circle of Security (COS) intervention, became foundational to our work. The course of projected history can be changed, one family at a time, but only if we understand and honor what children—indeed all of us—need to thrive.

Research and theory: An overview of attachment theory

...our attachments are a major source of what makes our lives
feel rich and wonderful or lonely, sad, and utterly wretched

Colin 1996, p.14

Not long ago child development experts believed that infants and young children lacked sufficiently mature emotional systems to feel the depths of human connection or the despair arising when those connections were lost or broken. Prolonged separations from primary caregivers were treated as routine, and the protest, sadness, and grief shown by infants during separations were overlooked or discounted.[4] Attachment theory, developed by British psychiatrist John Bowlby, changed those ideas. Based on his clinical work and early research, Bowlby understood that children have an essential need to be connected to their caregivers and develop deep emotional ties to these significant people.[5] During the course of our evolutionary history, developing these ties—or attachments—to our caregivers would have meant the difference between life and death. At its most basic level, attachment is about survival.

Starting from birth, infants show a wide range of attachment behaviors designed to capture the caregivers' attention and promote the development of the attachment bond: crying is the most profound initially but later comes smiling, clinging, following, and so forth. As the infant matures, these attachment behaviors become organized as part of a coordinated behavioral system. Under conditions of stress or threat—conditions that often provoke fearful arousal—infants' attachment systems are activated, motivating them to seek out their primary caregiver(s). Once their attachment needs are met, most often through contact, comfort, and reassurance, infants' attention and energy can be directed to other things like exploration and play, which are also important for growth and development.[6]

Mary Ainsworth, Johns Hopkins' professor and Bowlby's colleague, built her research career around the study of attachment through detailed observations of parents with their infants in their homes and in her research lab.[7] Through this work she recognized the caregiver's vital role as a secure base. She observed that when infants could confidently rely on their caregivers' availability, they were more—not less—free to explore their environment, just as Bowlby's theory predicted. Countering those who cautioned that "too much" attachment would create dependency, Ainsworth found that security liberates; it promotes exploration and supports autonomy. Ainsworth also found that not all caregivers were able to develop a secure relationship with their infants. The links she discovered between caregiving and attachment showed that *infants adapt their attachment strategies to match their caregivers' needs and behaviors.*

Ainsworth and her colleagues crafted a laboratory procedure that would allow them to observe the quality of the parent–infant attachment relationship. Now famously known as "The Strange Situation Procedure" (SSP), it included a series of brief separations and reunions between the parent and infant designed to activate the infant's attachment system. Using the SSP, Ainsworth and her colleagues identified three distinct patterns of attachment. They described the most common pattern as *secure*. Infants with secure attachments often were distressed upon separation, sought closeness and comfort upon reunion, and—once comforted—returned to exploration and play. Home observations[8] revealed that caregivers whose infants were secure tended to be sensitive and consistently responsive to their infants' signals. They were nurturing and attuned to their infants' emotional states, showing empathy, delight, and general warmth. They enjoyed close physical contact without being intrusive or overprotective. Above all, they communicated a sense of basic trust that they could be relied upon to meet their infants' needs.

Ainsworth and her colleagues identified two groups of infants with insecure or anxious attachments, recognizing that insecurity manifested in different ways. Infants with *anxious-avoidant* attachments showed little distress at separation but also little response toward the caregiver at reunion, sometimes avoiding the caregiver altogether. Ainsworth observed that caregivers of infants with anxious-avoidant attachments tended to reject their infants' attachment needs. They ignored their infants' cries and bids for closeness and were particularly uncomfortable with intimate physical contact. In contrast, infants with *anxious-resistant attachments* showed high levels of distress upon separation, mixed anger and avoidance with seeking closeness upon reunion, and had difficulty settling and returning to play. Their caregivers tended to behave inconsistently; they were very responsive at times but also anxious, overstimulating, insensitive, or non-responsive at other times.

Some years after Ainsworth's initial studies, researchers Mary Main and Judith Solomon, at the University of California at Berkeley, described a fourth pattern of attachment: *disorganized/disoriented*.[9] Observing unusual cases in the SSP, including infants with histories of abuse, they discovered a variety of odd responses from infants toward their caregivers. Some infants showed distress upon separation but then fell to the floor in a hunched or prone position when their caregiver returned. Some combined extreme distress with extreme avoidance while others seemed to freeze, as if in a dissociative state. Given the links to maltreatment, Main summarized these strange behaviors as indicating "fright without solution" (Hesse and Main 1999, p.484); the caregiver who was supposed to be the secure base was also the source of fear, placing the infant in an impossible approach–avoidance bind.

Research has shown that early parent–infant attachment matters; it predicts ongoing development in significant ways. Bowlby proposed that early attachment-related experiences are internalized as representations or working models of how relationships operate and act as non-conscious templates for future relationships. Internal working models include representations about the self (e.g. whether we are worthy of care), about others (e.g. whether others can be relied upon to provide care), and about relationships with others (e.g. whether we can risk intimacy).[10] Indeed, studies have revealed that children with secure attachment histories do better than their insecure counterparts, particularly in social relationships. Children with secure attachments show, for example, higher levels of self-efficacy, trust, and general social competence and lower levels of dependency and hostility.[11]

Although children with insecure attachment histories do not do as well when compared to those who are secure, of greatest concern are children with disorganized attachments.[12] Researchers have found that children with disorganized attachments develop highly disturbed internal working models characterized by deep mistrust, fear, rage, and often violence. They have difficulty in social relationships, showing higher levels of peer victimization and relational aggression, for example, and are at risk of a range of emotional, behavioral, and mental health problems.[13] Given their history of abuse, neglect, or otherwise significantly compromised caregiving, it is likely that many infants and young children in foster care have experienced early disorganized attachments. We believe that Rickie was well along on this pathway when he came into Janet's care at six months of age.

For Rickie and his mother, Laura, a comprehensive, relationship-based intervention, which might have allowed Laura to parent with more confidence and sensitivity, was not available to them. Instead, Rickie was returned to her well-intended but inept care and ultimately to the entire hostile family system. The early foundation of what was likely disorganized attachment, compounded by months of separation, would have returned in full force, particularly as Rickie became personified as "evil" within the extended family. And then, because later development is impacted by earlier development, and working models—both of Rickie for himself and of others for him—tend to resist change,[14] Rickie's pathway of behavioral challenges became further solidified.

In their book *The Boy Who Was Raised as a Dog*, child psychiatrist and trauma expert Bruce Perry and scientific journalist Maia Szalavitz discussed a case eerily similar to Rickie's. "Leon" experienced profound early neglect and went on to brutally murder two girls in his apartment complex. As they walked through the case, Perry and Szalavitz articulated the cascading effects impacting this child's development: early neglect, which led to the inability to connect emotionally with others, which led to peer rejection, which led to more intense hostility and rage, and so forth:

> In vain attempts to get the love and attention he desperately required, Leon would lash out, hit people, take things and destroy them. Receiving only punishment, his rage grew. And the "worse" he behaved, the more he confirmed to those around him that he was "bad" and didn't deserve their affection. It was a vicious cycle, and as Leon got older his misbehavior escalated from bullying to crime. (Perry and Szalavitz 2006, p.113)

Rickie's story bears a striking resemblance to Leon's—both ending in tragedy that probably could have been prevented if more support had been available and if helping professionals had better understood the critical nature of early relationships. Child maltreatment, including neglect—and its likely concomitant of disorganized attachment—place infants and children on pathways of developmental risk. Without intervention, these pathways may well predict tragic outcomes.

Chapter 2

RACHEL

A disorganized toddler[1]

Rachel, not yet two years old, stood looking at herself in the full-length mirror, a frown slowly overtaking her face. Deep in her throat began a low, grumbling growl. As the growl grew louder, she began hitting the side of her head and moving slowly toward the mirror, her eyes glued to her own image. The growling became yelling, and she began slapping at herself in the mirror. I sat stunned, unable to move or formulate a response. Her rage was palpable and deeply disturbing. Finally, I got up from my chair and went to her. I got down on my knees, gently held her shoulders, looked into her eyes, and said, "Rachel, this is not your fault! You are loveable, and you are loved."

After watching Rachel in the mirror, I was aware of pondering somberly how wounded she was. It was certainly clear to me that it was a dismal picture she carried in her head about how the world worked, whether or not she was valuable, how others would respond to her needs, and whether she could have any impact on her environment. Much of her rage seemed to be aimed at herself; somehow she carried the responsibility for the misery in her life. What, as a temporary caregiver, could I possibly do to help her?

I knew Rachel's story, and I knew her family, so it was not hard to imagine how her picture had evolved. Rachel's family had been involved with Child Protective Services prior to her birth. Rachel's father, who had sexually molested her older sisters, had been court ordered out of the house. Her mother suffered from depression and was fearful of and ineffectual with the older girls. As a result, Rachel's needs, even the most basic ones, often went unmet or were delegated to the sisters, who themselves were deeply wounded. Life was chaotic, inconsistent, unpredictable, often frightening, and punctuated with violence.

For the first 21 months of Rachel's life, she remained in her mother's care in an in-home placement under the supervision of the state. During the last 11 months of the in-home placement, Rachel and her mother participated in The Children's Ark when it was non-residential. As the difficulties and violence at home escalated, and it became clear that Rachel was no longer safe in her mother's care, she was placed in full-time foster care with me.

When Rachel came to me, she was an anxious and rage-filled little girl. Although much of her rage was aimed at herself, on occasion she also demonstrated aggression toward others. She often made menacing noises like growling and sometimes erupted into a nervous, haunting laugh, especially in response to an escalation in her caregiver's anger. Her activity level shifted easily into the frantic/frenetic range and often was accompanied by clumsiness and defiance. She showed a blatant disregard for her own safety, engaging with frequency in danger-seeking, or at least "adult-grabbing" behavior. She manifested a general anxiety, sometimes moving unpredictably into an exaggerated fear and startle response. She was extremely hypervigilant, as well as hypersensitive to the mood and availability of her caregiver. She demonstrated a very low tolerance for frustration, accompanied by no expectation that help was available. Occasionally, even a relatively minor frustration could lead to a real rage response. Her behavior was controlling in many ways, especially around eating. She manifested a general inability to regulate her emotions. She dismissed her own emotional responses and resisted others' attempts to comfort or soothe her. She was, in fact, resistant to relationship or any kind of intimacy at all and instead was extremely and compulsively self-reliant.

Between her history and her behavior, I could construct a pretty clear picture of what she would expect in relationship with others, particularly with me as her new primary caregiver. She would not expect me to meet even her most basic needs. She would expect me and her life to be unpredictable and chaotic. She would anticipate that I would be emotionally, and often physically, unavailable to her. She would assume that I could be either frightening or frightened and that I would allow, and perhaps even engage in, violence and aggression. She would not expect me to have any tolerance for intimacy, and she would expect to be alone in intense emotion. She would expect me to put my own needs above hers and to abandon her in many ways.

Conversely, I knew also how I wanted her to see me. If she was to recover and function effectively in the world, she needed to expect me to meet her needs, both physical and emotional. She needed to be able to count on the reliability of routine and relationship. She needed me to be sensitive and available and to be able to tolerate and validate her feelings. She needed to feel confident that I would support her exploration and provide her with comfort and protection, and she needed to trust that relational repair[2] was possible.

Rachel lived with us for 13 months. Over that time, I worked consciously and determinedly to shift her perception of the world in the direction of security. Some months later, upon reflecting with my clinical colleagues—Glen Cooper, Kent Hoffman, and Bert Powell, the founders of the Circle of Security (COS) intervention—about Rachel and the philosophy of their developing protocol, I realized that I had applied COS principles in my experiences and interactions with Rachel in the following ways.

Principle 1: "I am here. You are worth it"

This first principle was about framing everything I did and everything I said with the message: "I am here. You are worth it" (Jude Cassidy, personal communication). According to attachment expert Jude Cassidy, there are two things that secure children know: that their caregiver is available should they need them, and that they are worth it. Starting with the day she stood before the mirror attacking her reflection, I tried to wrap Rachel's entire life in the message "You are loveable, and you are loved." First, I was conscientious about reliability of routine and relationship, hoping to give her both a sense of security through structure and a sense of belonging. Bath time, for instance, was always at the same time and done in the same way. I always followed the same order of things. We always sang the same songs and played the same games. And, most importantly perhaps, we always followed the bath with the same ritual: finding my husband wherever he was so that he and Rachel could have the conversation they had every night in exactly the same way: "Did you take a bath?" "Bath." "Are you all clean?" "Clean." "Did you wash your hair?" "Hair." "What do you get now?" "BINKY!"

I filled Rachel's day with as many routine and ritual experiences as possible. I identified activities that she particularly enjoyed (with Rachel it was singing songs), and set aside at least one period of time a day to engage in them, no matter how difficult the day may have been. Rachel's life had included far too few of these connecting moments to date, and I wanted her to experience delight as a regular part of each day.

I believe that predictability became a lifeline for Rachel. If ever I doubted the importance of it to her emotional well-being, she was sure to remind me. My (usual) faithful practice was to carefully explain to Rachel everything that was going to happen, especially if it was at all out of the ordinary routine. One week about half way through Rachel's stay with me, I went away for a weekend. She was of course distressed and disorganized by my absence, and on Monday morning was struggling mightily to get it back together. I took her down to The Children's Ark with me, and as I sat down, she went off to play. Suddenly I remembered something I needed to do and so signaled a staff member to watch her and went upstairs. I didn't think to talk to Rachel as I was only going to be gone a few minutes. Apparently, in my absence, she came back to where

I had been sitting and noticed that I was gone. When I returned, I sat in the same chair, and as she came around the corner and saw me sitting there again, she burst into heart-wrenching sobs. I was stunned. As *her* experience became clear to me, however, it made sense. I picked her up and tried to soothe her while telling her that I was sorry I had not told her what I was going to do; that it must have scared her that I just disappeared when it was generally my practice to tell her what was going to happen next. I also told her that it must have been particularly frightening for her right on the heels of my weekend away and that she must have felt abandoned again. I had come to know that Rachel really needed her reality validated; to be seen, heard, and understood[3] by me were the beginnings of security for her. Like all children, Rachel needed at least one adult who "got it" about her.

Principle 2: Behavior as need

The second principle was to try always to view her "problem" behavior as the expression of a genuine need.[4] It is so easy to feel personally defied by the behaviors of children like Rachel; to see them as somehow inherently bad or flawed, or, at the very least, to see them as acting out in order to get attention. Instead, I came to see that Rachel was simply engaged in an ongoing attempt to get her needs met. Since we all come helpless into the world, we are all dependent upon others for our very survival. Yet we are handicapped early in life in several ways in the pursuit of getting those needs met. For one thing, in the beginning of life we are not very mobile and so pretty much have to count on whomever is already physically present in our environment. Hence as very young infants, we will work hard to find a way to stay connected that will work "good enough"[5] with whomever is available. Likewise, in the beginning of life, we have only limited ways of communicating with those who can help us. If we are not being heard, we have no choice but to "talk" louder. Some children, Rachel among them, have learned that they are generally not heard and that their needs will go unmet unless they can escalate their adult-grabbing behavior to the point where they cannot be ignored. Seeing all her behavior as the expression of a genuine need instead of as "acting out" allowed me as her caregiver to focus on ferreting out and meeting the need, rather than focusing only on stopping—or worse, punishing—the behavior.

One afternoon I was working late at the Ark, still engaged in a meeting long after our usual hour to head home. Our clinical director, Sandra Powell, was watching Rachel in another area of the house. She reported that Rachel was playing happily one moment and the next was racing around and around pulling magazines off tables and knocking over lamps. Rather than responding negatively to the onset of the behavior, Sandra recognized it as the expression of a genuine need (no matter how gracelessly expressed) and responded instead to that. She picked Rachel up, held her in her lap, and said to her, "I bet you are missing Janet and wanting to go home. You do not have to run around the room pulling magazines off the table and knocking over lamps to tell us that, because I am here. You can sit in my lap instead and tell me how much you miss Janet, and I will comfort you until she is here." Rachel settled right down and into Sandra, knowing in some way that even if her particular need to have me was not going to be met at this very moment, just having someone understand her was enough for now.

Principle 3: Cues and miscues

Not only will children like Rachel speak louder through their behavior if their bids to have their needs met are not heard, but they will also learn to speak their caregiver's specific, unique "language" in order to stay in proximity with their source of survival. Children who are generally responded to learn to cue their needs directly and anticipate that they will be met. When a child's caregiver is uncomfortable meeting or fairly consistently fails to meet a need, the child will adjust their behavior accordingly to stay in at least the approximation of relationship and will begin to miscue needs (see also Chapter 3). A miscue is a misleading or contradictory cue, diverting attention from or protecting the Rachels in the world from the pain of having specific needs exposed and unmet.[6] Essentially, children learn to pretend they do not need something because they have learned that it will be difficult or impossible for the caregiver to meet that need. My job with Rachel (and the third principle) was to be willing to override and say aloud miscues: to convince her that I was there and would meet her needs.

Rachel's miscuing was so firmly entrenched that it seemed like she was not even aware that she had needs or at least any expectation that they could be met. In the beginning, it felt like I was teaching her how to feel and how to cue. For example, several times she fell down hard enough to draw blood. It never occurred to her to cry out, look for a responsive other, or seek comfort. Under those circumstances, I would go to her and pick her up and say, "Oh, boy, that really looked like it hurt. Let me see. Let's go wash it off and find a Band-Aid. Let me hold you," and so on.

Whenever I thought Rachel was miscuing me, I tried to figure out what she really needed, what was really going on, and then reflect aloud what I perceived her to be feeling or needing. It was always of course a guess, but I had little to lose if I was wrong, and if right, a lot to gain. When I guessed right, I immediately had Rachel's attention. Sometimes that was enough to calm her down and regulate her. Other times I went on to move her to, and through, intense, genuine, and appropriate emotion, an important step in healing. And the bonus always was that Rachel had one more experience of someone "getting it" about her.

Toward the end of Rachel's stay with me, her new (adoptive) family made several visits to my home. During their third visit, we were all sitting in the family room talking and watching Rachel play. Her quality of play began slowly to deteriorate until I thought she might disintegrate completely. I picked her up and put her in my lap, facing me, and asked her what was going on. She first tried to tell me that she was fine and then that it was about a problem with a toy, but I took a fairly safe guess and said to her, "I don't think that you are fine at all, or that it is about the toy. I think that it is about those people sitting right over there, and what their being here means." Unfortunately, Rachel already had had one failed adoptive placement, so I was betting that a family visiting had meaning for her. She froze and looked deeply into my eyes. Then she looked over at them and back at me and burst into tears. She then could move both into expressing her feelings freely and talking about them, while allowing me to comfort her. I had the opportunity to begin in earnest the conversation about her move, to share with her my feelings about missing her, and to model for her new family how to help her grieve. All of this because of not letting a miscue go unchallenged.

Children like Rachel sometimes seem to regress temporarily, either in behavior or in skill level. Rather than a regression, I see this almost as a child taking back miscues; a way for them to say, "I didn't get this need met, and I want it." One day I was in the playroom with Rachel. She was playing with her dolls. Without initially attracting my attention, she brought a baby bottle over to where I was sitting and positioned herself on my lap as if she were a tiny baby. Once she was fully in my lap, she looked into my eyes and handed the bottle up to me and said, "You do it." Somewhat puzzled as to what she was up to, I did figure out that she wanted me to feed her the bottle...and so I did. After a moment she took the bottle out of her mouth and said, "Blankie too." Then I understood. I got a blanket, wrapped her up, and cuddled her, rocked her, and fed her the bottle while affirming for her, "You didn't get enough of this when you were a little tiny baby, did you?"

Principle 4: "Being with"[7]

I realized quite early on that the only way to get Rachel somewhere else emotionally was to be with her wherever she was. Not only was it important for her to know she had feelings and to be supported to feel them, but it was also important for her to feel met and held. Wherever she was, I wanted her to feel validated, understood, and even joined. Because this was not the dance she had learned as an infant and because she had learned to shut down her feelings very early on, I found myself actually actively encouraging these walks through intense emotion. Thus the fourth principle became to be willing to "be with" her in intense emotion rather than trying to make it stop. Not only was it important to her healing for Rachel to express her feelings, but it was also important for me to recognize that any discomfort I had with her distress was about me wanting to feel better.

I had learned early in my relationship with Rachel that when she was struggling internally with something that was difficult for her to manage, signals or cues became apparent if I was paying attention. Her play became less focused and her activity level more frantic and frenetic. She became clumsier, almost as if losing control of her external being as her internal being struggled. Often her posture with me became much more openly defiant. I always tried to catch these signals so that I could go about helping her sort out what was going on.

One particular evening I remember all of these signals happening one after the other, culminating in her standing on top of the coffee table, just a few feet from me, with her hands on her hips, looking right at me. After taking her down several times only to have her climb right back up, I finally put her on my lap facing me, held her firmly, against some resistance, and said to her, "I am going to help you figure out what is going on. Looks like you need some help. Looks like you are asking for help." Then I took my best bet as to what was going on. In this case, it was a pretty good guess that she was emotionally disorganized by a sudden and unpredictable increase in visits with her mother. So, I went on to say to her, "You saw Mom today; you have seen Mom a lot this week. That is confusing. You don't know what to think. You want Mom, but she is never there for you. It makes you sad. It makes you mad." I let her know that it was okay to have whatever feelings she was experiencing, that it was okay to let them out, and that I was there for her and would go with her. As my own voice and emotion intensified, so did hers, until she finally collapsed into my arms in shuddering sobs that lasted that night for 40 minutes. Interestingly, after these episodes, Rachel was always a different child. Her play became much calmer and more focused. She was less clumsy. She was not just less defiant but usually became quite affectionate. That night I got down on the floor because I knew she often returned to me with affection. The experience had been intense enough for me that I had tears in my eyes as I sat and watched her. She eventually came back and sat in my lap facing me, looked up into my eyes, and slowly wiped away my tears.

Principle 5: Repair

Despite my best efforts, there were times that I failed Rachel miserably, moments during which I disrupted our connection and challenged her trust. As a general rule, I like to consider disruptions in a relationship an opportunity to repair, the building blocks to intimacy.[8] Disruptions in a relationship as fragile as ours, however, with a child for whom trust is just emerging, can represent a major setback.

Rachel was a small child and came to me very thin. When she was sick, she seemed to stop eating altogether, and the pounds just fell away. So when she got pneumonia, lost her appetite, and started losing weight that winter, I naturally was very concerned. After several days had passed during which it seemed to me she had eaten absolutely nothing, my concern turned to worry, then panic, and eventually to something that felt a lot like anger. After trying every trick of the trade and all of her favorite foods to no avail, I recall making something of a conscious decision not to show her how angry I was becoming. In order to manage my own emotion, however, I chose instead to shut down, and I withdrew emotionally from her. I got her down from the highchair, moved with her to the playroom, and tried to move on. It took me a full 30 to 40 minutes, however, to regain my emotional balance; I recall not being able to even look at her during that period of time. I eventually rallied, but my reaction had apparently been enough for her to go to that old familiar place of, "You are not there for me. I don't need you. I know how this works."

From that moment on it seemed that all we had gained was lost. Rachel went far, far away, back to her old compulsively self-reliant self, and she did it in very concrete and specific ways. By this time in our relationship when I came into the house or into the room, Rachel ran toward me with her arms in the air shouting, "Up, up." Following this incident, she instead started toward me, but stopped abruptly a few feet away, turned her back to me, and walked away. She had also established a rhythm of coming in to touch base with me when we were in the same room together, then going out again. She stopped coming in to touch me at all. She returned my favor of gaze aversion and stopped looking at me or referencing me in any way as well. Every day felt like an eternity, and all the while I was working particularly hard to repair with her: giving her language to let her know that I was there for her, staying attentively focused on her hoping to catch and respond to her subtlest cue, and taking responsibility—out loud—for the disruption in the relationship.

Finally, after three long days, Rachel came back. And she came back as concretely and specifically as she had gone away. She began coming all the way in and up into my arms when I entered the house or the room after an absence. She re-established her rhythm of coming in and touching when we were in a room together. On one occasion, in particular, she came in, turned around and leaned against my legs, then picked up my hands and wrapped them around her and held them there tightly. After her bath at the end of the third day, I got her out and stood her up on a towel on the floor as usual. I was used to having to keep at least one hand on her at all times during bath time. Even when she was fairly settled, she was a very energetic little girl and into everything. That night I remember being aware of how still she seemed as I stood her on the floor, and I carefully took both hands off her and looked into her eyes. She stood motionless, returning my gaze until she fell totally into my arms. I remember thinking that it very much felt as if she were saying to me, "I am going to trust that this is different, that I can come back." I identified as the fifth principle "repair": to whenever possible manage and/or contain my own negative emotional state;

and when it was not possible, to acknowledge that difficulty to Rachel and work with her to repair the rupture in our relationship.

Principle 6: State of mind[9]

There is some question in my mind as to who benefited more from the 13 months we had together. My life changed in profound ways in relationship with Rachel. She opened up my heart: both to new ways of being and to very old painful wounds. She gave me access to parts of myself that I didn't even know existed and shook my sense of myself to the very core. This was, of course, not always an easy or comfortable process. Many of her needs stirred in me intense emotion related to my own history. As my colleague and trusted friend, Kent Hoffman, so wisely commented:

> **"My hunch is that Rachel touches you in a place that is both new and very personal, that is, deeply 'old.' Someone like Rachel is universal in her realness and her sacred goodness—a realness that is rarely responded to with the kind of sensitivity we require. I can't imagine that you had the kind of attunement that you deserved at this 'Rachel place' and hence your availability to her brings up the grief and emptiness of what you most needed."**

I couldn't help but wonder about and try to track how my own "stuff" was impacting my responses to her. Thus the last principle, "state of mind": when struggles continue, reflect on my own experience with a trusted other, especially the impact of my state of mind as a caregiver (see also Chapter 6).

After a long and carefully planned transition, Rachel moved to her permanent, adoptive home. The transition itself offered opportunities both for me to continue helping Rachel adjust and resolve and for Rachel to continue expressing her remarkable insight about her experience.

As I visited Rachel in her new home, I worked hard to acknowledge and approve her new reality while at the same time assuring her of our ongoing relationship, that I would always be "her Janet." Rachel's new parents showed a stunning capacity to understand Rachel and her needs, and the courage and wisdom to help her continue her journey. With their help, Rachel continued to grieve her losses (including her loss of me) and work through her pain. As she became more verbal, she talked with amazing competence and heart-wrenching clarity about her agony and the cost of the trauma she endured.

During a visit to her home, the summer Rachel was four, I was struck by how far she had come from that little girl raging at herself in the mirror. She came immediately to me and climbed into my lap. She started with, "I miss you, Janet." I told her that I missed her too and that every morning when I woke up, I wondered what she was doing, what she was wearing, and what she was thinking today. To each thing I mentioned, she responded, "I like that, Janet." Finally, she cuddled into my chest for what seemed like a very long time, then sat up and said, "That is my smell."

But perhaps most poignant of all was Rachel's comment during my visit the summer she was five. By then she was a little less sure of me, and it took a while for her to move in close. Eventually, she made her way to my lap. She then looked up into my eyes and said, "People give me away." I was stunned, and tears filled my eyes. Finally, I gathered myself enough to say to her, "Yes, Rachel, that has been your experience. But it was never your fault. You are and always have been lovable and loved. And nobody will ever give you away again."

Rachel is a classic example of the emotional and developmental impact on children of environmental deprivation and relational trauma. Fortunately she is also a symbol of hope and testimony to what a strong young human spirit and experiencing relationship in a different way can accomplish. Her struggle is far from over, but she is a survivor.

Research and theory: Disorganized attachment and foster care

> *Being-With, a deceptively simple term, represents a profound need that, when answered, paves the way for a lifetime of satisfying relationships, for a mastery of a raft of developmental tasks and adult competencies, for trust and self-regulation and even physical health. Being-With, when it is a need unmet, becomes "Being-Without," leaving the child bereft not only of an essential human bond at this formative stage of life but of the uninhibited ability to thrive in future relationships and as an (autonomous) adult.*
>
> Powell et al. 2014, p.38

At its core, attachment theory is about human connection; it is a theory about our most basic need to "be with." As described in Chapter 1, the predisposition to become attached is part of our evolutionary heritage—without it, we would not have survived. Because attachment equals survival, fear occupies a central place in attachment theory. Our attention to threat, our fearful arousal, motivates us to seek proximity to those who will protect us. In psychologist Arietta Slade's words:

> Relationships, after all, are a basic remedy for fear—of loss, of annihilation, of psychic emptiness—and offer us the deepest expression of our humanity. Ideally both proximity and safety in closeness are easily and readily achieved. When they are not, the child must *adapt* in whatever ways are necessary to achieve and maintain such proximity; in this, he will do what is necessary to survive. These adaptations form the essential contours of his psychic life. (2014, pp.254–255)

In their studies of disorganized attachment (see Chapter 1), Mary Main and her colleagues connected this disturbing attachment pattern to fear without solution, stemming from a relationship with a primary caregiver who was frightening. Their research also linked disorganized attachment to parents who are, themselves, frightened, particularly in the face of their children's distress—parents' own unregulated, and even non-conscious, fear overpowering their capacity to act as a secure base and only further triggering alarm in their children. Main's colleagues, Judith Solomon and Carol George (1999a), expanded the concept of disorganized attachment by proposing that it arises when a child's attachment system is repeatedly and strongly activated but rarely assuaged; a child who chronically experiences the terror of "being without."

Given the conditions under which disorganized attachment develops, the environments most likely to create disorganized attachments include those in which caregiving is chaotic or frightening (e.g. abusive, neglectful, chronically inadequate due to addiction or mental illness or the caregivers' own overwhelming needs); those in which children experience repeated and/or lengthy separations from caregivers, including the permanent loss of a caregiver; and those in which children suffer from profound deprivation of care over the first year and beyond, as in the case of institutionalized children. These are just the sort of environments from which children enter foster care. Imagining Rachel's experience of living in a chaotic and sometimes violent family environment, having a mother who was seriously depressed and potentially unresponsive much of the time, and then experiencing the separation from and eventual loss of her mother (who—even though an inadequate care provider—was still her primary attachment figure), it is not surprising that Rachel exhibited many signs of disorganized attachment that carried forward into her relationship with Janet.

As described in Chapter 1, researchers have discovered that children with disorganized attachments develop highly disturbed internal working models of self and other, models that reflect a fundamental lack of integration and coherence—models often born out of unmitigated fear.[10] Such disturbed psychic structures place these children on at-risk pathways for a number of relational, psychological, and mental health concerns. Researchers have found, for example, that disorganized attachment is especially predictive of externalizing problems, characterized by aggressive, unregulated, and generally disruptive emotion and behavior.[11] Researchers have also observed that children with disorganized attachments have a particularly difficult time with peers, engaging in socially withdrawn, odd, disconnected, and/or aggressive behavior, setting them up for peer rejection.[12] Some theorists further speculate that disorganization is a precursor to serious psychopathologies, including dissociative disorders.[13]

Likely to manage their own fearful arousal and perhaps also their caregivers', many young children with disorganized histories become compulsively self-reliant and controlling, in either a caregiving or a punitive way. Children who adopt controlling-caregiving strategies work very hard to cajole or appease their caregivers, often being especially polite or helpful. Children with controlling-punitive strategies attempt to manage interactions by being aggressive or hostile or by sometimes humiliating their caregivers.[14] Other children, disorganized in infancy, remain behaviorally disorganized, continuing to show some of the bizarre behaviors characteristic of the infant disorganized/disoriented classification (e.g., disordered movements, sudden shifts in emotion, confusion and apprehension with caregiver).[15] Some researchers speculate that this sub-group is more highly disorganized than the sub-groups who are able to adopt a controlling strategy.[16] At age two, Rachel was behaviorally disorganized as well as compulsively self-reliant.

Foster caregivers who do not understand the dynamics of disorganized attachment may feel especially challenged in caring for their foster children—by their children's attempts to control the relationship, their ongoing behavioral disorganization, or their otherwise disruptive behavior. Research and clinical accounts tell us that foster children with disturbing behavior may be moved repeatedly; may elicit insensitive, punitive care; and are sometimes abused, again, in foster homes.[17] Rachel's rage-filled outbursts, along with aggression toward herself and occasionally at others, almost certainly would have predicted very troubling outcomes in many foster care placements. It is not hard to imagine an ill-informed foster parent lashing out at Rachel in frustration, a response that only would have compounded her deep fear and distress. Fortunately, Janet had the wisdom, support, and training to see through Rachel's complicated behavior to her vulnerability and tremendous need. Janet understood Rachel's rage and other disturbing behavior to indicate her profound insecurity. Janet's patient, attuned care and her ability to understand the need behind the behavior gave Rachel her first experience of real security in relationship; an experience from which she was able to begin healing as she moved into her permanent adoptive home.

Chapter 3

BARBARA AND NATHAN

Repeating the pain of the past[1]

Nathan was a tall, slightly clumsy, blue-eyed blond, who came to
The Children's Ark at about nine months of age with his mother,
Barbara, from a small farming town. He was placed into foster care
because of domestic violence concerns; Nathan's older sister was
already living with their grandmother. Barbara's commitment to
her son and to doing all she needed to do to regain custody of him
was impressive. She was admitted to The Children's Ark program
while it was still residential, and so commitment to it meant moving
the 60 miles to Spokane, leaving behind everything she knew,
everything she owned, and her husband. Nathan had been placed
with a relative and so acceptance into the program meant a move
for him as well. But come they did, and they had much to teach us.

Although Barbara's husband certainly looked the small-
town, farm-boy type, Barbara herself seemed much more street-
life hardened; she was tough, rough, and savvy. Just beneath the
surface, however, was a tenderness and vulnerability that hinted
at the intense pain underlying it all. It did not take long for her
to reveal to us the tragic and deeply moving image that haunted
her: as a young child Barbara was molested repeatedly by her step-
father. When she was about eight years old and on a weekend visit
with her birth father, she finally revealed the truth to him. With the
young Barbara in tow, her father stormed to the home of his former

wife and her new husband and confronted them on the front porch. As Barbara described this scene to us, her voice dropped almost to a whisper and tears filled her eyes. Barbara's mother stood on the porch facing her with her step-father behind the screen door. She listened to her former husband's accusations, looked Barbara in the eyes, hesitated for a moment, then turned and walked slowly into the house and back to her husband, letting the screen door slam behind them. Her choice was clear.

As the months passed at The Children's Ark, the influence of Barbara's story on her relationship with her son began to unfold. Unbeknownst to her, she was passing on to her son her own picture of how the world worked. Nathan's normal need for closeness or intimacy from his mother stirred up in her the fear and anxiety of her own experiences. No matter how hard she tried not to show it to him, he read her anxiety and adjusted his behavior accordingly. We videotaped their interactions frequently and went over and over them in hopes of finding a way to capture "the relational dance" that had developed. One day I decided to watch a short tape in slow motion, and there it was: their heads moving in perfect synchrony! Whenever Nathan looked at Barbara, she turned her head away; conversely, whenever Barbara looked at Nathan, he turned his head away. It was a dance indeed. I decided to show the tape to Barbara in slow motion to see if she could see and, more importantly, tolerate it. She asked to see it again, and again. Finally, the fourth time her eyes lit up, her excitement escalated, and she exclaimed, "Oh my god, I see it, I see it." When I asked her what she saw, she said that every time Nathan moved his hand toward her, she moved her hand away, and vice versa. Heads *and* hands in perfect synchrony! I asked her what she thought it meant. Very soberly, she answered that she didn't know, but that she wanted to see it again. We started through again, and at a moment when the camera zoomed in on Nathan's face, Barbara asked me to freeze the frame. Barbara stared at her son's face, which seemed to register hypervigilance, hope, and fear all at the same time. Still staring and with tears running down her cheeks, she finally said, "I know how he feels. I never wanted him to feel the way I felt."

If the lesson wasn't clear enough yet, Nathan started demonstrating his dilemma in yet another—more dramatic—way. Nathan loved books. He often grabbed one from the bookshelf and ran to any available lap in hopes of getting it read to him. Luckily, he had a number of loving laps available to him most of the time. His typical form was to head—book in tow—with determination and at full speed directly into the arms of any willing "receiver," almost as if thinking to collect a hug along the way. When the receiver was Barbara, however, his approach was very different. He began to move toward her in his usual form, but once within about five feet of her, he turned around and *backed* into her lap!

Over the ten months Barbara spent at The Children's Ark, she came to see the cost to her son of her own unresolved grief and loss. But, for her, walking through the pain to the other side was too much. As she so honestly conveyed, "I want to parent my son, but I don't want to do what I need to do to be able to parent him."

Barbara was articulating an important and often misunderstood truth about what abusing and neglecting parents need to "learn" to care safely for their children: it is not an information issue! It is, instead, an emotional issue involving personal examination and awareness and often is a painful, courageous, and time-consuming process (see also Chapter 6).[2] We believed at The Children's Ark that traumatized parents have the right to the truth about what is involved in shifting to a place that will change how they parent (see Part 2 for additional discussion), and that they have the right to decide whether or not it is work they feel capable and desirous of doing.

Barbara's ultimate decision was to exit the program, leaving Nathan behind.

Research and theory: The Circle of Security intervention

The Circle of Security (COS), now an internationally recognized attachment-based intervention, was developed in Spokane, Washington, within a few miles of The Children's Ark, and the Ark was one of its early laboratories. In his Foreword to the COS book, child psychiatrist and infant mental health expert Charles Zeanah described the COS as an intervention that "translates attachment research more meaningfully and more directly than anything we have seen before" (Zeanah 2014, p.xii). Done in a group setting, the power of the COS lies in its ability to individually tailor intervention to the core or "lynchpin" attachment-related struggles between parents and children (Powell *et al.* 2014, p.133).

Using clear visual aids to translate abstract theoretical concepts to concrete ideas, COS therapists help parents understand some of the foundational ideas of attachment theory. One of the first visual images shared with parents is a graphic illustration of the "Circle," showing the child's basic needs for both a secure base from which to explore and a safe haven to which to return (see Figure 3.1). This illustration provides a powerful but simple image allowing parents to understand their children's primary attachment-related needs, behaviors, and emotions. The top half of the circle represents the innate need children have to explore their environment as they are developing a clearer sense of their own autonomy. As depicted in the graphic, the role of the caregiver is to watch over them, delight in them, and help support and encourage their exploration. The bottom half of the circle illustrates the complementary need for connection and support, particularly in times of distress. As shown, when children signal their desire to return to the safe haven, the role of the caregiver is to protect, comfort, and help them organize and regulate their sometimes overwhelming emotions.

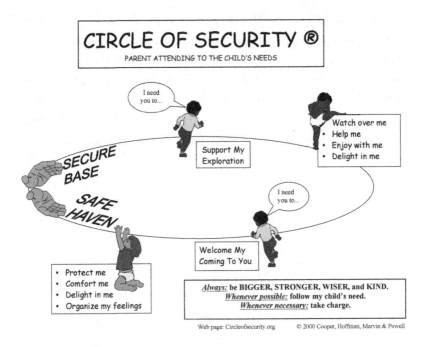

Figure 3.1 Circle of Security

As parents become aware of children's needs for support on both sides of the circle, they also begin to explore their own strengths and limitations in providing this support by watching carefully edited video of themselves with their child in the Strange Situation Procedure (SSP) (see Chapter 1). They learn that some parents are better at supporting autonomy (top half of the circle) whereas others find it easier to support intimacy and connection (bottom half). Understanding that children will do whatever it takes to build an attachment bond with their caregivers, parents also learn the costs to their children when they have difficulty supporting their children's needs. They learn that children will "miscue" their real needs in order to be in relationship with the caregiver (see Figure 3.2). For example, Barbara had developed an avoidant attachment dynamic with her son (difficulty supporting his needs on the bottom half of the circle); as Janet described, "Nathan's normal need for closeness or intimacy from his mother stirred up in her the fear and anxiety of her own experiences. No matter how hard she tried not to show it to him, he read her anxiety and adjusted his behavior accordingly." Nathan's behaviors (e.g. avoiding eye contact, backing into Barbara's lap) were miscues to divert his mother's attention away from what she found so uncomfortable.

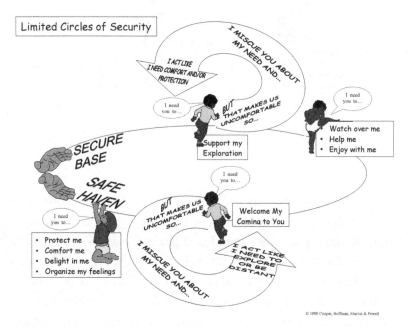

© 1999 Cooper, Hoffman, Marvin & Powell

Figure 3.2 Limited Circles of Security

Through the sensitive, "holding" environment provided by the COS therapist and group, parents begin to explore some of their own underlying issues that inhibit their ability to provide support on either—or both—sides of the circle, all the while building empathy for their children. The COS developers discovered that "shark music" (illustrated to parents using an adaptation of the score from the movie *Jaws*) was the perfect name for the psychological warning signals, produced by unconscious and deep-seated memories of parents' own unmet needs, which get in the way of responsive caregiving. "Over and over we have seen a whole new vista open up for parents once they can put a name—shark music—to the previously ineffable discomfort they have felt when faced with certain needs in their child" (Powell *et al.* 2014, p.89). As parents get better at identifying their own shark music, and at understanding how it triggers their psychological defenses, they also get better at managing those defenses in order to better meet their children's needs all of the way around the circle (see also Chapters 6 and 8).

Barbara's shark music was more than she could tolerate; she recognized the cost to Nathan of her inability to come to terms with the pain she had suffered as a child and made the courageous decision to relinquish custody voluntarily. Barbara was among a number of Ark mothers who made this decision. Although this was not necessarily the optimal outcome first imagined, the Ark staff quickly recognized that this outcome was far better for children than to have them languish in foster care while their parents continued to fight for custody. For Barbara, the realization that what Nathan needed from her as a parent was something just too painful to provide allowed her to relinquish with dignity, knowing that she was acting in Nathan's best interests. This decision took courage and Barbara needed support. She also needed to know that she was not "giving up" but instead doing what was better for her child. For Nathan, this meant that plans for a permanent home and caregiver could be pursued without further delay.

Nathan's transition

Nathan was in my care for a number of months. I eventually moved him several hundred miles away to his grandmother's where he joined his older sister. Nathan's transition to his new home and caregiver was carefully thought out and executed. And once again he was a master teacher.

Since Nathan's grandmother worked, she felt that she couldn't take time off to come to Spokane for a visit. I determined to make at least one visit there before beginning the transition in earnest. Nathan and I flew to his grandmother's for a weekend visit. Grandma had his room all set up with a crib. I took his favorite blanket, his favorite stuffed animal, and his pillow so that he would feel at home and have familiar things—and even smells—around him. Nathan went down for the night quite well, and I settled into the hide-a-bed in the living room. In the morning when Nathan awoke, he began calling my name. Grandma got him up and told him that she would take him to me. Before leaving the room, he pulled all his things—blanket, stuffed animal, and pillow—out of the crib between the bars, and dragged them all through the house as he padded along in his search for me. I greeted him happily and congratulated him on what a fine job he had done in his new room and his new bed. Ignoring my greeting, Nathan looked all around the room with determination and single-mindedness until he found what he was searching for: my suitcase. He stuffed all of his precious belongings into my suitcase and slammed it shut! He was not yet two years old, and just barely verbal, but his message was clear.

The following week I packed up all his belongings, toys, and some food and drove him the five hours to his new home. I had bought him a little duffle bag just his size and had him help me pack in it the sheets, blanket, pillow, and favorite animal from his crib. I had him carry it to the car and put it next to his car seat. When we arrived at Grandma's, I again had him carry his little duffle bag into the house, and together we made up his new crib with everything familiar, talking the whole time about how this was his new bed in his new home. I talked also about how his grandmother was going to take care of him now and always be there for him. Nathan had little to say that first day; but as the days passed in that first week, he increasingly commented with a resounding "No" as I talked about his new life.

I stayed in the area for a full five days, not in the house with him, but nearby. I came to see him each day but was careful to slowly affirm with my words and actions that this was now his home and I was the visitor. I was careful also not to assume the caretaking role but always to defer to Grandma. I didn't feed him, bathe him, or in any other way meet his physical needs but was there to support him emotionally and "approve" of Grandma. If he came to me asking for a drink of water, I took him by the hand and led him to her, saying, "Let's ask Grandma." If he needed help finding something or making a toy work, I suggested, "Let's see if Grandma can help us." I was careful always to include Grandma, and to give him the message that I approved of and enjoyed Grandma. Whenever possible I also slipped in the message that although I would always be his Janet, Grandma was the one who would be there for him from now on.

After this initial five-day visit, I returned to Spokane. I came back a week later, and then every two weeks, slowly reducing the number of days I stayed. Eventually I spread the visits out even further, coming twice a month and then only once a month. During my first 11 trips to see Nathan, no matter how much time had lapsed between visits, if I was present in the house Nathan sought me out if he was distressed, hurt, or needed help. He seemed increasingly comfortable over time with Grandma and his new home, but his persistent seeking of me when vulnerable told me that he had not yet really shifted caregivers. Patiently, we persevered.

The occasion of my twelfth visit to see Nathan was his older sister's birthday party. The living room was full of people: new aunts and uncles and cousins. Nathan seemed small and lost wandering among them. I was seated in my usual chair where I was available to Nathan, but in no way interfering with his access to Grandma. As Nathan stumbled about the room, he walked right into the legs of Uncle Fred. Although not hurt, Nathan was clearly startled and disoriented by the encounter and looked about for comfort. Seated in my chair I was but a few feet away and in direct sight. Instead of coming to me as usual, however, Nathan moved around Uncle Fred and a number of other new relatives *and* the dining room table until he reached Grandma's waiting arms. "At last," I thought, "finally he is home!"

Research and theory: Transitions that support children

Northern Arizona University nursing professor Caroline Ellermann explored the mental health of children in foster care and found that one of the primary factors influencing children's mental well-being was how transitions within foster care were managed. As one of the children she interviewed expressed, "All we do is get put into a car and drove [sic] to their house and then dropped off. And we are told this is where you are staying" (Ellermann 2007, pp.26–27). In fact, all three groups Ellermann interviewed for this study—foster children, foster parents, and professionals, themselves—regarded transitions as being poorly carried out.[3]

Compounding matters, many children in foster care experience multiple moves, sometimes reunited with parents only to be placed back into foster care sometime later. Multiple placements mean multiple separation and loss experiences, which only further compromise children's well-being.[4] The thoughtfulness with which Janet facilitated the transition for Nathan illustrates both the challenges of this process but also the potential for ultimate success.

Nathan's early experience in a violent environment, coupled with what appeared to be an insecure attachment relationship with his mother, certainly placed him at risk. The loving care he received at The Children's Ark allowed him to experience a basic sense of trust and security, which helped him learn new ways to be in relationship. The gains made while at the Ark, however, could have been erased by an abrupt transition; one that did not acknowledge the inevitable loss and grief young children experience with any change in caregiver. He had already lost his mother and now would lose Janet as well. Instead, the thoughtfulness of the transition allowed Nathan, even at age two, to have some understanding of what was happening, to be able to express and have his feelings validated, to receive support from a familiar secure base, and to eventually claim his new caregiver. Although not every foster care provider can take a week out of their lives to transition a child with frequent follow-up visits, recognizing the impact of transitions from the child's perspective helps us to imagine what we can do to make transitions less traumatic (see Part 2 for additional discussion).

Nathan: Follow-up

I continued to visit Nathan through his preschool years, though only when I was otherwise in the area. Grandma did a fine job with him, and he adjusted well. He saw both his birth mother and father on occasion, as both moved to the area. He was clear on who everyone was and where he belonged. Yet when I came for a visit he still ran to me with open arms and spent most of our time cuddled on my lap, long arms and legs draped around me, refusing to rise to any incentive to move. I believe that my presence stirred in him a whole body memory—perhaps his first—of what it means to be welcomed, held, adored, and safe.

Chapter 4

HANNAH AND ASHLEY

A story of two girls: Part 1

Prior to opening the doors of The Children's Ark, but while we were providing foster care in our own home, we received in care two adorable baby girls, born just six weeks apart. It was like having twins; they were alike in so many ways, and yet so very different.

Hannah came to us at six weeks of age, in the middle of the night: an adorable blonde-haired, blue-eyed cherub. She was the daughter of a very young mother who knew nothing about babies and was caught up in an abusive relationship with the father, an angry, aggressive young man who had grown up in violence and chaos. I have no doubt that Hannah's mother did the best she could to nurture her baby and to protect herself and Hannah from abuse, but by the time she sought medical attention her infant daughter was battered and bruised and her leg broken. Except for her injuries, Hannah was very much the typical cuddly and beautiful young infant.

A few months later, three-month-old Ashley arrived at our front door, also in the middle of the night, wrapped in a hospital towel: a skinny, dark-haired baby covered in bruises. It was clear even then that her trembling was out of terror rather than cold. Both her eyes were blackened, most of her body battered, and on each side of her face was a bruise clearly in the shape of a hand. She was stiff and very, very quiet. We learned that Ashley's parents were drug involved and struggling with alcohol addiction. As a consequence they were emotionally and often physically unavailable to her. She was regularly left alone in whatever precarious housing situation was available at the time and often went without food or comfort, her cries unheeded. She weighed just nine pounds when she came to us and, according to our pediatrician, would most likely not have survived another month. Ironically, it was probably an uncle, who escalated into rage at her distress and abused her, who ultimately saved her life. Had it not been for the bruising inflicted, she may not have come to the attention of Child Protective Services in time.

It became evident over time that these experiences, in the very first weeks and months of their lives, started each child down a path that in many ways drove and shaped their subsequent development: physical, social, and emotional. Hannah was abused, but probably not neglected. She was the victim of violence and chaos but was not ignored. When she cried, chances are someone answered. What she got was probably a mismatched response as often as not, and delivered tentatively, clumsily, and perhaps with anger, but at least it was something. As a result Hannah had learned, at just six weeks of age, that calling out in hopes of getting her needs met was unpredictable and sometimes frustrating, but worth it. When she came to us, she cried lustily when hungry and responded positively when picked up.

Ashley, on the other hand, during the short three months in her home of origin, was virtually deprived of human contact. She was primarily the victim of neglect and was for the most part alone in the world, sometimes only figuratively, sometimes literally. She was also the victim of physical abuse, but I believe it was the isolation and abandonment, her lack of access to a nurturing adult, that taught her early not to trust that her needs would be met. By the time she came to us she did not cry out for even her most basic needs, much less for comfort. She would lie quietly in her crib until a caregiver came and then would startle and shake as anyone moved into her line of vision. For Ashley the road to connectedness would prove to be a long and tortuous one.

One fall weekend both babies (Hannah, now about 11 months, and Ashley, 10 months) fell victim to the same nasty virus. Sharing symptoms and even the same exact 102 temperature, both were hot, miserable, and whiny. With resignation I settled into the family room with blankets, juice, and thermometers prepared to wait it out. Hannah wanted only to snuggle up with me, her blanket, a bottle of juice, and her favorite cuddly animal. I don't think I put her down in 36 hours. Ashley, on the other hand, arched and resisted my every attempt to hold her. After fighting for hours to finesse a way to comfort her, I finally negotiated sitting next to her on the floor while she wiggled and writhed in discomfort. I was allowed to sit there only as long as I did not touch her. It was as if the more vulnerable she felt, the harder she had to work to keep me at a distance.

This became Ashley's theme song: keeping people at a distance. Wiry and thin, she tensed and tightened at any human touch, never settling in or accepting comfort. As she became more mobile, she also became more independent and self-reliant. She carefully watched everything and everybody around her and was a quick study. If she saw you do it once, she knew how to do it and rejected help of any kind. She was strong and coordinated, and there were not many places she could not access. I pulled her off the top of the refrigerator more than once! In an odd sort of way she was also clumsy, as if not having a good sense of her body in space. Sometimes it was hard to tell if she didn't have good control over her body, or just didn't have any sense of valuing it, as when she repeatedly tried to ride her tricycle off the back deck sometime later, in her new adoptive home.

Ashley rarely referenced any human being and showed no preference for me, her primary caregiver. Hannah, on the other hand, was very relational and invested in keeping me near. A trip to the park was always a challenge. Ashley was off like a shot the moment her feet hit the ground. Hannah was much more cautious, hanging on to me until confident of her safety, then checking back in frequently as she ventured out to play. If there was an exit in sight, Ashley headed for it. She would leave the playground entirely if given the opportunity, with no regard for her own safety. Her behavior was risky in many ways. Clearly, she had no sense of what was too far to stray from a protective adult. And there is no question in my mind that she would have gone along with any stranger.

As Hannah continued to develop relatively normally, deepening her reliance on and trust in me, Ashley resisted stubbornly. Then, one spring afternoon, when I was in the playroom with both girls and both of my daughters, who were 12 and 17 at the time, I started out of the room to retrieve something. Ashley (about 15 months old) crawled after me, whining. Both my daughters broke into spontaneous applause, not exactly understanding what had just happened, but somehow knowing that it was important. In spite of these small moments when she let her need spill over, for the most part, Ashley remained distant and disconnected.

Another troubling difference in the girls we noticed quite early was Ashley's seeming lack of empathy. It made sense in a way: if she did not value her own safety and well-being, why would she care about anyone else's? She was not a mean or cruel little girl. She did not take pleasure in hurting other people, nor did she seem to enjoy others' pain. Rather, it was more like an ignorance of other people's emotional states; that she didn't notice or couldn't compute what those around her were experiencing or feeling. When in a group of children, if one child was crying Hannah tended to stop and look at the unhappy toddler and perhaps even mimic a "cry face." As she grew older and her social skills developed, she might even go to the child to offer comfort. Ashley, on the other hand, never looked up from what she was doing or seemed even to notice when another child was in distress, even if it was Hannah.

Although in many ways, Ashley did not seem conscious of the well-being of herself or others, there was also a way in which she clearly did not view the world as a safe place to be. One hot summer day I was dressing the girls for a trip downtown to visit Ashley's parents. I was on my knees in the nursery closet picking out little summer dresses. Ashley had crawled in after me. The girls were young toddlers and into everything. Hannah had discovered door shutting and pushed the closet door behind me. I was not particularly concerned as it closed behind me until it became stifling hot. It was also awfully crowded with both myself and Ashley, and a bit darker than was comfortable. I grabbed the door handle and turned it. Much to my surprise half came off in my hand, and half fell through onto the floor on the other side, leaving us locked in the closet with just a round hole connecting us to the outside and to Hannah.

Hannah had enough connection through the hole apparently to feel safe and enjoy exploring, while Ashley, who had me, was terrified. I ultimately succeeded in breaking through the door and reuniting us all, but only after interrupting my efforts multiple times to try to calm Ashley. The most interesting thing to me was not so much that Ashley was frightened by the ordeal, as my own anxiety and distress would probably have upset any child; but that my presence and attempts to soothe her in no way impacted her ability to calm down. Clearly, to Ashley, the world was a frightening place, and she was alone with her fear. Hannah, on the other hand, on the outside of the door and much more vulnerable to danger, found it all to be quite the adventure!

Research and theory: Trauma, attachment, and the developing brain

Research on brain development has led to some startling discoveries about just how much the immature human brain depends on the early caregiving environment for its organization and functioning and just how vulnerable it is to trauma. Bruce Perry and his colleague Ronnie Pollard explained the impact of trauma on the developing brain in the following way:

> Traumatic events modify an adult's original state of organization or homeostasis but may be the original organizing experience for the child, thereby determining the foundational organization and homeostasis of key neural systems. Experience in adults

> alters the organized brain, but in infants and children it *organizes the developing brain.* (1998, pp.36–37; italics added for emphasis)

The human brain develops sequentially and hierarchically, with the brain structures controlling basic, life-sustaining processes (e.g. breathing, temperature regulation) maturing first and the brain areas that allow for more complex functioning (e.g. planning, problem-solving) maturing later.[1] The areas of the brain most critical to human relationships, the areas of the brain psychologist Louis Cozolino calls the "social brain" (Cozolino 2014, p.3), include some of the early developing, lower and mid-brain structures (e.g. amygdala, hippocampus). The foundational structure and functioning of the brain—particularly the developing social brain—is critically dependent, then, upon the pre- and early post-natal environments, environments created in large part by infants' primary caregivers.[2]

Prenatal exposure to drugs or alcohol, poor prenatal care, high levels of maternal stress during pregnancy and so forth can all adversely affect brain development.[3] Although Ashley was not diagnosed with fetal alcohol syndrome at birth, she was later identified as fetal alcohol affected. Janet noted that Ashley struggled with certain cognitive processes, like linking cause and effect, and that she exhibited deficits in particular social skills, including empathy. It is likely that those deficits were exacerbated by the neglect she experienced, but it is also probable that prenatal alcohol exposure had an impact.

Following birth, whether a baby is held, comforted, delighted in, neglected, threatened, or terrorized matters a great deal in shaping the foundational brain wiring upon which ongoing development builds. Even though most of the approximately 100 billion neurons we will ever have are established by about five months' gestation, the neonatal brain is far from mature. The volume of the human brain more than doubles in the first year of life, a growth spurt unparalleled by any other time in development.[4]

This intense period of brain growth is due in part to the rapidly forming connections between neurons at microscopic spaces called synapses. These synaptic connections—up to 30,000 in some areas—allow neurons to communicate with one another. During sensitive periods of brain development many more synaptic connections than can possibly be used are spontaneously generated; those connections that are not reinforced by environmental stimulation (e.g. caregiving) recede, wither, and die. Other connections require environmental stimulation to be generated in the first place; these *experience-dependent* connections grow out of—and therefore reflect—our experiences within our caregiving relationships and in the broader environment.[5]

Another important contribution to our understanding of brain development is the recent discovery of aptly named "mirror" neurons. When we observe another performing an intentional action, the very same neurons active in the other person's brain are fired in our own, as if we were performing the action. Not only do mirror neurons help us learn through observation, but also it is likely that they facilitate a deep connection with others' emotional states.[6] As communicated by psychiatrist Dan Siegel, Executive Director of the Mindsight Institute, and child development specialist Mary Hartzell, "When we perceive another's emotions, automatically, nonconsciously, that state is created inside us" (Siegel and Hartzell 2014, p.63). By supporting the experience of shared states, mirror neurons have profound implications for the development of human connection and attachment. They also may help us understand the compromised development of infants whose caregivers are depressed, emotionally dysregulated, abusive, and so forth.

Over time, repeatedly activated neural connections form networks. According to Bruce Perry and Maia Szalavitz, reliable patterns of nurturing care stimulate the development of two major neural networks. The first network responds to all of the rich sensory perceptions—the caregivers' gaze, the soft voice, the warm touch—that comprise loving interactions. The second is a "reward system"—a complex set of neurological responses that create pleasure upon the relief of distress. Over time, these simultaneously activated neural networks become associated: "In the case of responsive parenting, pleasure and human interactions become inextricably woven together. This interconnection, the association of pleasure with human interaction, is the important neurobiological 'glue' that bonds and creates healthy relationships" (Perry and Szalavitz 2006, p.85).

Babies like Hannah and Ashley who are deprived of nurturing care or whose care is punctuated by periods of abuse form very different neural networks. In some cases, the normative, expected patterns of development, such as self-regulation and attachment, are disrupted. In other cases, developmental patterns are distorted, when, for example, sexual exploitation becomes associated with attachment and nurturing care. And, as horrific as abuse must be for an infant, neglect may exact a bigger toll. The understimulation of neglect causes more than the normal number of synaptic connections to recede, potentially leading to wide-ranging deficits in physical, cognitive, social, and emotional development.[7]

Neural networks also extend to stress-response systems. Because stress-response systems are regulated by early developing lower- and mid-brain areas, they are particularly vulnerable to early trauma. The overwhelming threat to survival and experience of terror invoked by neglect and abuse are likely to permanently sensitize the young brain and lead to the development of hyper-reactive neural systems. According to Perry and his colleagues, threat activates deeply engrained, total-body hyper-arousal responses, preparing—especially adult males—for fight or flight. Since infants can neither fight nor flee, their only response to threat is to cry, in order to signal to caregivers to act on their behalf. If crying elicits nothing or invites further trauma, infants move into hyper-arousal (e.g. frantic crying) and, eventually, to freezing and dissociation. The neurophysiological processes that characterize hyper-arousal and dissociation are very different; however, chronic activation of these states has the same effect: it sensitizes the developing brain so that even mild stressors can activate these states in the future.[8]

In sum, early experience, particularly in the context of primary relationships, organizes the developing brain. Early maltreatment—neglect and abuse—become building blocks in the brain's formation. For some children, traumatic experiences like physical and sexual abuse become inextricably woven together with care, connection, and attachment, potentially making them vulnerable to abusive relationships in the future. Maltreatment creates hypervigilant stress response systems that interfere with other aspects of functioning such as paying attention in the classroom. These systems may produce aggression as a young child's attempt to "fight," when even mild threat triggers a hyper-arousal response, or may lead to dissociation and paralysis, which may be interpreted as oppositional behavior.[9] And, as Perry and his colleagues (1995) noted, when these events happen during infancy, the cognitive and language resources that help older children and adults make sense of traumatic experience are not available. To heal, children need consistent and repeated reparative experiences in the context of safe, secure, and trusting relationships over the long term; experiences that will—quite literally—rewire the brain.[10]

A story of two girls: Part 2

Eventually both girls moved on to permanent homes (Hannah at about 15 months and Ashley at about 18 months). Both went to capable, stable families with adoptive parents who cherished them and wanted only the best for them. I expected that both girls' lives would continue to follow the trajectories they had already demonstrated: Hannah to continue down a relatively "normal" developmental path, and Ashley to continue to struggle in all realms. I also hoped that the gift of healthy environments might mitigate damage and maximize healing. However, over the years it is almost as if the girls' paths have crossed, and they have switched outcomes. Although Ashley remains in many ways physically and socially awkward, there is a huge way in which she is presently the more emotionally secure or grounded of the two. And it has been Ashley who has worked to maintain the connection between herself and Hannah over the years, referring to Hannah as her "sister" and always keeping track of her whereabouts.

Understanding that outcomes are complex and multifaceted and ultimately impossible to trace with certainty, several events or circumstances are most salient to me in terms of the possible impact on the lives of these little girls and their integration into their new families; factors that might help explain the change in outcomes given the apparent trajectories. Ashley went to adoptive parents who made a considered decision to add a child with special needs to their family. Once Ashley was placed with them, they claimed her completely, no matter what the future held. And, if their initial intentions were not enough, a rather surprising twist of fate certainly sealed the deal. After haggling for months, and once Ashley was already living in their home, her new family finally received Ashley's birth records. I'll always remember the phone call I got from Ashley's new mother that morning.

"Janet, you'll never believe this! I was the nurse who discharged her from the hospital following her birth! I'll never forget that baby. We were told that we had to discharge her even though it was in essence to the streets. I gathered clothes, supplies, and blankets and sent them all off in the dead of winter. And here she comes back to me!"

As her early experiences would dictate, Ashley did continue to struggle. The middle and early adolescent years in particular were difficult. She was plagued by poor social skills, exacerbated by her diminished ability to connect cause and effect. She struggled to set and maintain appropriate, safe boundaries. If she became frustrated it was as if she could not find a way forward and so succumbed to panic. Despite the challenges, Ashley's parents worked with her tirelessly and advocated for her relentlessly. In fact, following a number of the more troublesome years, a friend of Ashley's mother asked her, "If you had known that this is what it would be like, would you have done it?" The immediate, unflinching response was, "I would do it for Ashley again and again, but not for anyone else."

Ashley's lack of empathy, which had concerned us initially, was quickly replaced by an ability to develop and integrate a sense of compassion, lovingly reinforced in her consciousness by her determined new parents. The Halloween that she was three years old she came to visit us. We had in our front hall a toddler-sized Frankenstein who moved and spoke menacingly when plugged in. Most likely to hold her own fear at bay, Ashley practiced all afternoon scaring Frankenstein. When my husband, Paul, arrived home from work, she proudly demonstrated to him her loud and animated "BOO" directed at Frankenstein, complete with a scary face. Paul, innocently playing along, said, "Oh, don't scare Frankenstein. You will hurt his feelings." Ashley stopped cold, and it was almost as if you could see the wheels turning in her brain. Then she walked over, put her arms around Frankenstein, patted him tenderly on the back, and said, "I'm so sorry, Frankenstein."

Ashley, for her part, showed her own emerging determination to claim a place in her new family. By the age of ten, at a time when Ashley was beginning to understand her and her adoptive family's histories more completely, she announced that she believed she was actually the "spirit" of one of her adopted mother's miscarried babies, thereby cementing her place in the family.

Hannah's adoption experience was different. Although there were a number of typical twists and turns in reaching a "legally free" status for Ashley, it was not nearly the wait endured by Hannah's new adoptive mother, Beth, a single mother whose own story I knew. Hannah was an older toddler, with two brothers subsequently born and also placed in out-of-home care, before her birth parents' rights were terminated. There were many court hearings, and Hannah's birth parents were given many chances before a judge finally made the decision that would determine her future. Needless to say the waiting with their future hanging in limbo was hard on everyone, an anxiety-producing roller coaster ride during which emotions were never allowed to settle.

Additionally, visits with Hannah's birth parents continued up until the very end, even though her father's tendency to violence resulted in disrupted and frightening visits a number of times. Hoping to support Hannah in maintaining a tie with her birth family, Beth also endured Hannah's visits with her great-grandparents, who often were critical of Beth's parenting and sometimes threatened to go after custody themselves. And, as if things weren't already stressful enough, Hannah's younger brother, Daniel, was placed with Beth when Hannah was three, and it was another year before the parental rights to Daniel would be terminated, pulling Beth into continued contact with the birth family.

I suspect that the uncertainty and stress experienced over the two years it took for Hannah's case to resolve may have compromised Beth's ability to embrace her unconditionally as well as Hannah's ability to connect. Surely, consciously or unconsciously, they found a way to protect their hearts against the possibility of loss, at an inevitable, eventual cost to them both. Beth had already suffered the significant losses of her mother and her sister, probably rendering her particularly vulnerable and defended against further heartache.

Hannah's adoptive family grew with the addition of her brother, Daniel, and again when Beth married; these family transitions must have added to a sense of instability for Hannah. And, although both Beth and her new husband were certainly devoted parents, the relationships never seemed to reach the unconditional kind of claiming that Ashley experienced. I also suspect that Beth needed something from Hannah, perhaps for her to be the little girl she always dreamed of having. And when the unforeseen challenges arose, and reality did not meet her expectations, Beth, most likely operating out of her own unresolved longing, retreated into fear and defensiveness, responding out of her own history.

Unfortunately, Beth tended to protect herself by threatening separation, which on some level must have resurrected aspects from Hannah's painful early history and reinforced the story Hannah had begun to tell herself about her value and the possibility of people being there for her. Hannah, coming from her own place of fear and pain, increased the acting-out behavior that, in turn, continued to trigger her mother. These dynamics, likely operating at a non-conscious level, escalated over the years. Quite predictably, Hannah moved from defiance to lying and stealing to unmanageability, which became dangerous enough to move her to a special school in a nearby state during her teenage years. Now, in her 20s, Hannah has had one failed marriage and embarked on her second and has served in and been medically discharged from the military. She is now struggling to raise her own children.[11]

Research and theory: From foster care to adoption

The complexities of adoption are enormous. Although adoption presents a wonderful opportunity both for the adoptive family and for the adopted child, it may also expose a myriad of painful issues, including previous losses, needing resolution. The adopted child:

experiences multiple losses, though the exact combination will naturally depend on the child's individual history and the circumstances of the adoption: these include...the loss of the birth family (however bad the actual circumstances might have been); the loss of foster carers or other family carers; the loss in relation to the discontinuity of the child's "personal narrative"—the lack of the ordinary experience of a child's early history and development being known directly and held in mind by their primary attachment figures; the loss that may be involved in the painful recognition of what the child has missed in their early experience; and the loss associated with the reality that the adoptive parents may be less than the ideal parents the child might have hoped for or expected. (Hindle and Shulman 2008, pp.4–5)

One can imagine complementary experiences from the perspective of adoptive parents, particularly around loss of fertility or of previous biological—or perhaps, foster—children; carrying or holding the pain of their adoptive child's history—or carrying unanswered questions about that history; and even coming to terms with the reality that the adoptive child may not be what they hoped for or expected. Further, a particular challenge facing parents who adopt out of foster care is to understand their child's way of being in relationship and how that meshes (or doesn't) with their own relationship dynamics and attachment strategies. Not only, then, must adoptive parents cope with the possible remnants of early trauma but also they must adapt to, and quite possibly challenge, the ways their child has learned to be connected, all the while undergoing a huge family transition.

Even without the additional challenges that face adoptive families, the dynamics of parent–child relationships are indeed complex. As parents, we bring to the caregiving role our own history, whether it's a history of safety and security or a history of trauma and loss, and often we recreate aspects of our history with our children (see Chapter 6). According to Janet, Beth had suffered tremendous loss at a formative age, which most certainly left her vulnerable in ways she may not have even recognized.

Psychiatrist John Bowlby, the originator of attachment theory (see Chapter 1), discussed at length the painful nature of separation and loss on the developing psyche of the young child.[12] Indeed, even the threat of separation or loss can be overwhelming. For Hannah, with a background of early maltreatment and two separation and loss experiences (one from her birth parents and the other from Janet and Paul), it is not surprising that any threat of separation from her new adoptive family would have made her feel especially defensive. As she matured, Hannah enacted the pain she likely experienced in various ways, by acting out in anger, for example, and quite possibly by provoking the very response she feared. Unfortunately, it is likely that these "miscues" only served to further alienate Hannah's parents, who were trying to maintain some sort of stability in their home and lives.

In contrast, Ashley's experience of having parents who worked even harder to connect during the challenging times, giving her the unqualified message of "We are here, and you are worth it" (see Chapter 2), slowly overrode the deep insecurity created out of the trauma of her earliest months. Attachment researcher Mary Dozier and her colleagues have found caregiver commitment to be an important ingredient in positive development, particularly for children in the foster care system: "Perhaps just as critical as infants' expectations of whether their parent will soothe them when they are distressed...is their expectation of whether they can count on their parent's motivation to maintain a permanent relationship with them" (Dozier *et al.* 2007, p.92). Whereas the happy coincidence that Ashley's mom had also been her discharge nurse helped to cement their relationship, the tumultuous nature of Hannah's adoption— with the final custodial decision hanging in the balance—worked against an unqualified commitment from becoming established.

A story of two girls: Part 3

Reflecting over their life courses, I believe that both at the beginning and now, as Hannah and Ashley enter adulthood, the nature and quality of their relationships have been determining. Ashley's beginnings were in essence devoid of relationship. In those critical early months, her bids for connection went unheeded. It did not take her long to draw some significant conclusions about the world from her experience: that at best no one was there, at worst it was extremely dangerous. Hannah, on the other hand, learned that if you were patient and determined, your needs would be met, though life was often difficult and painful. She therefore did better through the early months and years as she knew she could find a way to keep her caregiver nearby and attentive if she tried hard enough.

As they moved into their adoptive homes, the tables turned. Hannah's sense of security was undermined by threats of abandonment, moving her into fear and preemptive acting out. Ashley's fear of abandonment, on the other hand, was slowly overridden by her family's single-minded determination and unquestionable commitment to her.

Did the struggle in finalizing Hannah's adoption move the whole family system to a place of insecurity? And, conversely, did Ashley's future family's ironic early connection to her somehow propel them into an unqualified claiming that may not have otherwise existed? We, of course, can never know the answers to these or other questions. What does seem clear, however, is that availability and predictability in relationship is a powerful positive force in the formation of healthy development across the lifespan. The presence of a caring, constant, and committed other can act both as a catalyst for early security and as an antidote to the later adverse effects of early trauma.[13]

In spite of some hurdles in navigating the world, Ashley now demonstrates a maturity and insight that is impressive. And, most surprising of all given her beginnings, she values and works to maintain the relationships in her life. I recently had a conversation with Ashley's mother. She told me that one day she asked Ashley, "What do you think my life would have been like without you?" Ashley answered, "Mom, I think you would have been lonely."[14]

Chapter 5

LUCY

We're all trapped in a body with limitations, even
the most able bodied among us. And we're all guided
by minds with limitations of their own... Our job,
regardless of our bodily circumstances, is to rise above
what holds us down, and to help others do the same.

Berg 2006, p.160

Lucy is special, but not in ways the world tends to understand, embrace, or value. Although she has acquired many labels over the years (fetal alcohol affected, bipolar disordered, autistic, attention deficit hyperactivity disordered (ADHD), oppositional defiant disordered (ODD), and so on), an accurate and complete diagnosis remains complex and largely elusive. Likewise her gifts and capacities remain mostly unseen or under-appreciated. But she has much to teach us. Every child's way of being can open doors to wisdom, compassion, and human connection. We need only to listen.

Lucy's history

Lucy was born to parents who, due to limitations of their own, were ill-equipped to provide her the care, nurturing, or even protection she required. She was hospitalized for ten days following her birth because of low muscle tone, not "knowing how to suck," not gaining weight, and jaundice. At two months of age, she was hospitalized for a week for "failure to thrive." Less than a month later at a routine checkup, it was discovered that Lucy had suffered fractures of both clavicles, several ribs, and her left tibia, apparently at the hands of her frustrated father. She was removed from the custody of her parents, and she and her mother were admitted as residential clients of The Children's Ark. In a matter of weeks, Lucy underwent surgery to repair a hole in her heart. She was not yet six months old, and already her life experiences were lining up to significantly impact both her sense of safety and her fear of abandonment: issues that would continue to follow and shape her.

It was immediately clear to us at The Children's Ark that Lucy was a kid with special needs. Her facial features suggested some as yet unnamed syndrome and her development lagged. When either upset or excited she twirled her feet and hands in circles. When angry she sometimes bit her hands or banged her head. But her smile came easily and often and charmed us all. It was also immediately clear that Lucy's mother's own needs were greater than her capacity to provide care and nurturance to her daughter. As my husband commented, "Tasha wants to be Janet's daughter more than she wants to be Lucy's mother." As a result the rest of us moved in with deliberateness to meet Lucy's many needs. I advocated for evaluations and genetic testing in an attempt to identify more precisely what her challenges might be. It was clear that her deficits were wide-ranging, and our doctor explained that she needed to remain in a very stimulating environment so that the gap between her and other children would not continue to widen.

Lucy's wisdom, in spite of her deficits, manifested early. When she was about 13 months old, her mother decided that it was time to "teach her independence." No matter what The Children's Ark staff told her about what her daughter needed, Tasha was determined that she knew best. One afternoon, when Tasha returned to The Children's Ark after being away all morning, Lucy crawled toward her excitedly, anticipating being picked up. Instead Tasha walked right past her and into the kitchen for a snack. Not easily thwarted,

Lucy turned and followed, but by the time she reached the kitchen door, Tasha was already walking past her in the other direction. This scenario was played out many times before Lucy finally gave it up. But rather than collapsing into defeat, Lucy moved toward what she needed. She clearly and decidedly "chose" me, understanding on some level that her mother was not up to the task at the moment. For several months, I became for all intents and purposes Lucy's primary caregiver. During that period of time, she demonstrated an unquestioning preference for me. After multiple interventions aimed at helping Tasha see her daughter's longing and real need for her, Tasha eventually returned her attention to nurturing her daughter, and Lucy, in turn, reclaimed her mother.

Tasha struggled on for a year at The Children's Ark and finally determined that parenting Lucy was not in her daughter's best interest, ultimately relinquishing her parental rights. As a result of the injuries he had inflicted, Lucy's father was not allowed contact with her. At 16 months, Lucy was placed with her aunt, Pam, and Pam's husband, who had been part of Lucy's caring team from the beginning. Because I had developed a relationship with the family, and because I anticipated that parenting her would prove to be a challenge, I resolved to stay involved with Lucy and her new family. My frequent visits turned to respite as Lucy began spending nights with us. Our contact was often weekly, sometimes biweekly, and remains consistent to this day, 20 years later.

The prediction of a widening gap between Lucy and her peers has proved true over the years. In addition to gross motor and social-emotional challenges, both sensory and behavioral issues have surfaced. It is as if Lucy's sensory world is so magnified and fraught with danger that survival itself is at stake. Her senses are all keen and on high alert, so that a garbage truck backing up or a darkening sky foretelling a possible thunderstorm can send her into a full-blown panic attack. Exactly when the sights, sounds, or even smells of a given environment might become intolerable to her has been frustratingly unpredictable; but once it happens, it is as if her life depends upon escape, and she becomes consumed with anticipating future disaster. Her primary defense has been to try to line up her world in a known pattern and then expend all her attention and energy in keeping it that way. Those of us in her life learned early, therefore, that the more predictable her world was—and the more she felt in control—the better she would cope.

Lucy had been spending nights with us for some time when we transitioned The Children's Ark from a residential program to a day treatment program, and my husband and I moved back to our home a few miles away. I spent months preparing Lucy for this change in her routine. I took her to visit our home, showing her where she would be sleeping on her overnights and where Paul and I would be sleeping. I talked about how everything in the room would be the same. When the time came, I carefully moved everything from her "old room" to her "new room," trying to set it up in exactly the same way. We moved the bed, bedding, stuffed animals, radio, clock, pictures, cup for water, and every other detail we could imagine was familiar to her in preparation for her first night in the new space. That first night I carefully followed our usual bedtime routine, tucked her in, kissed her, and headed for the door. Lucy immediately shot up in bed, looked frantically all around, and said, "Where is my blue glass?!" Even with my careful, conscientious preparation, I had inadvertently left beside her bed a little plastic *red* cup of water, instead of the usual blue!

On another occasion I took her to a local school playground so she could get some fresh air and run off a little excess energy. As I sat on a beam in the center of the play structure, she ran hither and yon testing her underdeveloped skills on various climbing and swinging apparatus, returning with regularity to check in with me. As she turned her focus to a jungle gym, struggling to climb beyond the first rung, I moved to the platform on the top so that I could be closer to supervise and encourage her efforts. As she moved around the structure in search of an easier toe hold, she kept saying to me, "Move over there," indicating with her hand to move to the right and then back to the left. Though I continued to try to accommodate her, she clearly became more and more agitated by my apparent inability to understand precisely where she wanted me to be. Finally, after many attempts, she managed to climb to a spot up near the top, just a foot or so from where I was. She looked at me with determination, patted a specific spot on the platform just inches from where I sat, and said, "Sit here, so I feel safe."

Although Lucy looked forward to our overnights, and the routine we had developed helped things run smoothly, her hypersensitivity and hypervigilance continued to invade her every experience. On one of our weekend overnights, rain had been forecast. Lucy was already anxious in anticipation of a storm. Just as I seemed to have her settled, the windows began rattling slightly. Lucy shot up and began escalating in fear. No matter how many times I explained that it was just the wind, that nothing bad was going to happen, and that she was safe, each round of rattling sent her further and further out of control. It was already very late, too late I felt to take her home. Finally, she was able to calm enough to sit on her futon holding tightly to her knees folded into her chest, occasionally crying softly. Each time the windows rattled she cried out my name and shook visibly. I remember looking at the clock at one point, noting that it was 2:00 a.m. and thinking what a long night this was going to be.

Then out of some reserve deep within her, Lucy suddenly found the energy and wisdom to begin offering solutions: strategies of survival. First, she asked me if the windows were all locked and could we check them? When affirming that all were secure did nothing to mitigate the rattling, she suggested moving the CD player in closer and turning up the music. When that also failed to assuage her terror, she begged to move us down two floors to the TV room. So, even as dawn threatened to break, we dragged futons, quilts, pillows, stuffed animals, and the CD player down two flights of stairs to a basement room in which indeed the windows did not rattle. Camped out anew, and with the music playing and the fire going in the fireplace, we both fell into a deep sleep. Upon awakening and reflecting on the night's events, I got in touch for the first time with what is must be like to live in Lucy's body and felt tremendous admiration for her ability to summon enough regulation, amidst circumstances that she surely experienced as terrorizing, to think her way to an answer.

Aside from this encounter with the weather, there was only one incident in all of these 20-plus years during which I felt that Lucy spiraled out of control in my presence, in spite of her escalating difficulties at home and at school. Lucy was particularly fond of the daughter of another former Ark client. Kendra is younger than Lucy, and with issues of her own, but Lucy worked hard to stay connected and asked about her often. When Lucy was 13, Kendra and her mother had just moved back to Spokane from the Seattle area. Lucy was anxious to see them, so I arranged for both Lucy and Kendra to spend the night. The early part of the evening went well, but as bedtime approached Kendra began to deteriorate emotionally. Unfortunately, she had just lost a beloved uncle in a tragic accident, and, in retrospect, it was probably too soon for her to be away from her mother. After assessing the situation, I decided that Kendra needed to go home and so called her mother to come get her. It did not take Lucy long to also want to go home. I knew, however, that Lucy's mother was unavailable—in fact, not even home—so I told her she would have to stay with me.

Almost instantaneously, Lucy escalated out of control. Immediately, she was in my face shouting and demanding to be taken home. She paced frantically about the room, stopping on occasion to kick her shoes off into the wall. Sometimes instead of shouting in my face, Lucy would drop her voice to a near whisper and hurl off a string of expletives. On occasion she took herself into the bathroom where she paced about frantically, whirling her arms in high anxiety. Several times she placed one hand right next to my face and with the other hand slapped hard the open palm, sending an awful smacking sound ricocheting through the room. At one point Paul came rushing in, afraid that she had hit me. I looked at him with as much calm as I could muster and said, "I am fine. Please leave the room." My fear was that his presence, especially if angry, would only escalate her further. I also feared that he would not be able to contain her without hurting her. Once, in a poignant moment revealing her underlying fear, Lucy stood way across the room from me and mumbled in a decidedly "little girl" voice, "You are going to leave me, aren't you?"

At 13 years old Lucy was already taller than me and certainly outweighed me. I knew at every moment that if she really went over the top and lost control completely, she could do some real damage. I also learned very fast that escalating at all myself—or even meeting her intensity—pushed her up quickly. I therefore stayed mainly at my desk, talking soothingly to her in a low, calming voice. I told her that I could not take her home, but that I would be happy to sit with her, to hold her, to lie down with her. I told her I would *not* leave her. I offered her a doll, a favorite blanket, all to no avail. Finally, after three excruciatingly tense hours, she lay down on the floor and fell into an exhausted sleep.

In the morning Lucy would not talk to me nor look at me during breakfast or on the ride home. I told her that what had happened the night before was not her fault and nothing to be ashamed of. The grownups in her life had just not yet found a way to help her calm down when she found herself in such an upset state. Once home, Lucy jumped out of the car and ran to her room. I explained to Pam what had happened. After I returned home, it was only a matter of minutes before Pam called and told me that I wouldn't believe what Lucy had just said to her. When she finally gathered herself enough to come out of her room and join her mother, Lucy had said, "I think I broke Janet's heart."

Although experiencing Lucy's rage was stunning and frightening, what I was really struck by was how hard she was working as she spun out of control. I never lost touch through every agonizing moment with the knowledge certain that Lucy did not want to hurt me and was fighting with every ounce of her strength and every weapon in her arsenal *not* to touch me. My compassion for her struggle was profound.

Our ongoing relationship

During our evenings and overnights together, I try to follow Lucy's lead, engaging in activities that will give her moments of delight and happy memories to savor. As is so often my experience with children, it is not unusual for her to teach me more than I teach her and to bring me as much delight as I bring her.

We almost always eat a meal out and on occasion take in a movie. She often initiates a creative plan of her own. Once around the Thanksgiving holidays, she asked if we could have dinner at her friend's church. It was a special holiday celebration dinner, she said. Two things I know about Lucy are that she sometimes doesn't have all the information, or at least doesn't have it all straight, and that she is very persistent and stubborn. This particular time I decided to put the responsibility on her for having all the information rather than trying to talk her out of her request. I told her that if she would get the address and write it down, we could drive by and check it out. I have to confess that I was counting on her not being able to obtain an accurate address or forgetting altogether, as Thanksgiving dinner at some random church was not my idea of a good time.

As soon as she climbed into my car, however, Lucy handed me the address written on a small piece of paper. Reluctantly, I headed across town, still counting on the possibility that she had the address wrong, or certainly that she had not coordinated with her friend. But, as soon as we were within a block of the address, I saw it: a huge sign proclaiming "Free Thanksgiving dinner. Welcome!" "Let's go, let's go," Lucy shrieked. "Wait a moment." I hesitated, still hoping for a reprieve. "Call your friend and see if she is here," I said, handing Lucy my cell phone. As soon as Lucy called, her friend came bounding out of the basement door at the back of the church, and the die was cast.

As we made our way toward the big basement room from which loud and boisterous noise was emanating, fear and anxiety had taken ahold of me. Walking into a roomful of people I did not know and joining their celebration suddenly felt overwhelmingly uncomfortable and challenging to me. Lucy, on the other hand—despite her tendency toward sensory overload—charged ahead with enthusiasm and joy, never doubting for a moment that she would be welcomed and embraced. Slowly and cautiously on a cold November night among total strangers, I walked into the midst of the sights, sounds, and smells of warmth and open-hearted acceptance. It was a diverse group. There were men and women who appeared to be homeless, wearing torn clothing and dirty from a life on the streets. There were young couples with numerous kids hanging off every lap. There were teenagers dressed in black and draped in chains. And there were two transgendered individuals done up in style complete with elaborate yellow and pink flowered hats. The room was packed, every table full and bulging at the seams. A table overladen with turkey and all the fixings stood at one end of the room, a Christian rock band shaking the rafters at the other.

As I wound my way through the maze, trying to keep track of Lucy's whereabouts, smiling faces turned to greet me, hands came up to meet mine. I was aware almost immediately of the tension in my body dissolving, the fear dissipating, and my heart softening and opening. It was as if the spirit of celebration and community that filled every inch of that room flowed into my body and transported me into a new, totally consuming, and amazingly comfortable world. A few hours later as Lucy, her friend (who was joining us for the rest of the evening), and I made our way back out into the cold and dark, I realized that Lucy had this night, in her naïve and unabashed enthusiasm, handed me a gift.

Perhaps the most touching experience with Lucy on an outing, however, was the afternoon we went to the amusement park. I resisted with every fiber of my being spending a day climbing on and off carnival rides and walking endlessly through crowds of overstimulated children and grumpy adults. But again my determination to offer Lucy some fun and happiness prevailed, and I devoted a weekend afternoon and evening to Silverwood, our local amusement park. By now I understood that Lucy would not tolerate me standing by and watching, so rather than thinking I could escape the rides, I was instead hanging onto the hope that we would avoid the bigger, more dramatic ones because of Lucy's fear and anxiety. I did not anticipate that such movement through space was actually soothing to Lucy with her funky vestibular system; in fact, in her mind the wilder, the better!

Faced with each new ride, each one more exciting than the last, I made a valiant attempt to distract Lucy or at least talk her out of going. But each time she not only stood firm but also determined to somehow assuage my fears. She assured me I could conquer them. She promised me the rides were safe. She offered to hold my hand and suggested that I close my eyes. And each time, with Lucy gently guiding and soothing me, I climbed once more into a tiny seat in a tiny box or car, swallowed my skepticism and discomfort, and abandoned myself to the experience. Later as we sat eating in a restaurant in the middle of the amusement park, I reflected on the day. How not only happy but also capable and competent Lucy seemed. How seamlessly and proudly she stepped up to help me overcome the same kind of irrational fears that normally hijacked her own experience. And how attuned she was to my emotional state. For just this one afternoon, we stepped into each other's shoes.

Lucy's future

There is no question that Lucy faces challenges in every realm of her life: physical, sensory, cognitive, social, emotional, and behavioral. Life will always be a struggle for her; but, based on my considerable experience with her over the last 20-plus years, I find her also to have incredible strengths. How we understand her struggles, and whether we appreciate her strengths, will have a tremendous impact on Lucy's future.

Consider, for instance, her sensory difficulties. Lucy's problems with sensory processing and integration distort her perceptions: how she sees the world and herself in it; how she interprets the behavior of others and therefore what she anticipates; how she moves in space; how she learns; how she communicates. Understanding how this is true for Lucy can inform us rather than limit her if we are willing to spend the time and energy it takes to know and adapt to her. It can enlighten us and direct how we see her and how we talk to her, what we expect of her and how we support her. Lucy herself can help and guide us.

Lucy's "flat" affective presentation in the face of emotion, in my experience, conceals a wealth of feeling. My experience with her is not that she cannot resonate with others' feelings—that she lacks empathy—but rather that she sometimes has difficulty recognizing or tracking the emotional states of others. When she does notice, or is made aware of, others' feelings, however, she cares a great deal. She does not always grasp the relationship "rules" or social mandates that organize most human interactions, and so her behavior often feels "off" or out of the norm. On the other hand, her unsophisticated, innocent approach to life allows her to walk into situations and relationships undefended, anticipating acceptance, in a way many of us often guard ourselves against out of skepticism and imagined fears.

Although interacting with Lucy is often awkward, she clearly has the capacity to be in relationship. In relationship with Paul and me, she has demonstrated the ability to communicate, negotiate, compromise, and to some degree regulate and integrate her emotional experience in order to stay connected. She clearly holds us in her heart and mind[1] when we are not together and can put our needs ahead of her own. Recently, when I called to finalize our scheduled overnight, Lucy asked in an apologetic tone if we could just visit without the overnight. After assuring her that I would always let her choose, I asked why she did not want to spend the night. Lucy then talked to me about how they were struggling to adjust a new medication and that she had been suffering from nightmares probably related to the current dosage. "Sometimes the screaming is inside my head," she described, "and sometimes the screaming is outside my head." She was willing to forgo her desire to spend the night in order not to risk a rupture in our relationship. She also feels remorse or regret when she feels that such a rupture may have occurred, as demonstrated earlier when she feared she had broken my heart.

I have been particularly touched by Lucy's attempts to make sense of her history and forge a future. She talks to me often about the Ark and her time there. She has reconnected with Tasha, her birth mother, and has established a relationship with her half-sister. She keeps and cherishes photo albums of her early years.

At 15, Lucy was moved into a group home. Even though this decision was made out of concern for Lucy's best interests, and with much soul searching and heartache, Lucy surely must have experienced it as yet another abandonment. She was sad, she was angry, she was depressed; but ultimately she put her mind to finding answers to survive and even thrive. She always manages to attach to people in her life in a way that elicits affection and devotion. Over time she has inspired a connection with and investment from the staff at her group home, just as she did with me at 14 months of age. She continues to demonstrate both the wisdom to recognize her need for security and the ability to seek relationship where she feels embraced.

I believe that Lucy, like all children, wants nothing more than to please the important adults in her life. She works hard to do the very best she can; and when things go awry, she never wants to be doing what she is doing. My wish for her is that we—the adults— find a better way to help her manage when self-regulation is beyond her reach. My wish is that we come to understand that it's not about "motivating" her to somehow "do better" in those moments, but that it is about staying in relationship with her no matter what. In other words, we want to help her learn to manage those things that will get her in trouble in the world or be dangerous to her while encouraging her healthy relationship-seeking behavior. It is telling, I think, that the trigger for Lucy's most significant "meltdown" at the group home, one which required police intervention, involved not being told that a group home staff member was leaving. Lucy, like all of us, is hardwired for relationship. She wants what we all want: intimate connection to other human beings. This is perhaps her greatest lesson to us: the knowledge that we are all more alike than different, no matter what our particular "disability."

Last summer was a busy one for me, with lots of traveling. One day when I was scheduled for an overnight visit with Lucy after having not seen her for a month, she called me early in the morning and said, "Janet, I was wondering if maybe you could come earlier today. I am empty." "Empty?" I replied. "What do you mean, Lucy—that you are feeling sad?" "Empty means I miss you," she replied. And I was struck once more at how eloquently Lucy speaks for us all.

Research and theory: Children with special needs in foster care

Referred to by advocacy groups as "the forgotten children," young people with special needs who are also in foster care represent a uniquely vulnerable population (United Cerebral Palsy and Children's Rights 2006, p.1). Infants and toddlers with special needs are at higher risk of being maltreated to begin with. They are also more likely to be removed from their parents and less likely to be reunified. Compared to their non-disabled peers in foster care, they experience higher rates of re-entry into care and spend longer time in care, with more placement instability. They are more likely to live in group or institutional care and are less likely to move into families. Following discharge from foster care, they are more likely to face homelessness, substance abuse, unemployment, violent or sexual assault, and a host of other concerns.[2]

By comparison, Lucy was fortunate; she was not, nor will she be, forgotten. Through her family's participation in The Children's Ark, she received comprehensive and coordinated services. She remained in one foster care environment until a permanency plan was developed. She now resides in a small, family-oriented group living situation, remains connected to her family and has forged significant, long-term relationships with people who are committed to her well-being. Her relationship with Janet continues to this day.

The challenges facing our overburdened child welfare systems are many. They are multiplied when trying to provide services to infants and children with disabilities. Front-line workers are insufficiently trained to accurately identify and assess disabilities, which compromises service provision from the start. Recruiting foster parents and providing them with the necessary training and support to adequately care for children with special needs remains a formidable challenge. Other concerns include the lack of access to quality health care, the lack of services tailored to individual needs, and delays in appropriate school placement, which further derail educational opportunities.[3] Additionally, a fundamental problem with the coordination of services leads to fragmented care; in the words of one advocacy group, "These gaps can result in poor health and well-being outcomes for nondisabled children in foster care and have the potential to be catastrophic for children and youth with disabilities in foster care" (United Cerebral Palsy and Children's Rights 2006, p.7). Underlying all of these issues, some argue, is a societal bias against individuals with disabilities.[4]

Strategies for improving child welfare services to children with special needs include efforts to build awareness of and reduce bias against individuals with disabilities; instituting comprehensive health care screening within 30 days of placement; better recruitment, training, and support of foster families; and stronger family preservation initiatives.[5] Every Child, Inc. is an advocacy group concerned about children with developmental disabilities growing up "in facilities instead of families" (Every Child, Inc. n.d.). Their first priority is to support families to allow them to continue to nurture children with special needs at home whenever possible. When children cannot be cared for at home, Every Child, Inc. works to recruit families in the community who, with training and support, can fill that gap.

Not only are infants and toddlers with special needs at higher risk of being maltreated, but also maltreatment causes or exacerbates certain disabilities. In fact, Nancy Rosenau, an

Executive Director of Every Child, Inc., recognized that "the list of behavioral consequences of maltreatment and attachment loss is suspiciously similar to the descriptions of many children with disabilities." She then asked, "If the behavior is assumed to be a manifestation of a disability rather than a traumatic experience, will we provide the right response?" (2005/06, p.3). Relatedly, one study found that children with special needs who enter the foster care system already have been faced with, on average, "14 different environmental, social, biological, and psychological risk factors before coming into care" (as cited in United Cerebral Palsy and Children's Rights 2006, p.5).

Children with disabilities have special needs, but they also have all of the regular needs of their non-disabled counterparts. As we discuss throughout this book, critical to all children is the need for relationship; the need to be connected, valued, and understood. These needs are sometimes overlooked or discounted in children with disabilities, particularly those who are viewed as deficient in social skills or who are placed in large, impersonal institutional care. In fact, behavioral approaches, which often focus on the modification of discrete, functional behaviors (e.g. increasing eye contact), have dominated the treatment landscape for children with special needs, whereas interventions described as relationship-based have received much less attention.[6]

Some may interpret Janet's decision to stay with Lucy when she had a significant, rage-filled melt-down as taking a risk. For Janet, it was the only way. Indeed, Lucy's comment in the midst of her meltdown, "You're going to leave me, aren't you?" gave away her underlying fear and tremendous vulnerability. Janet's summary of what she believes is going on for Lucy in these kinds of moments bears repeating here:

> She works hard to do the very best she can; and when things go awry, she never wants to be doing what she is doing. My wish for her is that we—the adults—find a better way to help her manage when self-regulation is beyond her reach. My wish

is that we come to understand that it's not about "motivating" her to somehow "do better" in those moments, but that it is about staying in relationship with her no matter what. In other words, we want to help her learn to manage those things that will get her in trouble in the world or be dangerous to her, while encouraging her healthy relationship-seeking behavior.

Understanding the fundamental attachment needs of all children, Nancy Rosenau echoes Janet's wisdom:

> Our collective response to children with disabilities is too frequently placement in settings to get "specialized treatment" to prepare them for community life. Treatment methodologies are written so they can be implemented by interchangeable staff. Treatment is seen as modifying the behavior of the child, rather than modifying the relationships available to the child. The relationships children need are not interchangeable, but rather require the security of a unique attachment to heal wounds of separation and maltreatment. The answer is not preparing for family life and the relationships it offers—the answer *is* family life and the relationships it offers. (2005/06, p.3)

A relationship-based way of proceeding in our work with all children and families in foster care is not only more humane but— as we argue—is also likely to be more effective. This is especially true for children who struggle with relationships, whether due to trauma or disability or both.

Chapter 6

DESIRAE AND HER CHILDREN

Discouraging reunification[1]

One September, in the early years of the residential program, a young woman showed up on our doorstep. She had just given birth to her second child, who had been removed from her custody because of prenatal drug exposure. She was currently in drug treatment and desperate to reunify with both her newborn and her older son, also in foster care. Because she could reside full-time with her newborn while participating in services, The Children's Ark was an attractive option. Typically, however, families were referred to the Ark by the Department of Social and Health Services. The kind of initiative that this young woman demonstrated by arriving without a referral was unusual, and perhaps our first hint that she had courage and wisdom well beyond her 17 years, buried beneath her tough exterior.

Desirae had a familiar history. She had been physically and sexually abused as a child and had been in and out of foster care herself. Her childhood experience of violence, deprivation, and abandonment had already played out in dramatic ways in her life. After being found guilty of second-degree manslaughter following the death of a fellow gang member when she was just 12 years old, she had served time in a lockup facility and was still on probation. Her first son, Isaac, was removed from her care when he was a toddler after he swallowed cocaine. When we met Desirae, Isaac was two years old and living in a local foster home. Desirae's second son, David, was yet a newborn, and it was with him that she requested entry to The Children's Ark.

Desirae and David moved into the Ark, together, a few weeks after she first knocked on our door. It was soon clear that Desirae was suffering from depression, struggling to bond with her infant son, and preoccupied with her older son. She was resistant, defensive, cold, and harsh, both with her baby and with the other parents and staff. Her tendency toward chaos and disorganization was problematic, and she and I were constantly in conflict as I struggled to find a way to connect with and help her.

Isaac began visits shortly after Desirae and David entered The Children's Ark. Under constant pressure from Desirae to allow him to join her, we relented in the early spring and transitioned Isaac into the Ark full-time. In retrospect it was probably much too early to include him, and things deteriorated quickly with Isaac also in the house. Desirae was stressed beyond her coping abilities trying to manage two children, go to school, and maintain even minimal living skills in the Ark environment. On May 1, she negotiated an exit. Isaac returned to his former foster home, David stayed on in care with us, and Desirae moved in with her boyfriend.

Over the next five months, we cared for David while trying to inform those in charge of this family's future what we had learned during our seven months living with them. In order to meet the emotional needs of her children, Desirae first had to learn how to manage her own emotions. Unfortunately and tragically, Desirae's model of herself in relationship was based on experiences with her own caregivers, characterized by abandonment, insensitivity, devaluation, bullying/belittling, and aggression. She thus had learned that the experience of being attached is unpredictable, chaotic, frightening, and dangerous. As she then entered into relationship with her children, these same dynamics played out.

Abandonment, or at least avoidance, was an issue from the beginning with David. There was little interaction between them.

She often placed him facing away from her, sat with her back to him, and spent long periods of time not speaking to him. She seemed to have the most difficulty when he needed her the most. The first night that Isaac spent at the Ark (after being in foster care for more than a year), Desirae took free time and was gone for the evening, leaving Isaac without her in his new surroundings.

Desirae devalued, bullied, and belittled both children in many ways. She carried David under her arm like a football even when he was a very small infant. She resisted soothing him when he was distressed. She mocked and teased him, once reportedly blowing a toy horn loudly in his ear and laughing at his frightened response. Desirae engaged in derisive name calling and frequently yelled at both boys. This alternated with periods in which she was flamboyantly affectionate, kissing them in a way that was overwhelming and intrusive.

Desirae's aggression toward both boys escalated as her confusing and sometimes frightening behavior (e.g. loud voice, threatening posture, sudden mood shifts) and failure to set appropriate and consistent limits involved them in frequent power struggles. Isaac's bedtime was a good example. Her lack of consistency coupled with a need to be obeyed led to a nightly screaming match. One incident of striking Isaac was reported to CPS. We then entered into a contract to stop the verbal and physical aggression and instituted a policy requiring continual supervision, a step we felt necessary to ensure the safety of the children.

Desirae's developing relationship with her children, then, mirrored her own experience in relationship with a caregiver. Her children also came to expect that closeness to her was unpredictable, chaotic, and often frightening. It was our opinion that Desirae would not be able to parent her children safely, and so we were persistent in discouraging reunification.

I believe that what happened to Desirae at The Children's Ark is that she became overwhelmed and "hit the wall," not only as a result of the circumstances of her life but also as she began to come to grips with her past in a way that exposed the pain of her own internal working model. She was perhaps not yet ready to confront that pain. It was our belief that if Desirae was ever to have access to her full potential as a parent she still needed to explore more completely her past relationships with caregivers and the role they played in her own emotional development. She needed to develop enough trust to allow her defensive armor to soften. She needed to grieve her pain and losses and find some resolution. All of that we knew takes time.

In spite of our concerns, after 12 months with us, 13-month-old David was returned to Desirae's custody and care, along with Isaac. Unbeknownst to us, she was pregnant when she left the Ark and so her life became even more complicated. She married her boyfriend and soon was also parenting both of his children from a previous relationship. The State of Washington then placed in their custody her sister's three children, so suddenly there were eight.

Desirae and her husband struggled over the years to create and maintain a home for themselves and the children, participating in drug treatment, parenting classes, and family preservation services. Sometimes the family was split up with some of the children living with relatives. Sometimes Child Protective Services was just a half step behind. Always they flirted with addiction, homelessness, poverty, and simply being overwhelmed by life.

Although we worked hard to discourage reunification after Desirae left The Children's Ark, we worked equally hard to stay in relationship with her, and not ambush, mislead, or abandon her. I visited occasionally during the first two years or so when I was able to keep track of an address. On occasion, they would contact us, usually when their backs were against the wall. Then one Halloween, Desirae, her husband, and all of the children in costume arrived on our doorstep, and thus began a tradition of a visit each year, something we looked forward to immensely. Over the years, we noticed that—in spite of their continuing struggles—Desirae and her husband were becoming more attuned to, and more sensitive and affectionate with the children, and the children were less chaotic, calmer, and more direct about their emotional needs.

Each Halloween we hugged them and told them to come and visit anytime. Each year they came only at Halloween. Then in January of 2010, in a follow-up to a promise for pictures of David in his football uniform, I received an email from Desirae, updating us on the children. Her "love you guys lots" salutation prompted a response from me including, "I think about you with such admiration, Desirae; you have hung in for yourself and these kids with such strength and courage and wisdom against so many odds at such a young age. I truly stand in awe." Several emails later, we set up a lunch during which we discussed her time at The Children's Ark, the events of the intervening years, and lessons learned.

The lessons[2]

Lesson 1: Safe parenting is not an information issue, but rather an emotional integration issue

Desirae came to us a charming, intelligent, strong, insightful young woman, who knew that hitting and yelling were not the way she wanted to parent. And yet, as her time at The Children's Ark demonstrated, she repeated with her own children many of the behaviors she herself experienced as a child. She was somehow unable to translate her insight into action but instead retreated into defensive withdrawal or hostile self-reliance. Clearly Desirae possessed a softer, more sensitive, vulnerable side. The challenge was in overcoming her fear of parenting from that sensitive place inside of herself. When faced with her children's need for open-hearted tenderness, whenever they cried out to be seen and held, Desirae's own emotional deprivation and longing were triggered. The pain was then too deep, the risk too great. Her only option was to protect her own heart.

What she needed was not instructions regarding the proper way to interact with children but some experience herself of how security felt. We cannot give our children what we have never experienced, partly because we cannot bear to acknowledge what we did not have and our yearning for it, and partly because only in receiving security are we able to open the heart enough to give it. So what Desirae needed were repeated overriding experiences during which she felt all the nurturing care her childhood lacked. She needed these experiences long enough to begin to trust them, to let them in. Only then would she be able to nurture her children in the same way. Providing her with opportunities to grieve what she did not get would also be essential in helping her integrate her own painful experience enough to operate from the more positive feelings generated by her new relationships. Desirae was able to begin this process at The Children's Ark, and, although she ended her work with us prematurely, her experience at the Ark gave her a foundation on which she was able to build.

Lesson 2: Being engaged in a caring, long-term relationship within the safety of a holding environment optimizes growth and change

> *One moment of unconditional love may call into question*
> *a lifetime of feeling unworthy and invalidated.*
>
> *Brach 2003, p.272*

Desirae, like all of us, seeks connection; even while she resists it. We all develop, and can change, within the context of relationship. In order to begin to trust new transforming relationships, however, or to embark on the important work of grieving what we did not have, we require a reliable, safe haven or holding environment.[3] Until we feel the safety of an environment that can contain the vulnerability of everything we think, feel, and are, we will not come out from behind our protective walls.

Though my relationship with Desirae was conflicted, each of us held onto a strong enough thread to keep the connection alive. Even as we fought reunification, we were careful to maintain enough relationship with Desirae that she always knew we were available to her and that our care for her was unconditional. For her part, Desirae contacted us just enough to stay "on our radar." I remember, for instance, a call from her several years after her exit from the Ark asking us how to cook an artichoke. For Desirae, maintaining connection with a nurturing other had never proved a satisfactory, or even necessarily safe, endeavor. To trust us enough to stay in any kind of contact, particularly given our determination to prevent her from having custody of her children, was in reality a huge display of faith on her part despite the seemingly fragile and tenuous nature of the connection. In the end, that thread of relationship was enough to make it possible for us to come together again in a significant way. When we did meet for lunch, Desirae talked, with warmth and wisdom, about how all we had to offer her at The Children's Ark was going in at some level, but she was just too overwhelmed in the moment to use it. She talked about knowing always that everything we did and everything we said, we did and said out of love for her and her children. She understood too that, even when she couldn't hear it, we cared about her. All knowledge that she could hold—because there was "enough" relationship—until she was in a place where she could access it, articulate it, and act on it.

Desirae also talked about how upon leaving the Ark she had to keep all that she had "learned" tucked away behind her tough, self-reliant front until she had tried many parenting "strategies" and had become more grounded. Then, years down the road, as she watched others all around her parent from defended, fearful places, she kept hearing our voices and could finally open herself up to the tender, real place in herself that knew what to do. What she was finally able to do, in essence, was meet her children's vulnerability with her own.

*Lesson 3: Meeting the needs of children and families
at risk requires an ability to hold with compassion
the ambiguity of good people doing bad things*

How easy it is to reach out to and love a battered baby; how much harder to hold compassion for the batterer. No matter how angry and frustrated the cruelty human beings inflict upon one another makes us, without the compassion that understanding another's pain brings, we can be of no help to anyone, including the children. Living with Desirae's abandoning, belittling, insensitive, devaluing, and aggressive behavior toward her children was never easy, making us want to scream out with frequency, "STOP IT!" As the stories of her childhood began to unfold, however, and her pain and fears were revealed, our hearts began to open in understanding and compassion.

Over one of the Christmas holidays at The Children's Ark, the mothers were sharing stories. Desirae started talking about how many agencies "adopted" her family at Christmas when she was little, and how as each stranger arrived bearing gifts, the pile of toys and goodies under the tree grew larger and larger. But then as her mother, who was an addict, fell into more depression and desperation—succumbing to her own painful ghosts from the past—the pile began diminishing. As Christmas approached, Desirae witnessed kids in the neighborhood riding "her" bike and playing with "her" doll. Tears rose in Desirae's eyes as she described the shame, humiliation, and deep pain of her mother putting her next "fix" before her children.

Suddenly, instead of wanting to respond with "STOP IT!" we were thinking, "OF COURSE." As Desirae was faced with her children's genuine need to be met and embraced, she could only be plummeted into grief and despair regarding her own unmet needs. In order to survive, she chose to protect and defend, at great cost to herself and her children.

Having compassion does not mean, however, condoning behavior that harms children, any more than understanding the genuine need behind children's difficult behavior means condoning their misbehavior. Having compassion also does not necessarily mean recommending that families be reunited. Compassion requires facing the truth. We did not support Desirae's children being returned to her, but we were honest with Desirae about what we were doing and why. We were clear also that we cared about her as well as her children, and that our position in no way diminished our care and concern for her. She was, in our opinion, just not ready. She had more work to do.

Lesson 4: Real change takes time

The walls that take a lifetime to build up, also take time to dismantle; there are no "quick fixes" or easy roads. The challenge, of course, is to give families the time they need—and deserve—to do the work, while not leaving children in limbo for too long. At our lunch Desirae talked about how it took time: time to try other, easier routes; time for life to get manageable enough to access and use her knowledge; time to allow herself to work through the pain and grief of her own experience so that her sense of self was more integrated; time to let fall her carefully constructed defenses enough that she could operate from a softened, opened heart; and so on. Anything less time consuming would probably have been compliance, and thus transparent and transient. In essence what Desirae was talking about was the beginning of a "rewiring" of her way of seeing the world and herself in it, giving her access to her full potential as a parent.

The implications

Desirae's story illustrates a number of implications for policy. These are discussed in more detail in Part 2 of this book but are worth mentioning here. How do we reconcile the need for timely resolutions for children with the time it takes parents to do the work they need, and should be allowed, to do, all within the constraints of an overwrought system? There are no simple or easy solutions, but there are things each of us can do to render interventions with fragile families both more nurturing and more effective.

First, the best interests of the children must always lead. In Desirae's case, decisions were too often made around the rights and perceived best interest of Desirae, not her children. Additionally, we must do a better job of considering the bigger picture in which children exist. Abuse and neglect do not just impact children, they impact whole families, and sometimes multiple families. Was it really in Desirae's best interest to return her children prior to the completion of her treatment, further burden her with the care and custody of her sister's children, and then in essence abandon her? Until we embrace the entire family unit, with creativity and compassion, we are not really helping anyone and in some cases are adding to the harm.

Embracing the whole family means treating the whole family. As stated in Rickie's story (Chapter 1), treatment needs to be centered upon the relationships: parents and children together. Really serving children may mean offering services to them, both with their birth parents and with their foster parents. Children will resolve and heal optimally if *all* of those with whom they are in relationship, past and present, are on board and aware of their own contributions to the relationship dynamics. The loss of the foster caregivers for both children when Desirae left the Ark was a significant blow both to Desirae and to her children. If those relationships had been encouraged to continue instead of represented as adversarial, how much smoother might the eventual transition home have been? Foster families and relatives can often be the best resource for a family in crisis. Had Desirae and I not been able to tolerate each other's imperfections enough to stay connected over time (in spite of the system's attempts to keep us apart), she would never have been able to use what The Children's Ark had to offer her.

Also in the interest of promoting meaningful change within the context of safe, stable relationship, we should strive to minimize changes in social workers, therapists, and other treatment providers during the course of a family's involvement in the system. Parents should be discouraged from treatment "shopping," except in the case of a truly inappropriate match. In Desirae's case, not only did treatment providers change but also several gaps in caseworkers allowed an advocacy group to take a stronger role in decision making than they were authorized to provide, which ultimately shifted the process toward reunification, despite our deep concerns.

Just as Desirae maintained enough connection to ultimately access the softer, wiser part of herself, so David held, on some level, the "knowing" of another way to be in relationship. One day, about two years after the family had left The Children's Ark, I encountered

Desirae, David, and the new sibling (who was now two years old) at a nearby park. David was playing in the wading pool. Desirae called him over to say hello to me. Quite appropriately, he first peeked out from behind his mother, then ran off to play on the climbing equipment with his sister. As I left the park, I walked by where David was playing up on a platform and stood eyeball to eyeball with him. I said hello to his sister, tousled her hair, and remarked, "You don't know me, do you?" as she stared at me with a bit of apprehension. David, however, was staring intently into my eyes. I said quietly, "But you do, don't you?" David nodded, slowly, almost imperceptibly, without taking his eyes off me. Finally, he fell into my arms and held on tight and long. Even after two years, something in his deeply rooted, perhaps unconscious, memory system allowed him to trust the safety and connection in my arms. That moment in the park floated through my mind some time later as I stood with Desirae on the sidelines of the then-14-year-old David's football game, cheering him on.

Research and theory: The intergenerational transmission of caregiving

"Shark music" was the metaphor developed by our Circle of Security colleagues to describe the psychological warning signals that get in the way of sensitive and responsive caregiving (Powell et al. 2014, p.82; see Chapter 3). These warning signals are thought to be produced by unconscious memories of parents' own unmet needs, deeply rooted in parents' internal working models. For example, parents whose attachment needs were rejected by their own caregivers may, in turn, feel uncomfortable or unconsciously threatened by their infants' attachment needs and may find themselves unknowingly perpetuating the rejection that they, themselves, experienced.

Selma Fraiberg, a child psychotherapist, called the unwanted influences from our past "ghosts in the nursery." She and her colleagues described these ghosts as particularly influential when they have "established their residence" over several generations:

The baby in these families is burdened by the oppressive past of his parents from the moment he enters the world. The parent, it seems, is condemned to repeat the tragedy of his childhood with his own baby in terrible and exacting detail. (Fraiberg, Adelson, and Shapiro 1975, p.388)

Their clinical research indicated that the isolation of and lack of access to painful emotion was especially predictive of the transmission of maltreatment. Parents could often recall details of the abuse experienced but until they were also able to remember and regulate the accompanying emotions—the terror, helplessness, shame, and so forth—they seemed doomed to repeat the past.

Research from an attachment theory perspective offers further understanding of the subtle psychological forces involved in the transmission of caregiving from one generation to the next. Mary Main and her colleagues, the same researchers who identified disorganized attachment (see Chapter 3), studied adult attachment and the connections between parents' own attachment representations and their children's attachment relationships with them. Using the Adult Attachment Interview (AAI), an interview they developed to identify parents' "current state of mind with respect to attachment," Main identified four patterns of adult attachment. These adult attachment classifications were found to be highly predictive of the parent–child attachment relationship in the next generation. In other words, how parents recalled their early attachment experiences, including memories of loss and trauma, predicted the quality of attachment they established with their own children.

Caregivers who valued attachment relationships, had resolved negative past issues with important attachment figures, and who presented coherent and believable interview narratives were described as *secure or autonomous* and tended to have children who were also secure. Parents who had limited access to attachment-related memories and tended to devalue attachment relationships (described as *dismissing with respect to attachment*) tended to have children classified as anxious-avoidant, and parents who were overwhelmed by attachment-related memories and remained caught up and sometimes angry about their early attachment relationships (identified as *preoccupied with respect to attachment*) tended to have children classified as anxious-resistant.

A fourth pattern was also observed—one that forecast disorganized attachment. Some parents talked about loss, abuse, or other trauma, experiences that would have been overwhelming to their early attachment systems. It was not the experiences, themselves, that predicted a deeply insecure state of mind; instead it was whether or not parents had come to terms with these early events, whether as older children or adults they had been able to develop an integrated and coherent understanding of their experience. Main and her colleagues identified this fourth pattern as "unresolved with respect to loss or trauma," and that unresolved state of mind was a powerful predictor of disorganized attachment.

Presumably parents' states of mind with respect to attachment are related to parent–child attachment in the next generation primarily through the parents' caregiving behaviors.[4] Researchers have, in fact, found that parents with unresolved states of mind behave in ways that are frightening to their infants (see also Chapter 3). Karlen Lyons-Ruth, a researcher at Harvard Medical School, and her colleagues identified two predominant caregiving patterns among mothers of disorganized infants: a hostile-intrusive and role-confused pattern and a helpless-fearful pattern. The "hostile" pattern was marked by a contradictory display of behaviors that simultaneously were rejecting and also attention-seeking. The "helpless" pattern was indicated by behavior that was withdrawn, fearful, and inhibited; sometimes these mothers were "particularly sweet or fragile" (Lyons-Ruth and Spielman 2004, p.324). Their research has led them to hypothesize futher that the "hostile" and "helpless" patterns represent a single, underlying dyadic internal working model, whereby the caregiver has internalized both the abusers' and victims' roles from early childhood relationships and can enact either or both sides of the relationship:

> For a mother who has experienced relationships of both harm and fear in her own early development, the responsibility for the well-being of another can be especially overwhelming…the new mother's response to her baby's distress can be impeded by her own memories of punitive attacks or abandonment from her own parents. The relationship carries both sides of a potentially highly polarized internal working model. (Lyons-Ruth and Spielman 2004, p.327)

In sum, whether in the form of shark music or ghost stories, the intergenerational effects on our caregiving can be powerful, explaining—at least, in part—why multiple generations of families are involved in the child welfare system.[5] Raised in a chaotic and abusive environment and in and out of the foster care system herself, it was no wonder that Desiree struggled tremendously as a caregiver. In a revealing comment, Desirae communicated that although she did not think her childhood had an effect on how she was as a mother, she wanted to do things "completely opposite" of how she was raised.

With a greater understanding of the subtle psychological processes involved in the intergenerational transmission of caregiving, researchers have also explored how to break dysfunctional cycles, a topic about which we have more to say in Part 2. In his book *Becoming Attached*, psychiatrist Robert Karen sums up some of the keys to change:

> An important lesson emerging from adult attachment research, then, would seem to be this: We cannot change our childhood. But we can let go of the defensive and obsessive postures formed at that time. We can make sense of what has been repressed and forgotten. We can re-experience dissociated feelings with a new appreciation for ourselves as we were as children, for the

situation that existed at the time, for the parents who may have caused us to suffer... To that extent it seems that in emotional life, much as in history, we are only doomed to repeat what has not been remembered, reflected upon, and worked through. (Karen 1998, pp.407–408)

As Janet so insightfully observed, until Desirae was able to soften her defensive barriers and openly reflect on her own caregiving history, she could not possibly parent with the sensitivity and nurturing her children required. Her experience at The Children's Ark provided her with the foundation to begin this work.

Part 2

REFLECTION

IDEAS FOR MORE COMPASSIONATE (AND MORE EFFECTIVE) FOSTER CARE

Fundamental change is possible in new contexts,
even though history is not erased.

Sroufe et al. *2005, p.150*

Introduction to Part 2

During a group therapy session early on in the residential years of The Children's Ark, a very insightful mom commented:

> **"I get it now that there is another way to be in the world, and I believe that I might succeed; but if I step over and leave everyone and everything that I have known behind and fail in your world, I will have nothing."**

This fear often became parents' greatest obstacle.

What we aspired to do at The Children's Ark was to enhance parents' capacity to be in relationship by entering into relationship with them and to give them a sense of feeling valued. Their most important job—and the most difficult—was to surrender to change. No matter what else they may have overcome, without trust, without both the courage to "step over" into an entirely new way of being and the belief that a brighter future was possible, long-term change remained unlikely.

According to Dan Siegel, "The brain acts as an 'anticipation machine' that continually prepares itself for the future based on what happened in the past" (2010, p.148). Such conditioning and the kind of despair and distrust that is generated by early traumatic experiences powerfully drive how we see and respond to the world. Overriding this personal history is a long and difficult process at best, and one which I believe can only be accomplished within the context of relationship: real, long-term, caring relationship, which is of course the one thing that asks the most of us as service providers.

If we really want to make a permanent difference in the lives and futures of children and families at risk, we need to ask ourselves if we are willing to do what it takes to meet this challenge. Do we have the courage to do what we have asked these struggling parents to do: take the time for and risk the vulnerability of genuine relationship? After all, "people, not programs, change people"

(Perry and Szalavitz 2006, p.80). The hidden gift is that if we too have the courage to "step over," and the belief that life can be different and are willing to open to the possibilities, the magic can flow in both directions.

Ted

Ted arrived seeking admission to The Children's Ark on a busy afternoon packed full of interviews. I remember clearly walking into the Ark living room to greet him, fear filtering rapidly through my body. My initial thought was, "We need to interview this man and get him out of here." A "Charles Manson" kind of spookiness emanated from him at this initial meeting. Though apparently sober going on 15 years, his long scraggly hair, what seemed to be a permanent layer of dirt, and a vacant yet wild-eyed stare all betrayed a hard life. Ted was a middle-aged Vietnam veteran who had survived the war only to face life on the streets at home.

It was not until the end of that busy day that Sandra and I had a chance to sit down to discuss the candidates and make admission decisions. After reviewing a number of candidates, Sandy inquired, "And what did you think of the single father?" Surprising even myself I answered, "I liked him; I think it is something about those sad gray eyes." Sandy returned, "So did I." For reasons we still are not clear about, and against our better judgment that day, we accepted Ted into the program and made arrangements for his infant son to join him for sessions at the Ark beginning the following week.

The first moment with Ted that caught my attention and perhaps began to open my heart and mind to promise and possibility was an infant massage lesson. In an attempt to catch Ted up to the other parents, I sat down individually with him and his infant son, Joseph. We both sat on the floor, I with a doll and Ted with his baby boy propped between our legs on a blanket, their little heads cushioned by pillows. I turned on a heater to warm Joseph, who was stripped to his diaper, and a little soft music to soothe us. I told Ted to look into his son's eyes and talk to him as I slowly demonstrated all the strokes. Ted's myriad questions eventually trailed off, and he became quiet, very quiet. As he fell into the rhythm of gently stroking his son's body while speaking in a soft, comforting voice, tears trickled down his cheeks.

Ted's sweet, gentle touch with his infant son was in stunning contrast to his rough exterior. He proved eager to learn and was clearly captivated by his son's engaging smiles. In the beginning, especially in the more academically rigorous trainings, Ted seemed confused and had a difficult time expressing his thoughts. We learned over time that the trauma he suffered sometimes compromised his ability to find the right words, but as we patiently and with persistence listened, waited, and occasionally offered assistance, it became clear that Ted indeed had insight and plenty to say.

Slowly Ted exposed his life to us, trusting us with more and more of himself. One day on his way out of a therapy session, he turned, his hand on the door knob, and said to Sandra, "Did I tell you that I have been arrested 67 times?!" That proved to be a particularly poignant revelation when a few months later he showed up with a shockingly short haircut and explained that he was tired of being stopped by the police just because he was Ted.

Day by day and week by week Ted's physical appearance transformed. Not only did his unkempt hair give way to cleaner, shorter hair, but also his clothes took on the look of someone who cared about his appearance, his eyes grew warm with just a touch of mischief, and his smile grew positively contagious. Between his sometimes unorthodox choice of words and his quiet "gotcha" sense of humor, he kept us all smiling gently and chuckling softly.

As Ted's confidence grew, those gray eyes began to twinkle and sparkle with love and humor. He emitted a sense of being "at home" within the Ark walls, claiming for himself a role as the kindly elder, and only, dad. It wasn't long before we all adored him, parents and staff alike. Over time the mothers of the Ark came to respect and support Ted, and to trust him enough to share their thoughts and feelings about what they valued and longed for in a mate. In return Ted's jaded vision of what women were all about shifted, a deep affection and caring for his fellow parents emerging.

Ted's presence at the Ark was consistent and reliable; his participation positive and enthusiastic. He learned to let his guard down and allow the gentleness at his core to lead. He integrated what he was learning into the relationship with his son. After almost a year Sandra and I could not think of any real reason why Ted's son should not be returned to his care. We transitioned them carefully to independence and encouraged ongoing contact with us. They returned often to The Children's Ark: for a visit or lunch or to share a proud moment. Life, of course, continued to throw obstacles their way. Ted's ambivalence about the presence of Joseph's mother, who struggled with drug addiction, in their lives periodically threatened to upset the delicate balance. Yet somehow something special continued to grow between Ted and his son. Their delight in each other was palpable, their understanding of each other intuitive. Although as Joseph grew older, he sometimes came to his dad's rescue—for instance in helping him find just the right word—it was always clear that Ted was in charge. Their visits always warmed our hearts and brought joy to our day.

There is no doubt that my life is richer for having known Ted. Had I followed my initial instinct that first day, the instinct to walk—if not run—away, had I not been willing to open my mind to the possibilities and believe that change is possible, and had I not also been willing to open my heart and risk the vulnerability of relationship, I would have missed the gift that was Ted.

Those of us responsible for protecting children are pretty good at recognizing danger. The struggle seems to lie in knowing how to think and talk about it, how to intervene, and how to assess change. This section will offer insights from our experience at The Children's Ark into some answers to these questions and—we hope—will also open a conversation regarding the possibilities for new directions in the child protection world.

Chapter 7

THROUGH THE EYES OF THE CHILD

We need to always keep in mind that as primates, attachment equals survival and abandonment equals death.

Cozolino 2010, p.285

Assuming that it is the intention of any service, agency, or society designed to protect children to base decisions on children's best interests, we must ask ourselves what truly serves children? To answer this question, it is vital to understand how human beings develop and to know what capacities support safety, security, and success. As we have described, children have a profound need for attachment to a caregiver in order to survive. This necessity is gravely disrupted by the separation from parents when we remove children for their protection. If we want not to lose children in saving them, we must start by considering their experience when making decisions at such a critical time in their lives. And we must remember Louis Cozolino's wisdom: in the minds of the children, survival itself hangs in the balance.

Considering the child's experience

Sometimes stopping to consider the child's experience is a fairly simple thing, like not scheduling visits during naptime. And yet even what seems so obvious can be completely disregarded. When Joyce and her son, Jeremy, were residents at the Ark, Jeremy was also visiting with his father. Without conferring with us, visits were scheduled at 1:00 p.m., right in the middle of naptime. Often after arousing Jeremy from a sound sleep and sending him off with a stranger, he was brought right back because Dad had not shown up. As Jeremy became increasingly distressed with this disruption in his schedule, I called the social worker and suggested that if 1:00 p.m. was the only time Dad's visits could be scheduled, perhaps we could wait until Dad had actually arrived before waking Jeremy and sending him off with a driver. This new plan worked a little better in that at least Jeremy could continue his nap if Dad was a no show. Children in care have already suffered for many of their parents' shortcomings; one of our most important jobs as providers and protectors of children is to minimize further harm.

Sometimes the impact of not seeing with a child's eyes is much more devastating. We knew that Luke (aged eight months) would be moving into an adoptive home as soon as his mother had finalized her courageous decision to relinquish her parental rights and give him a shot at a stable future. I was shocked, however, to learn that Luke's caseworker had made the decision to move him, with no preparation, on Christmas Eve because she thought he would make "a nice Christmas gift for the adopting family"! In what was clearly not one of my finest moments, I called up the caseworker and screamed at her, "Do you understand that you have ruined Christmas for this little boy for the rest of his life?!" Collecting myself to some degree, I then went on to relate to her the following story of Rachel (see Chapter 2).

After transitioning Rachel to her adoptive home in January, just months before her third birthday, I made the 560-mile round trip regularly to visit her. I had made plans to see her the weekend after Thanksgiving the following year. Early in November Rachel's adoptive mother, Katie, called me and asked if we could reschedule. "I don't know what's going on," she said, "but all of her old behaviors are back, she is in a really distressed state, and the whole family is in turmoil." "I know," she continued, "that seeing you is good for Rachel, but it is also hard. I don't think any of us can manage it just now until we figure out what is distressing her." I agreed immediately and told her that absolutely we could reschedule, just to let me know when they figured out what was going on. Katie went on to tell me that it had started in October and that no matter how much they tried to talk to her, they had been unable to get at the cause of Rachel's distress, and her behavior just continued to deteriorate.

Several weeks later I got a call from Katie. "You will never guess what Rachel finally said to us," she began. "What she said—in her own four-year-old way—was that the Christmas decorations were up in the mall, so it must be time to move!"

And then it struck me: she had moved to our house in December, and 13 months later I had transitioned her to her adoptive home. Both times the Christmas decorations were up. Rachel's unconscious mind, under stress, had come to associate seasonal decorations with the trauma of loss. As decorations started appearing in the malls, for Halloween, Thanksgiving, and then Christmas, this emotionally charged, implicit learning hijacked Rachel's more rational thinking,[1] and she moved into escalating panic and acting out. This, in essence, is what I tried to explain to Luke's caseworker.

Validating the child's experience

In addition to considering children's experience, providing validation of that experience and giving children the language to help them make sense of it has enormous healing power. Naming the unspoken exposes the fear and thus mitigates it. It also reassures children that we can understand and tolerate wherever their feelings take them. We can help children manage even difficult feelings by functioning as containers: "holding" them in their emotions.[2] We can't go back and change Rachel's experience of loss, but we can loosen the grip it has on her each fall as the decorations begin to appear, and we can remember the lesson in it for all children. Rachel's new family works to defuse the trauma each year by reminding her early in the fall that this is the time of year when she gets afraid that she will be abandoned again. They assure her that this is an automatic fear response that was once justified by her experience, but that it does not apply to her now, and she will never be left again.

Rachel's move to her adoptive home was carefully planned (see Chapter 2). After the move, I slowly lengthened the time between visits. The first day I arrived for a visit following the initial settling in period, I parked in the driveway, which was a story below the living room. From the living room, through a big picture window looking out over the driveway, Rachel could stand and watch the world go by. Upon seeing my car she got very excited, and once she had greeted me at the door, and we had all gathered in the living room, Rachel bounded to the window and exclaimed, "Go in Janet's car!" I walked over and knelt down beside her and very gently explained, "No, you are not going in Janet's car. This is where you live now, and Katie and Matthew will always take care of you. I will always love you and be your Janet, but you are not going home with me." Rachel, of course, resisted, first angrily, then falling quickly into wrenching sobs.

As I held her I tried to stay with her: resonating with her deep grief, affirming her intense feelings, yet standing firm in the inevitability of the truth. She had lost her mother, and now she was losing me; there was no way out for her but through it. From then on when I came for a visit I very consciously parked in that driveway in front of that window for the opportunity to once again help Rachel through her pain. How much easier would it have been to park down the street or around the corner and never have to face that distraught, heartbreaking plea, "Go in Janet's car?" But walking into it—again and again—was, I believed, the best way to help Rachel grieve her losses and dare to trust again.

Creating child-centered environments and interventions

Creating child-centered environments, for us, is about competent adults who can look into a child's world and recognize needs, whether expressed or suppressed, and fears, whether real or imagined. It means adults who can then respond with candor and kindness. It means adults with enough patience to honor a child's pace and perspective, and yet with enough confidence to take charge to maintain order and safety.

Child-centered also means focusing on the child's physical, social, emotional, and developmental needs. Often when infants and young children are taken into care, it is almost as if they are warehoused with a foster family while the system attempts to "fix" the parents. Seldom is attention directed or energy expended on identifying and attending to the critical impact the loss of family has on the child (see Chapter 10). Not only does this failure represent an additional insult to the child, but it is also a missed opportunity for effective intervention. Much of the potentially negative developmental impact to children that occurs as the result of even the temporary loss of their primary caregiving figure can be mitigated by increased time with their parents while separated and by involving the children in the treatment process.

When the children are included in the treatment process, there are benefits both to parents and children. Parents learn to parent by parenting, especially in an environment that also nurtures them. They participate in evaluations of their children, and, rather than being judged for any deficits, they are instead taught how to help their children progress. They have numerous opportunities to bond with their children and to create positive interactive memories, rather than the heart-wrenching and uncomfortable reunions and separations usually associated with visitation.

Children benefit because the connection to their parents is maintained while treatment proceeds. Attention is paid to developmental milestones and to the disruption to progress caused by the trauma of separation. The children are included in the process of repair, instead of being merely victims of the rupture.

We often said that our goal at the Ark was to do for the parents what we wanted them to do for their children. We believe that the most effective way for parents who neglect and abuse to learn to parent safely is to come to know their children, to understand that their children's needs were also their own needs. As parents focus on their children, while being held in compassion as they acknowledge the inadequacies and tragedies of their own childhoods, their hearts can open. They can experience joy with their children and want for them that for which they have always, themselves, longed.

Child-centered intervention thus serves children by acknowledging and helping them work through the trauma and developmental consequences of separation, abuse, and neglect and serves parents by encouraging the development of true empathy for their children's experience.

Carrie and Sean

Carrie, a young mother who participated in The Children's Ark when it was a day treatment program, was exposed to domestic violence, parental drug abuse, and sexual molestation during the first two years of her life. After her parents separated, the relationship between Carrie and her mother, with whom she was living, remained strained, primarily because of her mother's unpredictable and violent temper. This ever-present potential for physical harm coupled with the real trauma of her early years left Carrie scrambling to comply and to please and unable to initiate on her own behalf.

Carrie's coping strategies included detachment, avoidance, and the minimization of real danger, all in an effort to manage unpleasant emotion in herself and prevent conflict with others. She was prone to take on more responsibility than she could handle. When she became overwhelmed and then resentful, however, she was unable to articulate what she needed or to rely on others for support.

Upon becoming pregnant with her son, Carrie moved in with the baby's father and assumed most of the responsibility for making a living, managing a home, and parenting an infant. Unable to manage it all alone and unwilling to routinely ask for help, Carrie finally—out of desperation—negotiated an overnight away, leaving Sean with his father. Although unexplained bruising appeared on Sean the next morning, Carrie did not seek medical attention. The second time it happened she did call her mother. Sean was placed in Carrie's mother's care shortly thereafter upon the discovery of additional injuries at a routine baby exam. Carrie was allowed to continue to live with her son at her mother's, and Carrie and Sean were referred to The Children's Ark day treatment program.

Not surprisingly, living with her mother was difficult for Carrie. The constant reminder of what it was like to grow up in poverty with a single, overwhelmed mother in an emotionally dangerous environment only further activated her fear that she would end up solely responsible for Sean and living her mother's life. Unfortunately, the degree to which that fear kept her attached to Sean's father and in denial about his responsibility for the injuries to Sean was also the degree to which it was impossible for her to keep her baby safe.

Upon entering the Ark, Carrie presented as overwhelmed and anxious, both with her son and with staff. She was quick to comply and was hypervigilant regarding what she perceived others expected of her. She hovered anxiously over Sean, responding immediately to his slightest whimper. She demonstrated a limited ability to interpret his cues, often assuming he was hungry or tired when he was really distressed. As a consequence she was constantly insisting upon feeding him or putting him to bed. Additionally, it was clear that Carrie minimized the implications and possible consequences of the seriousness of Sean's injuries.

Sean presented with a number of developmental issues. He was easily distressed and difficult to soothe. Often he was rigid, frequently arching away, his arms splayed and his hands fisted. He had difficulty maintaining eye contact, and in fact seemed to struggle even to focus. He did not appear to respond to sounds. Although we suspected that many of these issues were related to the developing dynamic with his mother, we were concerned enough to recommend a full developmental evaluation.

For us, it was not hard to see the link between Carrie's response to Sean's distress and his perception that the only way to maintain proximity to his mother was to stay helpless. It was likewise not hard to imagine that Sean might decide to shut down and become non-responsive. The challenge lay in helping Carrie consider that her son's failure to initiate might be a reflection of her own struggle.

Indeed, as Carrie began to learn to regulate her own anxiety and to expose her previously unspoken grieving for both a lost childhood and now a lost young adulthood with the unplanned arrival of Sean, she was then able to be more present for her son. When she calmed, he calmed. When she slowed, his attention peaked. When she waited for the cause of his distress to become clear rather than rushing to the bottle or rocking him to sleep, he became more interactive and communicative. He began responding to sounds, especially his mother's voice, and initiating connection with her.

One by one Sean's developmental concerns dropped away until eventually only a difficulty or delay in focusing his eyes remained. Medical examination revealed that the abuse suffered by Sean had injured his brain and damaged his eyes, a fact that significantly and positively impacted Carrie's ability to step up as her son's protector. Ultimately, Sean was returned to her care, and they have done well together.

Carrie and Sean reaped the benefits of a child-centered intervention. It was clearly in Sean's best interest not to lose Carrie, but only if she was able to work through the issues and fears that interfered with her ability to protect him and put him first. By staying focused on Sean, particularly his developmental struggles, we were able to help both him and Carrie. As Carrie worked with Sean and began to see the reflection of her own lack of self-activation in her son's developmental lags, it served both as a powerful motivator and as a way to open her eyes to his needs.

When to stop intervening

Acting in children's best interests sometimes requires navigating the complicated balance between the benefits children derive from retaining their parents and the harm that can be caused them by exposure to their parents' ongoing lack of progress in treatment. If such a state of limbo goes on for too long children's emotional and developmental needs can be disrupted or even denied at a critical time in their lives. Thus, sometimes we need to know when to stop helping. These are hard decisions and should always be based on the needs of the child and not on what may be a desire to punish the parent.

Craig, Hilary, and Tim

The clearest case I have ever seen of parental fears manifesting in the behavior and development of the child ("ghosts in the nursery"— see Chapter 6) was the case of little Tim. Tim's parents, Craig and Hilary, were referred to Child Protective Services when it became clear that Tim was being neglected. Tim was moved into foster care, and the family was subsequently referred to The Children's Ark.

Tim presented as developmentally delayed due, it was assumed, to neglect. As Craig and Hilary's histories unfolded, however, the relational dynamics at work in this family became the focus of intervention. The relationship between these parents was misattuned and fairly volatile. Hilary's childhood had been filled with abuse, rejection, and lack of protection. She was disconnected from her own emotional experience and demonstrated a limited range of affect, her primary emotional response being anger. She was also unable or unwilling to let others help her self-regulate. For the most part, she abdicated Tim's care to Craig, while at the same time resenting the baby's preference for him.

Craig blamed Hilary for the neglect, even though it became clear that he also played a role in it. He felt therefore that he needed to monitor her constantly, often resorting to being critical and controlling. Both parents needed to be needed by their son and yet could not tolerate any emotional distress from him. As a result of these complex family dynamics, Tim—at just a year old—was caught in the middle, trying to manage the competition between his parents for his affection. As Tim moved into toddlerhood he was caught between his natural urge to assert autonomy and explore, and his perception that he was only safe and valued when he stayed close to his caregivers and remained helpless.

Curiously, it quickly became obvious that Tim's "delay" was most evident when in the presence of his parents, with whom he also displayed higher levels of distress. When alone with Ark staff, or his foster parents, Tim was much more capable. We first noticed this during a session with the physical therapist. With Craig and Hilary present, Tim became a helpless, pleading, resisting, screaming "infant" barely able to drag his weak and uncooperative body across the floor. When his parents left the room, however, the capable, confident toddler stood up and quietly walked across the room to the toy box.

It was apparent, therefore, that Tim's helpless behavior, including his developmental lag, was the result primarily of his attempts to accommodate his parents' complex needs for him to remain dependent. Understandably, he felt confused, dysregulated, and frustrated by his own desire for exploration and independence. This dynamic placed him in an overwhelming, disorganizing, and unsolvable dilemma. His delay represented a disruption in emotional development rather than a lack of cognitive or physical ability, a relational deficit so to speak.

It became imperative that Craig and Hilary embrace the challenge of recognizing the defensive barriers that prevented them from seeing and shifting the destructive family pattern that was interfering with their son's healthy development and putting him at risk for further abuse and neglect. Unfortunately, even though both Craig and Hilary demonstrated some willingness to open to vulnerability in therapy, there was little evidence over many months that there was any internalized change in the family dynamic. Both parents' capacity to reflect on their own experiences and how those experiences might impact them and those around them remained limited. As a result, neither could develop real empathy for Tim's experience.

In our opinion the cost was too great for Tim; for him time was of the essence. And so, with some sadness, we discharged the family from the Ark program. Unfortunately, in spite of our concerns, this family was allowed to continue to move through multiple services while Tim lingered in foster care. It was not until many subsequent professionals came to the same conclusion we had—and over a year later—that Craig and Hilary's parental rights were terminated, and Tim was allowed to move to permanency.

Knowing when not to start

Sometimes we need to know when to stop intervening, and sometimes, in the best interest of the child, we need not to start.

Connor

Ellie was referred to the Ark day treatment program upon the birth of her daughter, Jazmin. Ellie's two-year-old son, Connor, was already in placement with relatives. Connor was placed in care as the result both of Ellie's neglect and her failure to protect him from abuse by his father, with whom she remained involved. When she became pregnant with their daughter, Jazmin, Jazmin was placed with the same relatives, and she and Ellie began participation in The Children's Ark. Connor had been settled for some time, and we made the decision to assess first how Ellie would do moving forward without the children's father before further disrupting Connor's life by including him.

Ellie's history was horrendous, involving both physical and sexual abuse and abandonment. She had spent most of her life in the foster care system herself. She clung to what little power and control she had by manipulating those around her and could not imagine real connection. She was depressed and sometimes suicidal. At the time of Ellie's admission to the Ark she had already been involved in a number of services and had been prescribed antidepressant medications. Her ability to follow through with either was inconsistent at best.

The early months were a struggle, both in Ellie's relation-ship with Jazmin and in her continuing ambiguity around the relationship with the children's father. We allowed some visitation with Connor at the Ark, but the primary intervention centered around Ellie and Jazmin. At an early juncture, Ellie's public defender moved forward with a hearing asking for both children to be returned to Ellie's care. Ark staff testified that it was much too early in our process to make any recommendation. The court denied the request to return the children, but—perhaps in a misguided effort to appease Ellie—told her that maybe Connor could also participate fully at the Ark.

After careful thought and consideration, we made the decision not to include Connor in the full program. Connor had already suffered much disruption and trauma in his young life and was finally settled quite comfortably in the home of relatives. Ellie had not yet demonstrated either the capacity or the willingness to embrace the work that needed to be done if she was going to be able to parent safely. It did not seem in Connor's best interest to draw him into the intensity of the Ark program, further disrupting the security of his schedule and life, until a future direction was a little clearer. He already had generous access to his mother while maintaining a safe haven with relatives, and upsetting the balance at this moment felt more like a consolation to Ellie than a prudent plan for Connor. Ultimately, Ellie stopped attending services at the Ark, worked with her social worker to relinquish her parental rights, and both children were placed in the permanent care of relatives.

Connor's story is but one example of how the children can become almost irrelevant in the adversarial atmosphere of our judicial system. Rather than focusing on what children need, or even what might work best for a particular family, the very nature of the system dictates a context of winning or losing. Parental rights tend to trump children's needs. It is understandably difficult to mediate anybody's best interest, let alone resolution, in an atmosphere that often pits parent against parent, parent against service provider, and sometimes even parent against child. And so, in a system designed to protect children, the children often become the least represented and the least considered.

When children lose their parents

Making decisions in the best interests of children in care can sometimes mean making tough decisions that you know will cause pain in order to assure the health and safety of children. When children lose their parents, it can mean maintaining available familial ties and preserving and honoring children's histories or "stories." For us, always it meant considering the child's experience, working hard, for example, to minimize moves and transition carefully and thoughtfully when moves were necessary. The place we often started was to ask what does this particular child need and who can best provide it?

Tony

Tony was a beautiful, biracial toddler for whom we were asked to provide temporary foster care during the early days of The Children's Ark. He had spent the first six months of his life in his parents' care. He then entered foster care and was moved several times over the next year. As Tony's parents' rights were terminated, his paternal grandmother stepped forward and asked for custody. At about the same time his second set of foster parents also re-entered the picture. Those foster parents, the Randalls, had been a good match for Tony, and he had been in their care for seven months. They had only given him up when they were not allowed to take him on a temporary move out of the area.

Those responsible for Tony's well-being now faced the difficult dilemma of deciding where he might fare best: with his Caucasian former foster parents, who knew and loved him but who had now been separated from him for nine months, or with his African-American grandmother, who was of course family, but who had never met Tony and lived out of the area. At this juncture Tony's social worker asked us to take him while placement was determined, both because we represented neutral ground, and because we provided the opportunity and ability to observe and evaluate Tony in both of these relationships.

Tony was a delightful little boy and developmentally on track. We were told that he had struggled with some medical issues early on, but by the time he came to us he was no longer symptomatic. As Tony began to settle in we received a call from the social worker informing us that Mrs. Randall was in town and that she would like to set up some visits with Tony at the Ark. As we got to know Mrs. Randall and watched her reintroduce herself to Tony, we were impressed with her sensitivity and willingness to let Tony lead. Over time, we talked about her heart-wrenching bind: both adoring and wanting Tony back and understanding the value to Tony of being with family.

Ultimately, Mrs. Randall put forth a courageous and selfless proposal: If Tony's grandmother would travel to Spokane and spend time getting to know her grandson under the guidance of Ark staff, and things went well, she would withdraw her bid for custody. Accordingly, over a holiday weekend, Tony's grandmother arrived at The Children's Ark for a few day's visit.

Unfortunately, though understandably, Grandma moved in like gangbusters to Tony's personal space, wanting of course to swoop up her grandson in a loving embrace. She immediately felt an intense connection to this adorable little boy who was, after all, her flesh and blood. Tony, on the other hand, was puzzled and distressed by the sudden and overwhelming attention of this complete stranger. The weekend was a difficult one as we tried to slow Grandma down and faced the frustration of trying to obtain medical care over the long weekend in order to manage Tony's subsequent relapse into old symptomology. Clearly, he was stressed by this initial encounter with Grandma.

When Grandma expressed a willingness to do whatever it took to help her grandson, we recommended that she return to the Ark for a period of two weeks, work with our therapist, and begin to build a relationship with Tony before deciding whether or not to pursue custody. Grandma agreed, and a plan was put into place.

After a brief return home to organize an absence from work, Grandma then traveled back to the Ark and moved in. Over the next two-week period, she demonstrated the desire and the ability to see and meet her grandson's needs. She learned to slow down, back off, and allow Tony to come to her. By watching and waiting she came to know and understand Tony and of course fell hopelessly in love with him. At the end of her stay, we felt comfortable recommending that Tony find permanency with his grandmother.

This was a decision made in the best interest of a child. It would have been easy for the focus to develop around issues of race or previous custody and for the various adults to fight over their "rights." Instead, the families involved found a way to put their own personal agendas aside and join in discovering how to best meet the needs of the little boy they both loved.

Kraig

Based on homelessness and the drug and mental health histories of both his parents, Kraig was placed in foster care immediately following his birth after being referred by a public health nurse. The question was whether or not his father, John, had the capacity to parent his son, as Kraig's mother was quickly out of the picture. John was a first-time father in late middle age. He had a decade-long history of alcoholism and homelessness, though claimed upon interview several years of sobriety. His mental health diagnoses included post-traumatic stress disorder (PTSD) and antisocial disorder. John believed he was being penalized because he was a first-time father, and he saw the system as evil. Though his trust level was very low, he was nonetheless very invested in parenting Kraig and in being a good father. When Kraig was two months old, they entered the Ark's day treatment program.

In spite of his skepticism, John's participation at the Ark was enthusiastic. He was eager to take in and integrate information and feedback related to parenting his child. He clearly delighted in the very presence of his son. However, although John expressed pride in each of Kraig's developmental steps, his concrete thinking tended to interfere with his ability to keep up with, or in any way intuit, the rapid changes through which Kraig inevitably moved. He tended toward rigid compliance with whatever he believed he had once been told. As a result he demonstrated great difficulty in varying or changing what he had learned even when it was apparent that Kraig had moved on to another developmental stage.

Perhaps the most amazing change John made over time was a shift in his attitude toward his situation. He was slowly able to distinguish the difference between loving his son and being able to meet all his needs. He acknowledged and accepted the realities of his age, social and financial fragility, ill health, and lack of parenting experience or knowledge. He came to recognize that the system, rather than being evil, was looking out for his son and was actually on his side. Perhaps most importantly, he forged a cooperative and warm relationship with Kraig's foster family.

In the end, John himself negotiated an open adoption with Kraig's foster parents. They in turn also "adopted" John and made him a part of their family. Not only had they grown fond of John, but they also recognized that he had become a significant figure in Kraig's life and believed that it was important for him to remain so.

This, too, was a decision made in the best interest of a child. John was able to put his own desires aside in hopes of providing his son the life he himself felt unable to offer. Kraig's foster parents also were able to put Kraig first by acknowledging the importance of John's presence in their future son's life.

Research and theory: Reimagining foster care for infants and young children

In a 2011 research report, Charles Zeanah and his colleagues argued that the design and implementation of foster care for infants and young children should be fundamentally different from that for older children. They further recommended that this developmentally informed vision of foster care be grounded in "the decades of research on the science of attachment," to intentionally support young children's foundational needs (Zeanah, Shauffer, and Dozier 2011, p.1199; see also Dozier, Zeanah, and Bernard 2013). Among the key developmental tasks of infancy and early childhood are establishing basic physiological, emotional, and behavioral self-regulation; developing a sense of trust and security in relationships; and forming a healthy sense of autonomy and agency. These tasks are interrelated, and the foundation for all of them is laid in early significant attachment relationships.[3]

Taking an attachment-informed approach to foster care means understanding the developmental impact of loss and how it undermines emotional development and trust in relationships. It also means recognizing that the youngest children in foster care cannot maintain attachment relationships with parents from whom they are separated. Early attachments are emotional connections based on ongoing interactions with physically available caregivers. These early ties are not based on genetics, at least not from the perspective of the child. According to Zeanah and colleagues (2011), "Not until after early childhood are children able to sustain attachments over time and space to caregivers with whom they do not have regular and substantial contact" (p.1199). However, because stable attachments are vital for the healthy development of infants and young children, it is critical to support foster parents as the primary attachment figures in their foster children's lives. These realities were foundational in the development of The Children's Ark. The Ark limited moves and transitioned children carefully to minimize their separation and loss experiences; supported the growth of the attachment relationship between birth parents and their children, as long as reunification remained the goal; and joined with foster parents as important partners in their work with birth families.

Mary Dozier, the Director of the University of Delaware's Infant Caregiver Project, is a leading scholar on the development of attachment relationships between foster caregivers and their foster children. One series of her studies focused on caregiver commitment to their foster children.[4] Not surprisingly, Dozier and her colleagues found a range of emotional investment, from foster parents who thought of their foster children as their own to those who regarded the relationship as a temporary one in which they should remain uninvested. We think it likely that fully invested caregivers will better understand their foster children and be more likely to act in their children's best interests. Dozier and colleagues also discovered that highly committed foster parents displayed greater delight in their foster children than did foster parents who were less highly committed. Regarded as a key feature of secure attachment, delight is likely to communicate to the child something about their value, about how much they matter to the caregiver, and about how much they belong.

Dozier and her colleagues also studied the timing of placement into foster care as well as the impact of the foster caregiver's state of mind with respect to attachment (see Chapter 6) on the qual-ity of the foster caregiver–foster child attachment relationship.[5] Timing mattered. Infants placed prior to 12 months tended to organize a stable attachment strategy with their foster caregiver fairly quickly, whereas children placed after 12 months took longer to form a stable attachment pattern and often drew the caregiver into insecure relationship dynamics (e.g. "miscues" that elicited rejecting care). However, caregiver state of mind appeared to be the primary predictor of foster children's attachment. Infants and toddlers placed with secure/autonomous caregivers were likely to develop secure attachments with them. Notably, however, infants and toddlers placed with caregivers with *any* non-autonomous (insecure) state of mind were disproportionately likely to develop *disorganized* attachments. Based on these findings, Dozier and her colleagues underscored that infants and toddlers with disrupted early relationships are especially in need of stable, nurturing care. Further, they cautioned that without such care these children are likely to have difficulty developing organized attachment strategies, which places them on high-risk developmental trajectories.

Although it is unrealistic to screen all foster caregivers for attachment-related state of mind, we can do a better job of supporting foster caregivers as essential attachment figures and bolstering their commitment for the young children in their care.

As noted by Zeanah and his colleagues (2011), "Young children have no way of understanding 'temporary placements' or 'respite parenting.' They know only that they need someone who is fully committed to them" (p.1200). The Ark staff worked hard to develop partnerships with foster families, which enhanced foster parent commitment. They also helped birth parents to recognize foster families as valuable resources and as important caregivers in the eyes of their children.

If we want maltreated infants and young children to heal and to thrive, we must reimagine foster care by keeping their best interests at the center. Anchoring foster care in the science of attachment will help to provide a framework for this work.

Chapter 8

INSIGHTS INTO INTERVENTION

In order to grow up, we require a holding environment in which we feel we are loved and protected for all the time it takes to find out who we are. These are the COMFORTS that help us trust others. We also need a nudge from the nest so we can go out into the world and open to the full expanse of who we can be. This is the CHALLENGE that makes it possible for us to trust ourselves. We notice that we are ready and willing to accept the challenge to fly BECAUSE we were in a nest, a holding environment wherein we felt safe.

Richo 2008, p.129

We began at The Children's Ark with a number of assumptions. We assumed that all parents have an innate desire to be good parents and that each of us does the best we can in each moment with what we know. We assumed that children will engage in relationship-seeking behavior and will follow their parents' unique relational strategies, healthy or unhealthy, because they cannot afford not to be attached. Finally, we assumed that both parents and children long for intimate human connection.

Without the "holding environment" described by David Richo above, however, it is extremely difficult to override early experiences of disconnection enough to provide the safety and security for our children that we may not have ourselves experienced. Is it reasonable to expect parents to know how to give their children what they themselves did not receive? It became our intention at The Children's Ark to become that holding environment for parents so that they could then provide it for their children. The following elements are critical, we believe, to the creation of such an environment.[1]

Keeping the child's experience at the center

As discussed in Chapter 7, we need to make the child's experience central to intervention or treatment. The "problem" resides neither in the child nor in the parent, but in the relational dynamic between them. The first step toward repairing the relationship is in understanding the relational dance, and the first step toward understanding the dance is to help parents begin to see the world through their children's eyes. This kind of knowing on the part of a parent is almost always followed by a softening that can become the catalyst for change.

Tamera and Daisy

Once a week at The Children's Ark, all the children, parents, and staff participated in music therapy. Daisy, not yet two years old, seemed particularly delighted by the sounds and movement of the music hour. Her mother, Tamera, would gaily "complain" that her daughter would not sit with her during music but instead moved from lap to lap and danced and spun herself around the room with complete abandon, picking up the rhythm and tempo of each song.

Then during one particular session, instead of her usual behavior, Daisy hovered anxiously about her mother's lap, seemingly unwilling to venture out. Tamera and the staff worked to draw her out and into her usual enjoyment of the music. I remember all of us looking at each other in puzzlement, not understanding what could be dampening her enthusiasm. Then suddenly Tamera faced

Daisy and said, "Are you wondering where Shyre is?" Shyre was the toddler teacher assigned to Daisy, and the two of them had built a very special relationship. Shyre had taken the week off and so did not show up for music therapy, which took place first thing Monday morning. Nobody had yet thought to talk to Daisy about Shyre's absence.

In recognizing what was different and perhaps distressing in Daisy's world—and naming it—Tamera had spoken right to Daisy's heart. She had looked through her child's eyes, identified what her daughter was struggling with yet could not articulate, and in so doing gave her daughter a sense of being seen and understood. It was stunning to witness the calming effect those words had on that little girl. We followed up with an explanation of Shyre's absence, and Daisy was eased back into her usual delighted responsiveness.

Recognizing that parents were once children too

Just as we must consider the child's experience, we must also learn to look through the parents' eyes, to view life through their particular lens. Until we also understand each parent's experience, we cannot possibly hope to impact their relational dance with their child. The final question in our admission interview process was always, "What would you like your child to learn from being parented by you?" We were stunned and amazed at how often parents answered some version of "You can't trust people": a lesson they had experienced and internalized and felt necessary to communicate to their children. Such a belief system drives every interaction, shaping responses and limiting choices.

Exposing the conditioned beliefs and protective strategies parents have constructed in order to survive is tricky business, however. It demands of us that we set aside our judgments and take up genuine compassion, the kind of compassion that moves us through our own pain, reminding us of our commonality. It also demands that we treat parents as we wish them to treat their children and be for them what we want them to be for their children: a source of safety and support. We must be willing to model relationship.

One of the Ark moms once complained to Sandra about the inconsistency of the day and time of her therapy sessions. Sandra initially expressed some annoyance at being challenged in this way, especially since the very crisis-driven nature of day-to-day life at the Ark rendered consistency of any kind virtually impossible. As she thought about it, however, she realized that this young woman was actually asserting herself in the very way we had encouraged her to do. She was standing up on her own behalf and daring to claim her worth. Sandra met with her as soon as she was able, worked to repair the rupture, and remained diligent in the future about the consistency of her therapy sessions.

Only when we have joined in their journey can parents risk trusting us enough to consider the cost to themselves and to their children's social, emotional, cognitive, and physical development of continuing the dance. Carla may have said it best.

Carla

Carla is one of several Ark parents from the day treatment program whom I have stayed in touch with following discharge. She regained custody of her young daughter and is currently living in a nearby sober house for women and children. I see Carla fairly regularly, and at a recent dinner, we got into a discussion of the turning points on her life's journey. "Do you want to know my turning point at The Children's Ark?" she asked. "I certainly do," I replied. Carla reported feeling defensive and skeptical upon entering the Ark and not trusting or liking any of us. "Even when I could allow a momentary touch down into thinking I might like you," she went on, "I could not even imagine that I would be considered worth the effort." Carla described moving from outright hostility and a belief that she could "pull the wool over our eyes," to a more resigned sense of hopelessness and worthlessness. Until, that is, a group meeting that she detailed as follows:

"We were all in the training room in a group meeting of some kind. I can't remember if it was a group therapy session that turned to this particular topic, or if it was a meeting called specifically for this purpose; but we were processing the Ark's recent decision to recommend to the court that Janice's son not be returned to her. Sandra was probing after everyone's feelings and responses. I remember my first thought being, 'These people are serious about change...and not so easy to fool.' I then felt myself move into anger and cynicism and remember challenging Sandra by asking her, 'What about *you* guys; what do *you* feel?!'

Much to my surprise Sandra started talking about what it was like to spend so much time with families, enter into relationship with them, and then have to make these kinds of decisions. As she talked tears began to stream down her face. Her anguish was so genuine that I suddenly understood that she really did care about us, and care about us unconditionally, no matter what the outcome. That was it for me; I knew in that moment that I would work hard and do what I could to be the best person I was capable of being and the mother that my daughter deserved."

Once Carla knew unconditional caring, she was ready to tolerate investigating the very nature of her relational dance. She was ready to look through her daughter's eyes and see with clarity and kindness[2] how her own experience lived on in her daughter's experience. And she was ready to begin to learn how to break the cycle. Once parents understood and, often through the use of videotape, saw their own stories reflected in the behavior of their children, it was a powerful motivator. When they made the connection between that behavior and their child's development, it was even more compelling.

Bruce and Susan

Bruce and Susan came to The Children's Ark with their newborn daughter, who had been placed into foster care as a result of their drug histories. They were anxious to learn all about parenting, were quick to grasp concepts, and eager to act in their daughter's best interest. However, their own issues rendered them unable to act on their knowledge and good intentions: a dynamic that directly and negatively impacted their daughter's development. Both Bruce and Susan experienced childhoods in which their caregivers were not available to meet their needs. They were determined that their daughter would never feel as they had. This determination manifested, however, in the over-anticipation of her every "need." They were very quick to feed her or hold and rock her even with no indication from her of hunger or distress. As a result, over time she was denied the opportunity to communicate her needs, learn through trial and error, move about in her world on her own, or gain competence and confidence. She had little opportunity to impact her world or learn how to self-regulate. Consequently, as she approached six months, she was overweight and virtually motionless. She did not roll over, reach, track, or attempt to mobilize—though she was completely sound physically and on occasion leaned longingly from her mother's lap toward the floor where the other Ark infants were exploring.

Fortunately, over time as Bruce and Susan engaged in video reviews, therapy, and the Circle of Security intervention, as well as guidance during their daily interactions, they came to see the link between their fears and the cost to their daughter. They witnessed for themselves, both in video clips and in daily interactions, how their daughter was reading their discomfort with her autonomy and was adjusting her behavior accordingly, even when it meant forgoing her own needs. As Bruce and Susan worked through their own issues they were able to loosen their tight grip on their daughter. As she was allowed to move about more freely and explore, she advanced rapidly through developmental milestones and was soon functioning at age-appropriate levels. They ultimately regained custody and have done well.

Continuity and reliability of relationship

The necessity of establishing and maintaining genuine relationship is reiterated throughout this book. Both Desirae (Chapter 6) and Carla (above) beautifully articulated its significance to their healing and transformative process. But what does that mean about intervention? How does that look in the day-to-day operation of a treatment program? How does that translate within the formality and impersonality of systems?

Being who we are

First and foremost, personalizing systems means staff longevity and a client/staff ratio that renders real, consistent relationship possible. Trust develops when we feel free to expose the essence of who we are, when we feel safe enough to let down our defenses and reveal the truth about our vulnerable selves. Before that can happen, we must believe that we are not only in the presence of someone who will not harm us but also someone who will be there for us. Trust is difficult to develop when staff either rotate too frequently, when they are overburdened or undervalued, or when they are too hard to access emotionally.

To build trust, clients must have sufficient, consistent exposure to individual staff members and the ability to see them as "complete" people. We worked to accomplish that at The Children's Ark by having all staff present at all times instead of having rotating shifts, and by involving staff in all aspects of the program. Although each staff member had a title and particular responsibilities, and only the clinical director conducted actual therapy, all staff were involved in cooking, cleaning, transporting, teaching, participating in services, and providing guidance to all clients in all milieus all the time.

This kind of constant interaction with client families of course brings staff face to face with their own struggles. Competent reflective supervision is critical, so staff can recognize, own, and work through conditioned or defensive responses.[3] Staff will be challenged regularly in such an environment to model relationship, repair ruptures, and open to vulnerability. In other words, staff must be willing to do their own work while pushing client families to do the same.

Karen

Karen entered The Children's Ark with her daughters, Samantha and Rose. Over the course of the ten months that Karen participated in the Ark day treatment program, she struggled both with substance abuse and with significant ambivalence about her desire or competence to parent. Unfortunately, Karen's struggles manifested in frequent abdication of the care of her two young children, and sometimes in disappearing altogether.

I became aware over time of my own increasing agitation, irritation, and eventual anger at Karen for whom I had initially developed a deep fondness. I found myself distancing from her, feeling disappointed in her, and eventually even disgusted by her. Part of the time it was as if I had just given up on her and wanted to move on and be done with it. But part of my rage at her and my resulting dysregulation were so powerful, it was as if her shortcomings represented a personal attack against me.

Fortunately, I had the good sense to discuss my feelings with a trusted other who both knew me well and understood the environment at The Children's Ark. After guiding me skillfully to a precise description of my feelings—"I am angry at Karen because she abandons her children"—he gently invited me to replace Karen's name with my own. As the profound implications of the revised statement sunk in, tears streamed down my face. Something about this young woman and her struggles had deeply stirred my own early doubts, regrets, and failures as a parent. I had displaced the anger and disappointment I was feeling toward myself for what I perceived as the many ways I had let down or "abandoned" my own children, and had let Karen carry it all! I needed to be willing to recognize my contribution to this developing dynamic and refrain from continuing to act it out if I was going to be of any help to Karen or her children.

Maintaining the balance between entering into genuine relationship with a client and respecting the boundaries necessary to do no harm can be difficult. There are obviously behavioral and information-sharing boundaries that should never be crossed. Perhaps the key to determining the appropriateness of a boundary is in recognizing the difference between empathizing with and supporting a client, and taking care of or enabling them. The intersection between helping and hindering can be very fragile. Often what is most important and helpful to people facing difficult and distressing dilemmas is resonance, not answers. Staff members are most effective when they offer compassionate presence while following the client's lead in sorting out feelings and meanings and when they encourage the client's initiation of solutions.

The process takes time

Time is also a critical factor in relationship building. There are no quick fixes, and real relationship is built over time. It is a process: a repetitive cycle of attunement, rupture, and repair that builds, over time, a sense of being seen and a sense that things will work out—of hope for the future.[4] Since most parents at risk have been victimized in some way, such positive experiences are difficult to trust, let alone embrace. Consistent, long-term exposure to caring yet challenging staff for hours a day over weeks and months can gradually shift reluctant, fear-filled parents to more openness and vulnerability if they have the capacity to change and the willingness to work. Even then it is a slow, painful process, and one that was certainly never completed while under our roof. Desirae talked about how it was years later before she allowed herself to actually act from the tender, wise part of herself that she first uncovered at the Ark. Carla's wisdom and courage continue to this day to unfold as she meets and challenges obstacle after obstacle on her long road to recovery.

Carla: Part 2

After regaining custody of her daughter, Carla stayed in relationship with her daughter's foster family and has reconnected over time with her son (whom that same foster family had earlier adopted). At a recent dinner, Carla shared with me her increasing concern over the path down which her young adolescent son seemed to be traveling: "Ryan is starting to get in trouble at school and to lie and steal. I'm very worried about him. I know this road and where it leads. I keep asking myself how I can help him." She then went on to describe a recent weekend with him:

"I said to Ryan, 'I know you are struggling at home and at school, and that things are not going well for you. If you don't want to talk to anyone about it, you don't have to, but you need to find a way to get it out. If you don't, it will be toxic to you.' I then asked Ryan to go upstairs and write down everything that was in his heart and head. I told him not to worry about sentences or punctuation but to just get it down on paper. Much to my surprise he was upstairs for a very long time. When he finally came down he handed me three written pages and said, 'Nobody will read these, right?' I told him that was right, as I folded them and put them in my purse. 'We will burn these together later.'

Then Ryan handed me a single piece of paper and said, 'This is for you to read.' The paper was entitled 'That Day.' The first page was a heart-wrenching description of how it felt to the three-year-old Ryan to have the police come and take him away from his home and how he has wondered for the last ten years what he had done wrong. On the back was a short paragraph in which he inquired, 'And where is my dad?' As tears threatened to fill my eyes I knew the time had come to tell my son the truth.

I tried to use age-appropriate language and to be as kind as possible, but, for the first time, I told him the truth. I, of course, could not do that without crying myself.

As I finished, Ryan climbed into my lap and said, 'It's okay, Mom.' We then sat and held each other and cried together for a long time."

What greater gift could Carla have given her son than the truth? The kind of courage and compassion it took for her to give him what he so needed took time to develop.

Telling the truth

The kind of truth-telling that Carla was able to share with Ryan is another of the critical elements in relationship building. Just as we need resonance rather than answers, we need truth rather than unrealistic expectations or empty promises. We told parents the truth at The Children's Ark: truth about the work to be done, truth about the time involved, and truth about their progress. In the initial interview, we talked about the process we believed was necessary to effect real, lasting change (see section below) as opposed to ticking off a list of things to be accomplished. Throughout their time with us, we talked to parents about what their children needed and how their children might be experiencing them, and we challenged them to ponder what might be going on when the two did not match. We never suggested when they might be "done" or how much time had to pass or what "things" had to be accomplished before we would recommend to the court that their child be returned. Instead we focused on what their child was telling them, what was happening in the relationship.

It was our sense that parents appreciated the truth. We gave them credit for knowing it. Of course they knew things were not working for them. Of course they wanted to be good parents. Of course they wanted with their own child the relationship that they had longed for themselves all their lives. They just didn't know how to get there from here. We gave them credit also for understanding their child's needs once they saw them and for striving to meet those needs.

As a result of our honesty, I believe, parents were able to settle in and either do the work or, alternatively, participate in a different decision for their child's future. Because we never held out false hope, and because we tried always to be compassionate rather than punitive, parents were able more often than not to make wise—though sometimes tough—decisions in their child's best interest and make those decisions with dignity rather than shame.

Ashley

The truth can be a powerful force as we strive for resolution. With Ashley (see Chapter 4) newly transitioned to what we hoped would be her adoptive home, biological grandparents unexpectedly surfaced demanding custody. All our hard work to secure for Ashley what we believed was her best chance for continuing recovery seemed suddenly in jeopardy. On the other hand, an appropriate relative willing to step up is often the best choice for children whose parents have been lost to them. It seemed an impossible, heart-wrenching dilemma.

At this critical juncture, Ashley's social worker took a risky but brilliant step. She called a meeting of people who both had knowledge of Ashley and were invested in her future. The social worker, an attorney general (to answer legal questions that might come up), all of Ashley's providers (pediatrician, physical therapist, etc.), her Guardian ad Litem, my husband and myself, the prospective adoptive parents, and Ashley's grandparents all gathered around a large table in a Department of Children and Family Services conference room. One by one each of us shared what we believed Ashley's experience had been, what her needs were, and what her future was likely to look like.

At the end of two grueling yet poignant hours, Ashley's grandparents asked the social worker and me to step out into the hall. With tears welling in her eyes and her husband's hand on her shoulder for support, Ashley's grandmother quietly announced, "We want Ashley to stay where she is." This was a decision made by the right people for the right reasons. And it was a decision based on truth.

Underlying theoretical foundation

> *...we spend much of the first halves of our lives trying to build internal models that fit the world and much of the last halves trying to adjust the world so it fits our inner models.*

> Brooks 2011, p.209

A sound, coherent, evidence-based theoretical practice helps guide intervention and also normalizes behavior by giving us a way to understand it and a language to describe it. The theoretical foundation of The Children's Ark was attachment theory, enriched by the latest in brain research, all within the specific context of The Circle of Security language and philosophy. A significant part of our initial interview with parents consisted of our explanation of how we believed the relational world worked, what we thought had to happen to shift particular, destructive trajectories, and how we aspired to help. We began by explaining to parents the following presumptions:[5]

- We are all born helpless infants, hardwired to seek relationship in order to survive. Thus, very early, we read our parents' emotional signals and learn what brings them in and what drives them away. We then adjust our own behavior—even if it means forgoing a genuine need—to accommodate the needs of our parents.

- Out of these early relational experiences we develop strategies for being in and maintaining these significant relationships, and a broader view of the world, including whether our behavior matters, whether we can rely on others, and whether we have value.

- Two of children's most basic needs that must be met within the context of their early caregiving relationship are the need for exploration, which facilitates learning, and the need for comfort and protection. When parents' own unmet needs are stirred by their child's bid for the same need, the result can be a plummet into grief and defensiveness that feels to the child like fear and rejection. The child will then learn to suppress or "miscue" this need in order to maintain proximity to the parent, and a relational "dance" thus develops.

We explained to parents that this is what we all do. We suggested that the "dance" they developed with their own caregivers may have helped them adapt as children but had not served them well in the long term. We assured them the development of this dynamic was not their fault. It was a dynamic, however, that—without intervention—they would continue to play out with their own children. What we aspired to do, therefore, was to help them see and understand their particular "dance" while watching it unfold with their children, and to provide the environment and relationships within which they could override these relational strategies and learn to trust a different, more vulnerable, way of being in the world. From within this framework, everything else flowed.

What ultimately became clear to parents was that the counterproductive or destructive behaviors that contributed to them losing custody of their children were really cries for help, or "clues" about what had been missing in their own childhoods, evidence of what they themselves had needed and been denied. Once parents understood this link, the possibility of opening their hearts to their children's longing for connection increased. In relationship with staff, the hope was that parents would come to feel valued enough to begin to consider that they might be worthy of their children's love after all.

Jonathan, Heidi, and Rose

Rose was removed from her parents' care at just a few months of age following a doctor's visit for a swollen ear. During her examination it was discovered that Rose had sustained multiple injuries over time. Several incidents of failure to seek medical attention, or medical neglect, also came to light. One particularly troubling incident involved Rose being submerged in very hot water. Rose was placed in care with a relative. Two months later Heidi and Rose entered The Children's Ark day treatment program. Heidi's husband, Jonathan, was allowed to join them the following month in spite of the belief that he was the cause of Rose's injuries.

This family's course of treatment, particularly as it exemplifies theory-driven intervention, is an interesting and clear one because they were not encumbered by the usual additional burdens we were accustomed to seeing. Neither Jonathan nor Heidi had histories of drug or alcohol abuse, criminal activity, or even unstable relationships. In fact, this marriage was the first significant relationship for them both. Although their financial stability was fragile due to unemployment, they were both bright and educated and did not seem destined for poverty.

Jonathan's childhood, however, was spent in significant poverty, and he was subjected to physical and emotional abuse and neglect. He was the third son in a family of four children. His mother had been the ongoing victim of sexual abuse perpetrated by her own father, and she imbued Jonathan with the notion that he too would grow up to be a sexual victimizer. His experience was of having to fight for a place in the family—to be seen—while, at the same time, feeling blamed and punished for everyone's transgressions. Only flawless performance guaranteed security and safety and asking for help felt dangerous.

Jonathan eventually became highly anxious, rigid, and controlling in an attempt to manage his own and other family members' emotional states. As a result, it became difficult for him to separate his own experience from the experience of others, and, although he desired it, he came to see connection as dangerous. He anticipated that his needs would not be met and believed that he had no value outside of what he did for others. Underlying it all was resentment and anger, the only emotions to which he had access. What he ultimately feared, of course, was abandonment.

Heidi was an only child whose family lived in relative isolation. Both of her parents were immensely shy. Her mother saw Heidi as more of a companion, and her father was so uncomfortable with relational interaction that after a social engagement of any kind he would need to be totally alone. As a result Heidi viewed herself as a burden to her parents, particularly if she needed anything. She, too, learned to be hypervigilant to her parents' emotional states and to put aside her own needs in order to meet theirs. This belief that the needs of others were more important than her own left her unable to recognize or express her own feelings or to function autonomously, believing that if she voiced or put her own needs first, she would be abandoned. She was thus left with little ability to function effectively within the context of a relationship or to act on her own or, eventually, on her daughter's behalf. She had very little tolerance for disagreement or conflict and saw anger as particularly dangerous. When distressed she managed her own emotional state by "going invisible" or by becoming passive aggressive.

As a couple Jonathan and Heidi entered into an unspoken agreement whereby Heidi would be dependent upon Jonathan, letting him lead so that he felt needed. As he took control of more and more of the care and attention of Rose at the Ark, however, Heidi withdrew from interaction, feeling dismissed and irrelevant, further escalating Jonathan's anxiety and controlling behavior.

Unfortunately, neither Jonathan nor Heidi displayed much capacity to communicate or negotiate: Heidi because of her fear of speaking up on her own behalf and Jonathan because of his fears both of appearing incompetent and of asking for help. Rose was thus caught in the middle, with neither parent available to attend to her emotional needs. As this pattern became apparent, so did the combination of relational elements that had led to the abuse and neglect of Rose in the first place.

Jonathan and Heidi's parenting strategy during the first few months of Rose's life was to share caretaking, by which they meant "equal time." When Jonathan returned to work after Rose's birth, both of them became even more focused on whose "turn" it was, at the expense of their daughter's needs or, for that matter, their own needs. The evening of the bath incident was Jonathan's night to put Rose to bed. Heidi's resolve not to interfere with Jonathan's time was likely further strengthened by her presumably unconscious rage at his return to work, leaving her to manage alone with the baby much of the time.

Jonathan felt uncomfortable changing Rose's diaper or bathing her. Lingering always in the back of his mind was his mother's prediction that he would become a sexual predator. He also struggled, as do many new parents, with the awkwardness of handling a tiny infant. The night of the fateful bath, Rose had a bowel movement in the bathtub. Jonathan, feeling frustrated and angry, picked up his wet, slippery daughter with one hand while changing the bath water with the other. He then plunged her back into the fresh water without checking the temperature. Rose was thus submerged in scalding hot water for long enough for her skin to turn bright red, causing her to scream out. At no time did Jonathan ask for help and Heidi, sitting just in the next room, never responded to the ruckus. In the aftermath of this incident, neither parent sought medical attention for Rose.

It is not hard to imagine how Jonathan and Heidi's beliefs, needs, and fears—created out of their early experiences and exacerbated by their interactions with each other—came together that night in ways that put their daughter at risk. It was those same beliefs, needs, and fears that then dictated their treatment plan and led to concrete treatment goals encouraging the emergence in each of a "real self,"[6] free of the limitations and distortions of their early relationships.

Jonathan's treatment goals were centered on developing an awareness of his own feelings, differentiating them from the feelings of others, learning to express them appropriately, and building the capacity to regulate them. Within the context of therapy, he began fairly quickly to track his desire to organize and control others as a way to soothe himself, for instance. As he became more aware of his own feelings, he was more capable of identifying and expressing his needs. As he came to recognize that others' experience was different from his own, the relationship with both his wife and his daughter began to shift. He even came to see asking for help as a positive, daring to open himself up to the vulnerability of criticism.

Heidi's goals were to find her own sense of power and believe in her ability to influence things in her life. She needed to address feeling like a burden by beginning to feel comfortable stating what she wanted and needed. She needed to learn not only to connect with her feelings but also to trust them and let them guide her in making judgments. As Heidi slowly came into her own power, she began to recognize and acknowledge that her passive aggressive way of managing her own angry feelings set Jonathan up to be the family's bearer of anger. She also realized that managing the way she did had resulted in her failure to act on her daughter's behalf.

As a couple, Jonathan and Heidi's primary goals were to learn to trust each other, be direct with each other, and support each other. Success depended upon each being willing to take responsibility for their own emotional state and daring to believe that even strong feelings could be safely expressed and eventually worked out. Heidi needed to find the confidence to voice her true opinions, and Jonathan needed to support her in making decisions. They each needed to be sensitive to the defensive patterns of the other and be willing to compassionately challenge behavior that was potentially risky to their relationship or to their daughter's well-being.

With a better understanding of their relational dynamics, they made good progress. After several months, however, old patterns reappeared. As Rose moved into toddlerhood and pressed for greater independence, Jonathan embraced his daughter's move toward autonomy while Heidi's anxiety escalated. Operating out of her own separation and safety fears, Heidi began to intrude into and interfere with her daughter's normal exploration. Rose naturally responded by disengaging from Heidi and seeking Jonathan. Rather than supporting Heidi's competence in Rose's eyes, Jonathan fell into familiar controlling behavior. Once again the individual pieces of this family's puzzle came together leaving the youngest and most vulnerable member feeling unsupported and clearly at risk. One particular day, in fact, the dynamic escalated into a heated conflict in Rose's presence.

Out of the intensity of this incident, however, with Sandra's competent coaching in-the-moment came new and deeper insights: insights further defining the very nature of the danger for this family. Jonathan really came to understand how he actually manipulated the environment in order to feel valued, and how when his manipulation failed he could move quickly into anger. Heidi came to see that when she got anxious about disapproval or anticipated conflict, she made arbitrary or revenge-driven decisions, further angering Jonathan, or withdrew and failed to protect herself or her daughter.

As Heidi and Jonathan increasingly appreciated both the patterns they repeated and the cost to their daughter, the question that moved to the forefront of treatment became whether or not they could remember and stay with newly developing strategies for interaction in the heat of conflict. Could they, in the face of fear, recognize the difference between history and reality in the present moment? Could each stay with their emotions, even allow their emotions to inform their decision making, while also staying regulated? Ultimately, could they parent safely?

Several months later, after further progress, Rose was moved home while their participation at the Ark continued. One particular incident as reported by Jonathan highlighted again both the strength and tenacity of deep-seated responses and the life-altering shifts that can occur when we choose to confront and challenge them. In order to prepare dinner for the family one evening, Jonathan put Rose in her highchair with some toys in a spot where she could see him but not be in harm's way. Almost immediately Rose protested, resisted, and, in Jonathan's eyes, defied his wishes by trying to climb out of the highchair. Jonathan struggled to regulate his escalating anger in response to what he perceived as Rose's challenge to his competence and control.

As Heidi became aware of the situation, she chose to face and override her fear and confront her husband. She challenged his lack of empathy for the experience of their daughter. Jonathan was able to hear Heidi's concerns without moving immediately into defending himself. He recognized that he was playing out his own story with his daughter. When activated by her normal developmental opposition he had become enraged and felt the need to punish her for "breaking the rules." He also recognized that in the moment he had identified his daughter as his sibling and felt the familiar anticipation of being blamed for her misbehavior. Jonathan reported feeling real empathy for his daughter as a result of these insights and, perhaps for the first time, saw her as her own person. The difference between taking charge and punishing became clear to him.

Heidi and Jonathan have a lifetime ahead of them of learning to compromise, negotiate, and co-parent. Coming to terms with their own anger, fear, and grief was an important beginning, however. The world changed for this family because of their courage and willingness to recognize, reside in, and eventually override the emotional conditioning that blocked access to their parenting wisdom. A cohesive and coordinated theoretical foundation gave them the context in which to do this work.[7]

Focus on reflective functioning

> *Our awareness of another person's state of mind*
> *depends on how well we know our own.*
>
> *Siegel 2010, p.62*

The capacity for reflective functioning is crucial to treatment because, as Dan Siegel suggested above, parents cannot understand and meet the needs of their children without also having insight into the origin and meaning of their own thoughts and feelings. Quite simply, reflective functioning is the capacity both to see into your own mind and to imagine the mind of another. Initially, we come to know ourselves as reflected in another. When we are very young infants, the faces of our parents act as mirrors, informing and defining us, determining what we think and feel.

Over time and in the normal course of development, the capacity for reflective functioning emerges. First comes the revelation that what we think and feel is separate from what others think and feel. Next comes the understanding that what we think and feel is closely linked to what we do or how we behave. Finally, it becomes clear that this process is reciprocal. What I think and feel impacts what I do; what I do impacts what you think and feel; what you do as a result impacts me, and so forth.

Trauma tends to distort this interdependent interaction and solidify destructive, defensive patterns. Promoting the ability to track and translate emotional responses and reactions can lay the foundation for the possibility of real change in wounded relationships. At The Children's Ark, just as staff were asked to face their own presumptions, prejudices, and predispositions, so were parents challenged to notice what their expectations were in relationship and how they protected themselves when feeling vulnerable. They were invited to become aware of how those relational patterns and defensive strategies affected their parenting and how their children might be experiencing them. As empathy begins to develop, parents can learn to reflect both backward and forward, tracing the implications and impact of ancient wiring from their parents through themselves to their children.[8]

Reflecting backward, as parents see how they operate in the world, they can choose to change it. Once they make sense of it all, come to understand that reasons once existed for the way they think and how they protect themselves, reasons that are no longer relevant, they can then consider a different path. Grieving what should have been and was not then becomes possible, as does understanding, compassion, and forgiveness for those responsible. With grieving comes healing and with healing, resolution.

Reflecting forward, by resonating with their children, parents can break the cycle of dysfunction and help their children learn to develop healthy relationships, including how to regulate their emotions. Reflective functioning allows parents to step back from their own experience long enough to observe with clarity the experience of their children. In this reflective place, parents are more able to be present and emotionally available to their children, more able to "hold" their children in distress, and more able to model emotional competence. Children then learn that all feelings can be named, tolerated, and shared.

Anna and Kendra

Kendra was removed from her young parents' care at two months of age when a doctor's visit revealed five to seven broken ribs and healing fractures of both femurs. Although Anna admitted that Kendra's father, Roger, could be violent when drunk and tended to lie, she tenaciously resisted believing that he might be responsible for Kendra's injuries. Instead, she put forth a litany of possible scenarios in explanation: from a rare bone disease to the play of a rough three-year-old living in the house to Roger rolling over on her in his sleep. She insisted, "Even though he has a bad history, he would never hurt Kendra."

Anna's own history was horrific. Her father, who struggled with both schizophrenia and drug addiction, was an imposingly large man who controlled the family through intimidation. He terrorized Anna and her siblings with threats of violence and most likely physically abused them on occasion. Although Anna never accused her father of sexually abusing her, there was the suggestion that he subjected her at an early age to sexual activity with other men. She also reported being molested by a friend's father at age nine and being raped at 16.

Anna's mother was dependent on and enabling of Anna's father and did not intervene on Anna's behalf. When Anna was eleven, she was taken out of school allegedly to be home-schooled. In reality, as the oldest child, she was given the responsibility of caring for the other children and her increasingly incapacitated father. Anna reported being virtually held housebound for three years. Her mother was usually out of the house, working to support the family, leaving Anna to run the household and care for her siblings and at the mercy of her ill and demanding father.

Anna escaped her particular hell by leaving home at 16. By 17 she was pregnant, and at 18 a mother fighting for custody of her child. Not surprisingly Anna suffered from depression and anxiety. She anticipated not only rejection but also humiliation in her close relationships. She imagined impending danger constantly. In order to survive she aligned herself with those around her upon whom she depended and adjusted her behavior to accommodate them even if it meant distorting reality or turning a blind eye to the truth. Anna also developed an elaborate system of strategies for distancing herself from others in order to protect herself and in an attempt to maintain some control over her world. She sometimes used an angry or harsh "edge" or preemptively moved into dismissing or rejecting behavior in order to avoid being attacked or shamed. She sometimes escaped into "spaciness," losing focus and going inside or invisible.

As a result of these defensive postures, and in spite of her obvious high intelligence, Anna lacked judgment. She involved herself in relationships with abusive partners and struggled to maintain even the most basic of boundaries. Her fears and distortions made negotiating tasks or making decisions extremely difficult and stressful for her, and yet once she came to a conclusion, she tended to hold to it rigidly. It didn't take long for all these pieces to come together in ways that put herself and her daughter at risk, leading to the same failure to protect that Anna suffered at the hands of her own mother. Whether or not Anna had the ability over time to reflect honestly on the impact of these patterns would determine whether she could ever parent safely.

In the beginning Anna simply played out her familiar story with Kendra, with me, and with other parents and staff at the Ark. In all her relationships Anna anticipated old patterns of interaction and responded out of her history. With Kendra she assumed a certain resistance or willfulness on her infant daughter's part and shut her down before any connection could take hold. Anna also demonstrated an ambivalence toward Kendra that must have left her daughter confused. Sometimes she was playful with Kendra, but at other times she was harsh; sometimes she ignored Kendra, while at other times she was intrusive; and sometimes she was so "spacey" that she was unable even to notice what Kendra was doing. Kendra, in response, was often extremely fussy and anxious, resulting in a decrease of her natural exploration and ultimately a delay in her normal developmental progress.

Anna also played out much of her reactive drama with me. She held me at a distance in many ways and clearly did not trust me to care about her. She often displayed an angry, critical, or skeptical edge, sometimes devaluing me, sometimes dismissing me. At the same time, there existed an underlying longing to be my special "child" and an accompanying sadness or even bitterness in the knowledge that it was not to be.

One incident that stood out in particular followed a group therapy session. I was in the office debriefing with Sandra when Anna suddenly burst in the door and challenged the hours I had tallied toward her allotted free time. She insisted that I had miscalculated the total and was shorting her time. She stood ready to argue the point. I pointed out that I was currently engaged in a conversation with Sandra and was not able to discuss the issue at the moment. Anna moved immediately into an escalating rage, screaming at me with a vengeance significantly out of proportion to the situation, and stormed out of the office.

Shaken and grateful that Sandra was with me, I spent a good part of an hour calming myself, processing with Sandra, and trying to make sense of the outburst. Finally, I found Anna and simply said to her, "I am not your father. I want you to consider what your experience has been with me." Slowly over time, after many interventions of a similar nature, Anna began to reflect and to relate her present behavior both backward to its origins and forward to its implications for Kendra.

Two videotape interventions in particular impacted Anna's relationship with Kendra. The first, which we called the "kiss off" tape, demonstrated the link between Anna's behavior and Kendra's, the dynamic dictating their "dance." In the video Anna buffers herself from real connection with her daughter, as was typical. She stays engaged with Kendra only when both are focused on a toy or task. Then in a moment in which Kendra undeniably reaches out, seeking intimacy with her mother, Anna shuts down her daughter's bid for closeness with a perfunctory kiss on the top of the head that unmistakably signals "go out" rather than "come in." Kendra responds by quickly giving up, which then feels to Anna like rejection. As Anna became willing to track this pattern we were able to cue her when it occurred with the gentle reminder, "Are you kissing her off?"

Through the second video intervention, Anna was able to begin to come to terms with the very roots of this dynamic. As Anna sat watching video of her daughter sitting in the middle of the floor unmoving except for waving her arms helplessly as she wailed in distress, I asked her, "Who do you see?" We moved one by one through the descriptors that came to mind: big, fat, loud, stationary, demanding. Anna finally dropped into a soft, sad place and replied, "I see my dad." She went on to describe how he used to sit in his chair and scream at her to come empty the cup into which he had just relieved himself. Once Anna realized that she "saw" her dad in her daughter and that her fears of being overwhelmed and overpowered by her baby were displaced feelings, she was able to hold her daughter with more compassion.[9]

Over time Anna's increasing willingness to reveal her vulnerability and the resulting softening and dismantling of her defensive barriers not only allowed for more relationship with her daughter and others but also permitted her keen insight to surface. She came to see that living in the fear and anxiety she experienced as a child produced her hypervigilance and hypersensitivity to perceived danger that no longer existed. She came to recognize her father as a very powerful "ghost in the nursery" (see Chapter 6) intruding into her relationship with Kendra. As her work progressed, she identified her experiences with him as responsible for her feeling criticized, incompetent, unheard, unvalued, and manipulated in all her relationships. She began then to slowly separate the person she really was and aspired to be from the person she had needed to create in order to manage the relationship with her father. As Anna came into her own, she acknowledged, "I never realized that I mattered." She even was able to open to her longing for a real family and to own her jealousy toward my children, "the real children."

But shining the light in this way into Anna's wounds, all that had hurt her and all that was missing, also deepened the pain and moved her into what I call the "in-between place." In the work of recovery, this is a crucial place, a place that sends many a struggling parent running back to the comfort and familiarity of old ways. As they begin to recognize and lift their protective armor, the exposure for many is too great, the risk in "stepping over" too costly. It is in the "in-between place" that parents come face to face with the anticipated loss of all they have known and the terrifying void that remains. Anna described it beautifully:

> "I feel sadness when I look back. I have gained a new life. It feels scary because I have left everything I know behind, and I still want some of it. Being in between is harder than being either place. Being in between feels like I don't have a place to be."

Following a visit with her family who were here for her graduation from college, Anna's musings to me were particularly heartbreaking in their clarity:

> "My family tree is sick and dying. I feel like a seed that blew off and has to start over, all alone. I have to mourn that I cannot have my mother. I have to mourn that she was and never will be there for me. And I have to mourn that you are not my mother. I will never be the most important, special one."

Although Anna's longing for her family remained, her need to step away from the forces that bound her to them had also become painfully apparent to her.

Translating insight like Anna's into change and moving beyond the "in-between place" takes courage. Bridging this gap requires a willingness to both "refrain" and "reframe."[10] Once the stories of her past that drove her current behavior were clear, the task became to refrain from indulging the defenses she evolved to help her manage the pain. It is not enough to just see clearly. Only by refraining from her usual protective patterns and instead actually stepping into the fear thus revealed would she ever be released from its grip.

In order to move forward and transform behavior, Anna also had to reframe her experience to its present context. Again her capacity for reflective functioning was key. She came to see, for instance, that her drive to help others and her "panic" when she perceived that others were doing things wrong grew out of an early, too young responsibility for everybody getting everything right. As she reframed this compulsion for perfection to her present context, she realized that others might experience her behavior as intrusive, controlling, devaluing, and degrading and so worked hard to override her anxiety and both trust others' competence and let go of others' failings.

The ultimate hoped-for consequence of such reflective insight can be the natural emergence of empathy, again in both directions: backward for the imperfect and sometimes significantly wounded adults in our young lives who are responsible for how we see and function in the world and forward for the experience of our children.

Anna and Kendra lived with us at The Children's Ark for two years. Their transformation was inspiring to watch. This kind of life-altering change is fragile and tenuous, however, without a future to walk into that promises enough safety, security, and hope to encourage staying the course. For Anna and Kendra, that meant staying close to us. After Anna regained custody, their first move was to an apartment across the street from the Ark and up on the second floor so that, as Anna put it, "We could sit in our new home and watch the Ark family gathered around the dining room table for dinner." Her ongoing connection with us became, I believe, a lifeline for her.

Research and theory: Attachment-based intervention with at-risk families

"Angels in the nursery" was a concept offered by clinical psychologist Alicia Lieberman and her colleagues as a counterbalance to Selma Fraiberg's notion of "ghosts in the nursery" (see Chapter 6). Lieberman, a leading expert in child–parent psychotherapy who had witnessed the power of "ghosts" in her therapeutic work with children and families, also recognized that some parents were able to break negative cycles. Often, these parents described moments of connection, joy, and caring that made them feel loved and valued. With this realization came the insight that—even for parents with horrific pasts—some intergenerational influences were benevolent and that drawing on those benevolent influences might have therapeutic value.

> In ideal circumstances, self-affirming influences move silently in the lives of children, wrapping each successive generation in the security that comes from being loved, accepted, and understood. In darker moments, these "angels in the nursery" square off against their more famous siblings, the ghosts (Fraiberg, Adelson, and Shapiro 1975), doing battle with them to keep intact the protective shield of parental love that surrounds young children and endeavoring to repair the damage when malevolent influences from the past break through. (Lieberman *et al.* 2005, p.506)

Child–parent psychotherapy (CPP), the therapeutic approach developed by Lieberman and her colleagues, built on many of Selma Fraiberg's early insights. Fraiberg is well known for her pioneering work in infant mental health and infant–parent psychotherapy. Her therapeutic approach—often taking place in the home—was designed to observe, directly, how parents' pasts ("ghosts") played out in their caregiving. Through this approach, she helped parents gain insight about their ghosts and worked with them to ultimately resolve early past traumatic experiences, so that they could build healthier relationships with their own children.

Rooted in psychoanalysis and attachment theory and informed by developmental psychopathology as well as stress and trauma research, CPP has become a rich and effective therapeutic intervention.[11] Essential to this approach is to have the child and parent present together during sessions and to focus on the emotional quality of their relationship, while also attending to how each individual affects the shared emotional tone. In addition to ferreting out the "ghosts" of the parents' past, exposing positive memories of feeling loved and valued is central to treatment: "Uncovering of angels as growth-promoting forces in the lives of traumatized parents is as important to therapeutic work as the containing, taming, and exorcizing of ghosts" (Lieberman *et al.* 2005, p.506). When a parent's early relational experience is so bleak that very few positive memories are available, as was Anna's experience, the therapist works to create new relational experiences that are supportive and affirming.

The Children's Ark was initially developed as a residential approach to foster care, a place where parents could co-reside with their children while getting the help they needed, so that they could both become self-sufficient and parent safely. In this way, children and parents together could be the focus of intervention. This focus was maintained when the Ark became a day treatment program. The philosophy of The Children's Ark, with genuine relationship at the center, provided parents with an environment that challenged many of their expectations. Janet and her staff became the "angels" that helped open windows to new ways of being in relationship that parents could then carry forward with their children.

In addition to creating a general therapeutic milieu that brought parents together with their children and in which all felt safe and valued, The Children's Ark was imbued with the philosophy and practice of the Circle of Security intervention (see Chapters 3 and 6). As one of the first laboratories for the COS, The Children's Ark was deeply influenced by this developing intervention; the language of the COS became the language of The Children's Ark. As Janet described, "Operating out of a sound, coherent, evidence-based theoretical practice helps guide intervention and also normalizes behavior by giving us a way to understand it and a language to describe it."

A central premise of the COS intervention is that what gets in the way of responsive caregiving is not a lack of desire to be a good parent but rather one's experience:

> None of these parents lacked the desire to do right by his or her child… They just did not know how, largely because the parenting they received had not taught them. What their caregivers did teach them—in some way or another—was that certain needs around the Circle were precarious to express: asking for them to be met resulted in driving the caregiver away, physically, emotionally, and/or mentally. The distance that resulted left the child vulnerable, with her survival at risk, or at the very least left the child subject to the isolation of Being-Without. It left the child, now grown into an adult, afraid of being devoured by sharks that no longer existed. (Powell *et al.* 2014, p.84)

Giving the negative emotion evoked by unconscious memories of traumatic experience a name—"shark music"—and helping parents to identify the "shark music" that put their relationships at risk became a powerful part of the COS intervention. This concept was embraced at The Children's Ark: parents came to speak openly of "their shark music." The therapy room even had a sign on its door that read "Shark Crossing"!

The use of carefully edited video to help parents observe their relational dynamics with their children more objectively is another potent technique utilized by the COS and, as Janet described above, was powerful in creating awareness among the Ark parents: "Seeing themselves react to their children's needs in ways that are both harmful to their children and unplanned, previously unrecognized, and unintended is a shocking eye-opener" (Powell *et al. 2014,* p.90). Just as Anna was able to recognize that she was playing out her own history with her daughter, so too were many parents able to identify a familiar pattern being enacted with their children once they could see those patterns from the outside.

Improving parents' capacity for reflective functioning is also central to the COS intervention and was a daily aspiration within the Ark environment. According to psychologist Arietta Slade (2005), reflective functioning (or mentalization) can be "understood narrowly as the capacity to understand one's own and other's behavior in terms of underlying mental states and intentions and more broadly as a crucial human capacity that is intrinsic to affect regulation and productive social relationships" (p.269). As Janet explained above, initially we come to know ourselves as reflected in another, with our parents' faces acting as mirrors of our experience. Caregivers with high reflective functioning can mirror for their infants their infant's affective states while also acting as a container for intense emotion. Disruptions occur, however, when caregivers' mirroring either misrepresents or is not connected to the infant's emotional experience or when it is too real: "For example, a mother might herself respond with fear to her child's fear, rather than acknowledge and frame his own experience without taking it on herself" (Slade 2005, p.273).

Reflective functioning was identified and studied by British psychoanalyst and clinical psychologist Peter Fonagy and his colleagues as being critical to the intergenerational transmission of secure attachment: "Reflective functioning, in fact, consistently emerges as a cornerstone capacity within the state of mind of those who are able to support secure attachment" (as cited in Powell *et al.* 2014, p.115).[12] As Anna's ability to understand herself and her child grew so did their connection and Kendra's feelings of security. Whereas early in their relationship Anna and Kendra were on a pathway toward disorganized attachment, just after they were discharged from the Ark, Kendra was assessed as secure.

Over the past several decades, relationship-based interventions focusing on the parent–child attachment relationship have been shown to affect transformational change, putting at-risk families on healthier developmental pathways. The ghosts and sharks may linger, yet with insight and enhanced reflective abilities, parents learn to manage and regulate these threats to their caregiving. The "quick fixes" characteristic of many current approaches to child welfare (e.g. parenting and anger management classes) are likely to do little to promote lasting change, as evidenced by what some describe as a "revolving door" in contemporary foster care. Although initially more resource-intensive, interventions that focus on parent–child relationships while also providing comprehensive support for at-risk families are not only more humane but also are likely to be both more effective and cost-efficient in the long run (see Chapter 10).

Chapter 9

THE MEANING AND MEASURE OF CHANGE

Frequently in the heat of an Ark staff meeting while being grilled by a public defender as to when we would be recommending that a client's child be returned, I found myself saying, "First, I suggest that we have a discussion about what is different and how you know it." This inquiry captures, I believe, the essence of the distinction between compliance and change: what is different?

The first task for us always was to identify the problem. There could be no answer until we knew the question. The second task was to assess, following intervention, whether or not genuine change had occurred and to be able to describe it.

Defining the nature of change is a complicated and elusive endeavor. Our experiences at The Children's Ark over a 15-year period, however, gave us some insight into both what seem to be some of the important prerequisites to change (what the client brings or develops in treatment) and significant indicators that change has occurred (what it looks like).

Prerequisites to change: Resilience

It is particularly challenging to capture the essence of resilience or to attempt to define what creates it with specificity, but its role in promoting change is undeniable.[1] Two things seem clear. First, resilience is developmental rather than inherent, suggesting that it can be enhanced or cultivated through effective intervention. Second, resilience at any given time depends upon the current balance in one's life between stressors and supports. This also implies that the ability to endure and recover in the face of adversity is a fluctuating process. Certainly, the more resilient parents weathered the challenging and painful work at the Ark best and ultimately resisted transforming their lives the least, whether they came with this particular characteristic or developed it in treatment.

One of the most universally recognized factors in the lives and histories of individuals demonstrating resilience is the presence of at least one caring person with whom they felt seen and understood. An experience of being known and valued, even for a relatively brief period of time, seems to open up the possibility of a future different from the past or the present. Possibility—even a very small peek into another way to be—can be a powerful rationale for hope, and the ability to understand that another might see you differently than you see yourself can lead to a shift in self-image. As psychotherapist Irvin Yalom (1999) states, "People love themselves if they see a loving image of themselves reflected in the eyes of someone they really care about" (p.197).

Several of the more resilient Ark mothers were able to identify someone to whom they felt connected. Anna, highlighted in Chapter 8, remembered, "I have a flash of a teacher that comes to mind." Two other moms had fathers who, though with troubling issues of their own and not always reliable, nonetheless adored them. Carla (Chapter 8) spoke of her former foster parents and also of a Guardian ad Litem assigned to her when she was a child. In fact, she was able to describe to me in astounding detail a day she spent as a child with her Guardian ad Litem, Carol; a day during which she felt like she mattered. She talked of going to church, a big, fancy house, and swimming in a lake. She then went on to describe two memories from that day that speak with such wisdom to the tremendous redeeming effect of a moment of sensitive caring and empathy. When noticing the table set for their meal, Carla felt overwhelmed by its formality and demoralized by her ignorance of even which fork to use. Carol, sensing Carla's discomfort, gently led her through the rules of table etiquette in a way that felt nurturing to Carla and allowed her to feel that she fit in when lunch was actually served. Later Carol's daughter gave Carla clothes from her closet. Carla was often ridiculed at school for the shabby way she dressed, so the clothes were a godsend. Carol's daughter managed, like her mother, to see and empathize with Carla enough to create in this gift the sense of friends sharing possessions rather than an act of charity.

Tenacity

Part of resilience seems to be tenacity. In spite of seemingly insurmountable odds, clients with resilience push on with a resoluteness that suggests a belief that they can impact their environment. They tend to move toward challenge rather than away from it. They set goals and move toward them with uncanny single-mindedness. They can, of course, hold just as obstinately to a misguided or illusionary goal as to a sound one, but it is perhaps the stubbornness itself that allows them to persevere long enough to ultimately consider alternate paths.

Anna, for instance, showed fierce determination in spite of her initial conviction that she was not in need of intervention. Driven by the desire to defend herself, she demanded access to every evaluation and service of which she became aware. She was the only client ever at the Ark to ask both for extra sessions with our therapist and to attend sessions with the therapist who supervised my use of videotape. The very relentlessness of her pursuit eventually allowed her mind to open to enough information that her insight could kick in and as her insight evolved her defensiveness gradually receded. Anna was also the client at the Ark who worked the hardest to maintain the relationship with us upon exiting. As mentioned before, she initially moved across the street from the Ark. Then when we transitioned to a day program and moved back to our home, she followed us to our neighborhood, renting an apartment just blocks away.

Capacity for relationship, reflective functioning, and empathy

The general capacity for relationship seemed another important component of resilience and prerequisite for change. A client who valued relationship on some level, who clung to a thread of connection with significant others in spite of the pain, who allowed the longing to spill over on occasion, was able to enter more easily into a therapeutic alliance. That, of course, did not mean that the therapeutic road was smooth or that there wasn't resistance, but the emotional struggle of trying to reconcile the gap between what was and what should have been was at least a familiar one, rendering intervention somehow less complicated.

A more developed capacity for relationship usually also meant easier access to both reflective functioning (which was usually also indicative of a higher level of intelligence) and empathy: more willingness to look at and talk about the self and more ability to find some softness and forgiveness for others. In such clients the hunger to connect tends to keep hope alive, and so the bitterness of disappointment is less likely to lead to defeat. There was also a sort of compassion for or resonance with vulnerability in others. As Carla said to me at a recent lunch, "I am totally drawn to the forgotten child; perhaps it takes one to know one." I believe that it is that sense of connectedness to others, that sense of feeling part of a greater whole, that serves as an antidote to the fear and pain of feeling alone and abandoned, and that thus contributes to the courage to persist.

Hope

Finally, Ark clients with resilience demonstrated a sense of hope, an expectation of something better, an ability to step back and recognize that although their lives were in shambles, it was not the essence of who they were. They could envision another path. They believed in the possibility of choice. This faith in possibility encouraged perseverance. Hope also manifested as trust and the willingness to allow others to be with them and believe in them, indeed, the grit to fight for connection.

Angie and Charlie

Angie was imbued with all the qualities or capacities of resilience, and although her road has been long and arduous, her resolve has remained steadfast.

When Angie arrived at the Ark with her toddler son, Charlie, the odds were already stacked against them. She suffered from a significant addiction to cocaine and methamphetamine and had dropped out of or been discharged from a long line of treatment programs. Her son had been in foster care since birth. The Child Protective Services social worker on the case feared that if the bond between mother and son was not established soon, reunification would become unlikely.

Angie's struggles were numerous. Focus and consistency eluded her as she fought to bring some order to the chaos of her life. It was extremely difficult for her to maintain enough structure to keep herself on track or to stay in charge with Charlie. Her troubling relationship with Charlie's father remained unresolved. Though now sober she continued to demonstrate a multitude of addiction-related behaviors: from diverting attention away from herself to pushing the limits to flirting with the need for lesser mind-altering drugs like painkillers. Every week felt like one step forward followed by several steps back.

Yet Angie radiated promise. In spite of her addictive acting out she was charming and relationally competent in many ways. She maintained close ties with her family, including a brother and sister with whom she regularly visited. Though imperfect with troubles of their own, Angie's parents stuck by her, and Angie managed most of the time to hold a balanced view of them even when they disappointed her. Angie befriended the other Ark parents easily. When small skirmishes inevitably occurred between them, Angie knew how to and was willing to work at repair. She demonstrated a clear capacity for relationship, which drew people to her and ultimately encouraged them to invest in her success. Because of this capacity for relationship, Angie's response to therapeutic interventions—and even confrontations—was open and receptive. She welcomed feedback and reflected thoughtfully.

She also understood the impact of her early experiences and the present costs of them to herself and her son. Part way through her stay at the Ark, Angie—referring to her mother—commented, "Our relationship plays out a lot with Charlie...ever since I was little she basically gave me the message that I couldn't go out and do anything without her." She could see the link between the lack of boundaries and structure in her own upbringing and her parenting of Charlie. She overindulged Charlie, could deny him nothing, but then moved quickly to anger as he spiraled out of control. When asked what that was like for her, Angie replied, "To make myself feel better, I do not discipline him." Angie clearly demonstrated the capacity for reflective functioning. Her ability to translate her insight into acting in her son's best interest, however, was often confounded by her guilt at having let him down.

Angie understood that she was "running from her own anger," frequently transferring it to or directing it at another. She had an opportunity, for instance, to be a model for a hairdressing event which would earn enough money to pay off a substantial part of the debt owed her mother. To everyone's surprise she turned it down. Reflecting later in conversation with me Angie disclosed feeling that "paying her off would mean forgiving her." Softening a bit she continued, "or perhaps I'm just not ready to feel worthy." She also expressed anger at other Ark parents when she perceived their behavior as neglectful or abandoning of their children. Angie came to see in these cases also that much of her anger at others was displaced and that really she was angry at herself for all the times she chose to get high instead of visiting her son.

Angie was also tenacious. Even as she stumbled and fell back, she stayed focused forward. And stumble she did. Her months at the Ark felt like a roller coaster ride: accomplishing goals and progressing forward one moment, falling back into old habits the next. But she stayed sober, passed her high school equivalency exam, and enrolled in college classes, and ultimately demonstrated enough stability and competency in parenting to gain custody of her son and move out of the Ark and into her own apartment.

An exit plan that kept them tied to Ark staff and services was put in place.

It was not long, however, before we began noticing a gradual but undeniable deterioration in her demeanor and behavior. She sometimes didn't show up for services or lunch at the Ark or showed up late. She began looking more and more unkempt and uncared for, as did Charlie. She started losing weight. One day as we watched Charlie romp in the park I confronted her and asked her if she was using drugs. She initially denied it, inquiring as to why I asked. I remember saying to her, "You taught me well, Angie," and recited all the symptoms of relapse I learned from her that she was now displaying.

Angie lost Charlie again, this time for good. But after one more spiral downward into the throes of addiction, she checked herself into an intensive inpatient treatment facility followed by outpatient services and eventually found her way back. She has since given birth to a second son (Brian), continued her pursuit of a higher education, and remained gainfully employed. She has avoided unhealthy entanglements with men. She has remained clean and sober for going on ten years. She works hard to be the strong, consistent, confident parent for Brian that eluded her with Charlie.

Through it all Angie never gave up hope. She always kept one eye focused forward, understanding what she needed to do to create a future for herself and her son, "I really, really need to stay in school… I'm not going to have any sort of future for Brian or myself if I don't have a career." She understood also that "everything's a choice; everything has its repercussions." Perhaps most important of all, Angie knew that "the life that I did lead before wasn't who I am."

Angie's reflective capacity continues to this day. At a recent lunch she said to me, "I need to get back into therapy. As Brian grows I realize that my delight in him triggers my grief at having failed Charlie. I need to begin to resolve my guilt, despair, and shame over his loss." Angie's insight is imbued with a softness and sensitivity that allows her to resonate with the feelings of others and even on occasion offer herself gentle kindness and forgiveness.

Prerequisite to change: Surrender

Some kind of surrender usually precedes real life-altering change. To surrender is to cease fighting, to stop resisting.[2] That may mean a client owning her part in the "dance," acknowledging the negative impact on her child, and taking responsibility for her behavior. It may mean recognizing and stepping out of the protective armor that distances a client from uncomfortable feelings and walking into the pain. It may mean the dismantling of carefully constructed "rules of the universe" and dysfunctional strategies of survival.

But because surrendering means stripping away the blinders and seeing more clearly it also means exposing the underlying pain and fear. When a client drops, as a result, into profound grief and remorse, it is critical that the hand of a trusted other be available. To surrender without such support can lead to despair and desolation instead of healing; but, in the words of psychiatrist Mark Epstein (2013), "Trauma becomes sufferable, even illuminating, when there is a relational home to hold it in" (p.197).

Surrender is about trust and courage because, as one Ark mom so insightfully described (see Part 2: Introduction), once that line is stepped over there is no going back. There is both fear and loss in change: fear of the unknown and of stepping into the suffering one has so meticulously shielded oneself from, and loss of the known and familiar and comfortable. It requires a leap of faith and perhaps some promise of safety and salvation at the other side of the chasm.

"The Shift"

We called this leap of faith, this stepping over the line into another way of being, "The Shift." It was often felt rather than seen and was more like a softening and an opening than a capitulation. It was clearly a process, but often there was a moment in time at the Ark when we suddenly became aware of readjusting our own internal emotional response to a client; sometimes it was only years later that surrender was evident.

Tamera

Tamera, Daisy's mother (see Chapter 8), was particularly anxious to regain custody of her child and live independently. She was familiar with the system and, in hopes of speeding up the process, put herself on the list for every supervised living facility in town. Tamera was tough and savvy and used to getting her way. The day she received a letter from one of the supervised living facilities informing her that she had moved to the top of the list and housing was available for her and her daughter, she marched triumphantly into my office, paperwork in hand.

I responded to her that although her social worker might support such a decision, if it were up to me the answer would be no. I then invited her into a conversation as to why I felt she was not yet ready for such a step. Tamera flew into a rage and slammed out of my office yelling that she would be calling the social worker. Before long I received a call from Tamera's social worker assuring me that such a move would only be allowed at our recommendation. I breathed a sigh of relief, believing we had dodged a bullet and that the issue was resolved, not yet understanding that I had miscalculated Tamera's determination.

The following week Tamera was at my office door again having come to the top of another list. Mustering all the therapeutic patience of which I was capable, I announced once again that I did not feel that she was ready. This time Tamera was quiet though clearly fuming. Without saying a word she turned her back on me and walked out of my office. I could feel both anger and anxiety well up within me: anger that she was making me take this position and disappoint her again, and anxiety about my right to even be making such decisions about people's lives.

A couple of days later I was sitting at the dining room table paying bills. Staff, parents, and toddlers milled about both in the dining room and in the adjacent kitchen and living room. I suddenly became aware of the presence of someone standing directly in front of me. I looked up to see Tamera's somber face just as she placed in front of me a letter of acceptance from a third supervised residency program. This time I was unable to contain my intense feelings, feelings that were fueled I'm sure by my own escalating self-doubt. I spit out angrily, "If I didn't think you were ready last week, and I didn't think you were ready two days ago, what makes you think I would think you were ready now?!"

Tamera's face fell, and she turned and walked away. Shaken, I tried to return to my work. Within minutes she was back. I could feel myself stiffen and prepare for yet more resistance. As I looked up, however, Tamera softened into vulnerability and said quietly, "But why are you so angry with me?"

When Tamera's investment in the relationship with me took priority over what she wanted so desperately, it felt like surrender. I could feel my heart shift. Without her defensive need to manipulate me and aggressively push her agenda and without my defensive need to assert my authority, we were ultimately able to meet and negotiate real, reasonable solutions, and, eventually, when we felt Tamera was ready, we did support her moving into a transitional home.

Heidi

Heidi (see Chapter 8) was very slow to engage meaningfully in therapy. For many months it seemed she could not tolerate thinking about her own experience enough to allow a real therapeutic alliance with Sandra. She eventually made several fairly superficial shifts and was able to talk about her childhood but was still unable to stand up for herself in the relationship with Jonathan. Sandra recalls a particular couple's session during which she pushed Heidi to try to get her to take a stand with Jonathan. Heidi was never able to take the risk to assert herself on her own behalf.

Not long after this session Sandra had an individual session with Heidi during which she brought up the couple's session and asked Heidi what it had been like for her. Under fire again, Heidi finally dared to walk into the unimaginable. She exposed to Sandra her violent fantasies, revealing to her all the things she had felt like doing when feeling "attacked" in the couple's session. When

Sandra did not flinch, become angry, or abandon her something shifted in Heidi.

Once Heidi found the courage to surrender to her most vulnerable truth, she stepped over that line from which she could never return. When the punishment she imagined did not come to be, she was then invested with the strength to do what had previously seemed impossible: stand up for herself.

Carrie

Although Carrie (see Chapter 7) understood that moving Sean into foster care, and thus getting them both out from under her mother's control, was a necessary step in her own individuation and ultimately toward reunification with him, her longing for her son was significant. In order to minimize Sean's time away from her and expedite their reunion, we decided to hold full staff meetings monthly. We assigned everybody tasks and each month we all sat down to discuss our progress and deal with the inevitable setbacks.

I recall month after month feeling some annoyance as each staffing began with some version of Carrie bemoaning what wasn't happening. Then one month instead of sounding like a maligned victim, Carrie started talking about what she still needed to do to adequately provide for Sean. And instead of minimizing or denying the disabilities Sean faced as the result of his abuse, she inquired as to services that she might pursue to help him recover. And something shifted. I remember saying to Sandra, "Why do I feel like returning Sean to Carrie today?"

When Carrie shifted from being the person to whom all this bad stuff had been done to taking on the responsibility for being Sean's mother, it was a kind of surrender. Once her focus shifted to helping her son by making use of the resources available to them instead of blaming the system, those of us around her were motivated to help her get what she needed and get out of her way. She ultimately regained custody of Sean, and they are doing well.[3]

My conversations with Desirae, Carla, and Angie over the years have demonstrated that surrender can happen at any time and is always possible. Although each of them left the Ark under different circumstances, they all took something away that they continue to be able to access years down the line. Their ongoing growth, courage, and willingness to surrender are a tribute to the human spirit and the innate yearning for healing.

Understanding change

To the degree that we look clearly and compassionately
at ourselves, we feel confident and fearless
about looking into someone else's eyes.

Chodron 1997, p.76

Change takes time, and it rarely follows a straight line. It takes courage to surrender to the process, and those with resilience are probably more likely to endure the journey. But to return to the original question: what does real change look like? What is different at the conclusion of a successful intervention?

At The Children's Ark we measured change by tracking clients' increased capacity for relationship and intimacy or the maturing of their emotional development. We tracked clients' ability to self-activate, to initiate on their own behalf. We saw change when clients could ask for what they needed, could negotiate in good faith, and could problem solve. We saw change when clients demonstrated and could regulate a wide range of emotions and could tolerate the same in their children. We saw change when it was clear that clients understood that not everyone's experience was the same as their own, and when they could acknowledge and take responsibility for their behavior. And we saw change when clients could take the next step and fully engage in a therapeutic relationship and make effective use of the resources available to them.

Change was reflected in how clients saw and were with their children. We saw a new layer of commitment that was based on unconditional acceptance and a willingness to put their children's needs ahead of their own. We saw an intimacy that came from being available, aware, and attuned to their children. We saw a willingness to assume responsibility for parenting and to stay in charge of the relationship,[4] and, at the same time, a deep compassion for even the most tender and fragile of emotions.

Perhaps the most striking indicator of change was this tendency to deep compassion or empathy for the experience of another; the ability, in American Buddhist nun Pema Chodron's words, to "look into someone else's eyes." But as Ms. Chodron also suggested, we dare to open our hearts in resonance to another only to the degree to which we have looked into our own heart with clarity and kindness. Client stories of empathy therefore are stories of transformation, stories of growth manifesting in an increased ability to open their hearts to their children, to others, and to themselves.

Desirae: Empathy for her children

The day Desirae came to review the chapter about her family I asked her how all the kids were doing. She told me a story about David that rings in my memory still as an example of astounding advocacy and empathy. David had been medicated through the years for a number of ADHD and related symptoms. Desirae worked with David's doctor to find the ideal balance between minimal medication and manageable behavior. The summer that David was between grade school and middle school, he was taken off all his medication to assess his ability to regulate his emotions outside the school environment.

Desirae's plan for the upcoming school year was to slowly reinstate only that level of medication that was necessary for David to manage his behavior, again in consultation with David's doctor. Understanding that school personnel could not focus on David's needs and accommodate his fluctuating moods like she could at home, she hand-delivered the first day of middle school to every teacher David would encounter a several-page letter entitled, "What you need to know about David," including information on how to reach her.

"We got through a couple of days," Desirae related to me, "but on the third day of school I got a call from the band teacher." The teacher told Desirae that he had suspended David from class, that he was distracting the other kids by tapping drumsticks on everything in sight and would not stop when asked. "And then," the teacher went on, "he just went crazy turning over his chair and leaving the classroom."

"Did you reprimand him?" Desirae asked. "Of course," the teacher told her. "Did you reprimand him in front of the whole class?" she asked. "Yes," he answered. Desirae then went on to explain to the band teacher that, as she had stated in the letter, David is easily triggered by situations in which he feels humiliated in front of others and that if it is possible to take him aside and quietly correct him for inappropriate behavior, he responds more positively.

I remember thinking as Desirae related this story to me how attuned to this child's experience she was and how invested in his success and well-being. Desirae is a young, struggling woman, raising eight children, in a world stacked against her in so many ways. Yet her knowledge of, commitment to, and compassion for all of her children represent a profound change from the harsh, insensitive, punitive young mother who knocked on the door of The Children's Ark all those years ago.

Carla: Empathy for others

Several years following Carla's exit from The Children's Ark we were having lunch together at a local restaurant. We got into a discussion about my retirement from the Ark, and Carla was commenting upon how hard it must have been for me to walk away. I certainly concurred that leaving what had consumed my life for 15 years was difficult and carried much sadness for me. I told her that it was also clear that the time had come to retire for many reasons. I then dropped into a very quiet, vulnerable place as I shared with her that there was a way in which it was actually harder and harder for me emotionally to be at the Ark toward the end.

When Carla asked me what it was that I feared, I teared up and said that it felt like I couldn't do what I was asking the clients to do: be totally honest. I told her there were things about my own life that I felt were not appropriate to share and yet refusing to do so had made me feel like an imposter. I feared that if any of the parents served at the Ark subsequently learned these things about me, it would feel to them like a betrayal of trust and thus cause them to call into question or repudiate all the tough work they had done.

In a moment of profound empathy, Carla reached across the table, took my hand in hers, and said, "Oh, Sweetie, don't you see? You couldn't tell us." A response of such sensitivity and sympathetic support required Carla to reach past her own pain and feel into my heart with wisdom and compassion. This was a remarkably transformed Carla from the cocky, resistant, devaluing young woman I first interviewed.

Anna: Empathy for self

As I have learned walking through my own pain, kindness and compassion directed toward ourselves always seems the hardest. This was also true for clients of the Ark. Anna articulated particularly well her struggle over time from feelings of shame through increasing understanding toward eventual empathy.

Anna revealed early on in therapy her sense of feeling criticized, devalued, and taken advantage of by others. She came to understand that in anticipating such behavior—and responding accordingly— she was closing herself off to relationship. Even though she also came to see the link between her present perceptions of others and her experiences with her father, she carried alone an enormous burden of guilt and shame.

Anna longed for family, to belong, to be delighted in but could not imagine that she could be worthy of such care: "Even the things I'm proud of have bad memories. I'm ashamed of so many things. Part of me can't forgive myself. The voice I hear is my dad's. I can't forgive myself because I anticipate others can't."

Over time as Anna came to see more clearly the painful dynamic at work in her family of origin and had repeated, overriding experiences of unconditional caring in the Ark environment, she dared to consider that her story wasn't her fault, that she "mattered," that she deserved better: "I had no control and no boundaries. I wanted something to hold onto. I didn't have enough information to make better decisions."

Insight followed compassion, and compassion, again, followed insight. So the more kindly Anna held her experience, the more precise became her reflection and vice versa: "I think I need to try to help people I perceive as powerless because no one helped me. I wish someone had fought for me. I wish I could have grown up here. I would have been free to be myself and would have had the guidance I needed. I never had a real home."

Success

Perhaps the real test of change is whether or not experiences in intervention get translated into the bigger arena, into life outside treatment, and whether change is maintained over time. Many of the incidents and conversations in this book took place years after treatment, and still the ends of these stories have yet to be written. How then—and when—is success determined?

Yet we cannot escape a conversation about success. If it is change we are after it would seem we have to be able to measure success. When dealing with the many changing dynamics of lives at social, economic, and relational risk, however, assessing success can be elusive and confounding. Life is complicated. What looks like success today may fragment in a million ways tomorrow, and then look like success again sometime in the future. What feels like failure today may morph into an amazing success story years down the line.

Although I understand the necessity for evaluating outcome, I always felt myself cringe when questioned about success rates at The Children's Ark. I don't believe that my discomfort was based on a fear of poor outcome—indeed we were proud of our record[5]—but rather the nagging conviction that the wrong question was being asked. Perhaps rather than "Was it a success?" we should be asking "Was it worth it?" It is my belief and experience that every client who passed through the doors of the Ark was changed in some way. So also was every staff member changed by each client. The value lay in what happened between us. When one human being genuinely and openly touches another human being, change happens. And as Father Boyle, founder of Homeboy Industries, suggests, if we get too caught up in the ending, we miss the story: "Salivating for success keeps you from being faithful, keeps you from truly seeing whoever's sitting in front of you" (Boyle 2010, p.168).

Success: The children

Always included in my response to questions about outcomes was that we measured success by the children. Were the children included in the treatment process and given adequate visitation? Was permanency achieved as quickly as possible and with minimal further impact to the children's emotional well-being? Were placement decisions made carefully and transitions handled sensitively? Did they, ultimately, end up in the best caregiving situation available to them, even if it was not what we would have wished for them? And what did the children take away from their foster care experience?

As stated elsewhere in this book, foster parents can be a tremendous source of comfort and strength to the children in their care. Even temporary caregivers can make a lasting difference in the life trajectories of children at risk as they support them through the trauma of separation and loss. I recall a conversation with a colleague at a time I was deeply grieving the return of a foster child in my care to a situation that I was concerned would be detrimental to him. My colleague gently reassured me that I had given this young child a gift, an experience of being valued, that he could choose to access and act from at any time in his life. If Rachel, Nathan, and David carried memories in their hearts of my caring presence, I was comforted by the thought that so could this little boy.

Success: The parents

We never talked to the parents at The Children's Ark about "graduation" or being "finished" and never considered anything like a "Certificate of Completion." We told them instead that change and healing took a lifetime of work. We also knew that we could not really guarantee them success, we could only convince them that they had choices. So perhaps a better way to think about success is that it is relative and an ever-evolving process.

Desirae

Life for Desirae and her family has recently taken a tragic turn. Isaac, David's older brother, is serving time in prison for the senseless killing of a family friend. Desirae and the rest of the family have disappeared behind a wall of their own making, perhaps too filled with fear and shame to accept the love and support awaiting them.

During that discussion with Desirae in which she showed such empathy for David, she said something else that now feels hauntingly prophetic. In a moment of painful truth-telling, she revealed to me her most honest and vulnerable fear: "I do the best I can. I have always done the best I can. But I fear that giving me my children was not the best decision for them." As I complimented her on her knowledge of and compassion for her children and stated that I thought they were lucky to have her, she replied, "Yes, but it took me so long that I'm afraid it was too late for most of them."

Apparently, as the boys grew older and spun out of control and into defiance and aggression, Desirae did the only thing she knew to do in hopes of protecting the younger children: she first kicked Isaac out of the house and then David. I don't know how long Isaac had been on the streets before his fateful confrontation with the young man he shot, nor do I know where David is. What I do know is how my heart aches for them all.

So where do we place Desirae on the success scale? Certainly, we did not consider it a success when she left the Ark. We, in fact, fought long and hard for her children not to be returned to her after her departure. It was our belief that she was far from ready to parent safely. And yet as we watched her over the years we came to consider her one of our greatest successes in terms of how we define change. So now, with this turn of events, do we again consider hers a failed outcome?

Desirae is a poignant example of both the relative and the shifting nature of success. I concur that she did (and continues to do) the very best she could with what she knew in the moment and under whatever the current circumstances of her life happened to be. The obstacles and challenges have been many, and yet never has Desirae stopped reflecting honestly and integrating courageously the lessons she learned while moving bravely, cautiously, and slowly forward. Has the pace been too slow to save her children from having to repeat history? Perhaps—at least for some. But was it worth it? In the end it is my firm belief that whenever one imperfect human being stays present with another imperfect human being through all the successes and failures, not only is it worth it but both human beings are the better for it. And Desirae's story is far from over.

One final note about Isaac

Isaac's former foster mother and I have visited him several times in prison. He seems to be making the most of his time there. He works out to stay fit and healthy, takes classes to prepare himself for employment, and is staying out of trouble. He faces more years behind bars and then an uncertain future, but he can choose how to use his time on the inside and what path to take once outside.

What really gives me hope is what I have observed between Isaac and his aging former foster mother, Sarah, during our visits. Sarah and her husband have consistently been available to Isaac wherever he is and through whatever is going on in his life. Desirae, for her part, wisely allowed the relationship between them to continue even after Isaac was returned to her.

It is clear that Isaac views Sarah as a secure base, that he values her deeply. He is also willing and able to articulate to her his most vulnerable feelings. During one of our visits when both Sarah and her husband were present, Isaac expressed his gratitude to them, acknowledging their constant and loving presence in his life. He then went on to say:

> **"I feel that I have let you down. I made a promise to you that I'm afraid I can't now keep. I wanted to be there to help you as you aged, but instead I'm here. If one of you dies while I am locked up I will never forgive myself."**

We cannot know what lies ahead for Isaac. Only time will tell if he can find a way forward in which his past does not dictate his future. But what we do know is that he has received from Sarah what my colleague spoke of: a window into another way to be in relationship and an experience of being unconditionally loved, both gifts that may well sustain him through whatever his future may hold.

Research and theory: The seeds of change

While many parents experienced transformational change through their experience at The Children's Ark, identifying and measuring success, as Janet notes, is a complicated and elusive endeavor.[6] One measure of success is captured by recognizing that the Ark opened a door to a new way of being in relationship; by recognizing that— even when parents continued to struggle—they were less likely to parent out of their own pain and destructive defensive strategies. Not all parents regained custody but, as exemplified by Angie, their relationships with any future children had a better chance. Many Ark parents stayed in touch with Janet, even when the outcome was not in their favor—testimony to the connection they felt with her. She has witnessed their ongoing struggles but also how the seeds of change planted at the Ark continued to develop. Janet's experience with Desirae (Chapter 6) is worth repeating here:

When we did meet for lunch, Desirae talked, with warmth and wisdom, about how all we had to offer her at The Children's Ark was going in at some level, but she was just too overwhelmed in the moment to use it. She talked about knowing always that everything we did and everything we said, we did and said out of love for her and her children. She understood too that, even when she couldn't hear it, we cared about her. All knowledge that she could hold—because there was "enough" relationship—until she was in a place where she could access it, articulate it, and act on it.

Researchers have identified a number of factors related to change; two of the most powerful are resilience and resolution. Most scientists agree that resilience is not a trait; although some temperamental or personality characteristics may be related to resilience, there does not appear to be a "singular, 'master trait' of resiliency" (Masten 2014, p.167). Expanding on this point, resilience researcher Ann Masten offered the following caution: "At worst the idea of a resiliency trait carries the risk for 'blaming the victim' who does not show resilience...as somehow deficient" (p.167). Likewise, Bruce Perry and his colleagues identified resilience in children as nurtured instead of inborn and described the tendency to assume resilience in children as "an ultimate irony...at the time when the human is most vulnerable to the effects of trauma—during infancy and childhood—adults generally presume the most resilience" (Perry *et al.* 1995, p.272).

Although resilience is a developed capacity, it is not an extraordinary one. In her recent book, *Ordinary Magic: Resilience in Development*, Masten described resilience as "common": "Most of the time, the children who make it have ordinary human resources and protective factors in their lives," including things like "a healthy human brain in good working order; close relationships with competent and caring adults; committed families..." (2014, pp.7–8). Many of the mothers, fathers, and children represented in this book, of course, did not enjoy these ordinary resources and protective factors in their lives. Many were chronically threatened by those who were supposed to be providing them comfort and support. Indeed, Masten regarded abuse or neglect in the family as grave threats to children and recognized that maltreatment "can disturb the development of major adaptive systems that promote competence and resilience, including cognitive skills, the stress response systems, and the capacity for close and secure relationships" (p.201).

Nonetheless, the parents with whom Janet worked who demonstrated or developed resilience were also those most likely to realize the greatest change. At the top of Masten's "short list" of factors related to resilience—those that, in study after study, have predicted resilience—are relational factors (e.g. nurturing primary attachment relationships; close relationships with significant adults other than parents, particularly when parents are not available; close friendships). Anna was able to draw on a close relationship with a teacher. Angie had a father who adored her and, perhaps as a result, valued connection and worked to be in relationship, drawing others to her from whom she could derive support. Intelligence and problem-solving abilities are also on the short list as are self-regulation and a sense of agency or effectiveness. Anna's high intelligence supported her developing capacity for reflective functioning (see Chapter 8), and many of the parents were able to develop stronger capacities for self-regulation as well as a stronger sense of agency.

Tenacity was one of the characteristics Janet identified in a number of the mothers that seemed related to resilience and ultimately to change. Psychologist and MacArthur Fellow Angela Duckworth recently developed the concept of "grit," summarized briefly as a combination of passion and perseverance. In her recently released book on grit (Duckworth 2016), Duckworth depicted numerous studies in which she found that grit predicted success more than any other personal asset. She also described several psychological characteristics contributing to grit, all of which can be developed, nurtured, and honed; included among these is hope, which is also on Masten's short list. Quoting a Japanese saying, "Fall seven, rise eight," Duckworth identified a different kind of hope than casting our chances to the universe: hope meaning "I resolve to make tomorrow better" (p.169). This kind of hope was exemplified by Angie; in Janet's words, "Through it all Angie never gave up hope. She always kept one eye focused forward, understanding what she needed to do to create a future for herself and her son."

Duckworth also recognized that hope could be crushed under the weight of ongoing suffering, particularly suffering experienced as the result of circumstances we cannot control. Duckworth's research mentor, Martin Seligman, is credited for identifying a phenomenon he called learned helplessness. Learned helplessness occurs when we are repeatedly exposed to bad outcomes outside of our control—when nothing we do matters. More recent research on the neurobiology underlying learned helplessness suggests that it is not the helplessness that is learned. Helplessness, along with passivity and anxiety, appears to be the "default mammalian reaction to prolonged bad events" (Maier and Seligman 2016, p.364). It is, instead, the expectation of control over aversive outcomes that seems to be learned. Perhaps developing that expectation of control—developing a sense of self-efficacy or agency—within the nurturing walls of The Children's Ark was part of the change that Janet witnessed: "When Carrie shifted from being the person to whom all this bad stuff had been done to taking on the responsibility for being Sean's mother it was a kind of surrender."

Interestingly, much of what Janet describes as evidence of change aligns with Masten's description of resilience and Duckworth's conceptualization of grit. However, perhaps the most striking indicator of change, as experienced and described by Janet, was a "tendency to deep compassion or empathy for the experience of another," enhanced by honest and open self-reflection: looking into one's heart "with clarity and kindness." Gaining insight into the impact of past relationships on those in the present, coming to terms with previous hurts, and moving toward resolution helped parents gain greater empathy for themselves and, in turn, for others, including their children. Indeed, it is when past trauma remains unresolved that it exerts its power on the next generation.[7]

Perhaps the most important measure of success lies with the children. The Ark children were in stable, nurturing placements— either at The Children's Ark, when it was residential—or with foster families, many of whom became important partners to their birth parents. As long as reunification remained the goal, children had much more access to their parents than in traditional foster care so that the early bonds of attachment could develop. Because of the intensive nature of the program, a number of parents made the courageous decision to relinquish custody, allowing their children to find permanency more quickly and with much less stress than was typical in traditional foster care. Presumably children's experience of a stable, nurturing environment in their early years helped to lay a foundation of security, supporting more optimal development. As attachment researcher Alan Sroufe once said, "Early security is like money in the bank, paying lasting dividends over time" (Sroufe, personal communication). One ultimate hope is that—with an early experience of being welcomed, held, adored, and safe—the Ark children will be in a better place to parent their own children so that future generations will be less encumbered by the pain of the past.

Chapter 10

FINAL REFLECTIONS

The lives of children and families at risk are complicated and fraught with obstacles and setbacks. Interventions involving them are challenging and carry heavy responsibilities, the first of which is to do no further harm.

Putting children first

Even the temporary loss of a primary caregiver can profoundly impact how a child comes to understand the world, his sense of trust and security, and his identity formation. That reality encourages us, first and foremost, to focus on prevention and early intervention rather than trying to pick up the pieces when families come apart. Removing children should be our last resort and should be done only when the cost of leaving children is higher than the trauma of moving them.

When it does become necessary to remove children for their protection we can minimize the trauma to them by including them in treatment. Treating parents and children together not only minimizes separation and thus increases the potential for successful reunification, but also serves to focus interventions on the relationship itself. Learning to parent a particular child in the absence of that child is rather like learning to swim without any water; you might understand the theoretical technique but staying afloat really depends upon being immersed in the experience.

Relational struggles within families tend to be intergenerational in nature, leading us to direct treatment to the entire family unit. What is in the best interests of the children is dependent upon the needs of the whole family. A family represents an intricate interconnected and interdependent whole. Traumatize one, and you traumatize all. To heal one, you must look to heal the whole. Most of the parents we served had histories not unlike those unfolding for their children. In other words, the parents also had suffered early trauma and loss and the resulting developmental and emotional consequences. Not surprisingly, as they struggled to connect with their children, they kept bumping into their own pain. If a parent lacked someone to stay or stand by her or delight in her as a child, if a parent never gained enough trust in early relationships to dare to care, if a parent knew only pain and fear and loss at the hands of her own caregivers, how was that parent to know how to relate to her own child, let alone address the pain her child has suffered as a result of the pattern having been repeated?

The destructive emotional and psychological wiring created from early trauma that compromises the ability of at-risk families to parent safely is not undone or overridden easily or quickly. At the same time, children cannot afford to wait in limbo for long periods of time while their parents heal. This seemingly insolvable paradox further challenges us to look to programs like The Children's Ark that keep families together through the treatment process.

When families cannot be kept together, there are other ways that we can mitigate the harm done to the children. Moves can and should be minimized. Too often children in foster care are moved from foster home to foster home, compounding their trauma and loss experiences. Perhaps even worse, children are often moved into and out of foster care as parents struggle to succeed. Establishing and adhering to clearer guidelines regarding meaningful progress would allow permanent decisions to be made in a more timely manner.

When children must lose their family of origin, it is important to help them maintain contact with birth family members when possible and to give them access to their history without shame.

Children are not served by erasing people or events from their story. Children in care, especially, need help putting all of the pieces of their lives together into a coherent whole, including the losses. Unfortunately, when children are denied the truth, often the only way they find to make sense of their traumatizing experiences is to make it their fault. We can help children heal and resolve early trauma by acknowledging and honoring all of their history and narrative.[1]

Parents' need for ongoing support

When parents leave treatment, even if they succeed in regaining custody of their children, they are often still recovering from substance abuse and are usually undereducated, unemployable, living in poverty, and sometimes plagued by criminal records. The road forward will be tortuous, and all it often takes is just one small setback to bring carefully constructed future plans crashing down. It is important to remember that newly gained perspectives and fledgling self-esteem are fragile, especially when parents return to the relationships and environments that produced them.

We must also keep in mind and respect the reality of their lives. If our interventions have been successful, we have softened some of the protective barriers that parents have built around their hearts in order to manage the trauma of their early experience. How foolish would it be to divest a soldier of his armor and send him back into battle? Can we expect parents and children to continue to respond in a gentler, more sensitive way if the environment to which they must return cannot reciprocate? How can we, as providers, convince wounded parents that they have worth, that they matter, and then expect them to walk away from perhaps the only nurturing they have ever known and face the world unsupported and without a safety net? It is critical, therefore, that we make a long-term commitment to families at risk.

We can increase the odds for success by offering continued treatment following the return of children to their families. Treatment should not end with reunification, nor for that matter should it end with relinquishment. Parents need ongoing support to resolve the issues that compromised their caregiving to begin with, both for themselves and for any future children. We can help prevent a return to old ways and old connections by providing support and new environments in which families can survive and thrive. We talked often about incorporating a kind of halfway house, close to the Ark, where "graduates" could reside together, support each other, and continue to have access to our services.

And we must be willing to allow them a future. Far too often parents who overcome troubled pasts to fight their way through treatment to health and hope are only confounded again by criminal and child protection records that follow and haunt them for years to come, precluding them from obtaining everything from a driver's license to an education to a job. This injustice is not only a setup for failure but also represents a tremendous loss of potentially productive citizens to our communities. Both Jonathan and Carla, for instance, are fighting to be allowed gainful employment as a direct result of records related to their Child Protective Services involvement. Ironically, both aspire to give back to their communities by choosing fields that serve families at risk. Both believe, as do I, that they have something positive to offer based on their own experiences.

Support for foster families

It is imperative that we educate and support foster families. They are entitled to effective training and to information, not only specific information about the children placed in their care, but also general information about all traumatized children and what helps them heal. It is well established, for instance, that children move through developmental stages within the context of relationships.[2] When that relationship is disrupted, optimal development can be compromised until a new intimate relationship is established. It is critical therefore that foster parents be encouraged to invest in and bond with their foster children to provide not only a sense of security for their children but also to maintain developmental progress.

When it is safe and appropriate to do so foster families and birth families should also be encouraged to know each other and work together. Foster parents are often birth families' best teachers, mentors, and advocates, as well as an ongoing safety net for the children and parents alike. Indeed, it was not uncommon for Ark parents whose parental rights were terminated or who relinquished custody to request that their child be adopted by the foster parents. Such resolutions occurred fairly frequently at The Children's Ark, I believe, because of the interaction and cooperation between birth parents and foster parents that we promoted. In any case, it is never in a child's best interest to have to choose where to place his loyalty and love: with foster parents with whom he has formed an affective bond or with birth parents for whom he longs.

Systemic change

If given the power and opportunity to change just one thing about child protection systems, I would choose to move them out of the judicial arena altogether. As stated earlier, child protection cases are about entire families. It is not a process that should be either adversarial or punitive. It should not be about winning or losing but about resolving. It should not be about punishing but about helping. The judicial system by its very nature is adversarial, which in a child protection action just increases the barriers to solutions. Although we profess to be about reconciling families, putting solutions in the hands of an adversarial system simply pits party against party and increases discord. Instead all parties should be encouraged to work together, to negotiate, and to compromise. Finding common ground toward a common goal is a key to healing families.

It is also very difficult to be a party to a judicial action without feeling somehow judged. Carla once again articulated the experience beautifully. She recently shared with me another pivotal moment at The Children's Ark that shifted her way of thinking. She described holding, bouncing, and trying to soothe her screaming infant, Kelsey, one evening while attempting also to organize the dinner that was her responsibility. She recalled keeping her back turned away from staff and other parents, feeling certain that we were all watching, disapproving, and denouncing her in some way. As her anxiety escalated and her attempts to calm her distressed baby became more frantic, the situation only spun further out of control. Finally Emma, our infant lead staff member and resident "baby whisperer," walked over to Carla and asked her for Kelsey.

Carla handed the baby over and moved immediately to her kitchen tasks, but her sense of failure, of even having been condemned, only heightened as her baby settled immediately into Emma's competent embrace. Once dinner preparations were under control, Carla stepped out on the back porch to smoke a cigarette and try to collect herself. As she returned to the kitchen, Emma took her aside and asked her if she was all right. At this point Carla's resolve to resist the vulnerable feelings overwhelming her cracked, and she broke down in tears insisting to Emma that her baby hated her, it was all too hard, and that she just couldn't do it.

According to Carla, Emma's reply was, "Yes, you can. And in those moments when you feel that you can't, I'm here to help you." Something changed for Carla once she realized that we were with her, not against her, and that she didn't need to fight us. When the energy she was expending to struggle against her perceived enemy could be freed up and directed toward making the most of the support offered her, she felt joined rather than judged.

Finally, we need to consider our use of language as we strive to support and assist children at risk and their families. Sometimes even a small change in the language we use can create a paradigm shift in how we think and talk about things. Can we, for instance, think of what children want as "connection" rather than "attention"? Can we see their acting out as the expression of a genuine need as yet unmet rather than a personal attack or an attempt by children (or their parents) to manipulate us? Can we talk about "struggles" or "challenges" in families rather than "problems" or "failures"? Can we think in terms of "joining" rather than "fixing"? In fact, rather than thinking of "serving," can we think in terms of "being with"?[3]

Such a reframing can not only nudge us toward a kinder approach to intervention but can also remind us of the commonality of the human experience. We are all more alike than different. We all operate out of similar fear and pain. We all build up walls and devise strategies for keeping us safe. We all persist in keeping these safeguards and ways of being in the world largely intact, even when they no longer apply to our reality. And, underneath it all, do we not long for the same intimate human connection? The facts and degree of woundedness may differ, but our stories are really the same. Looking through the eyes of children and families in distress can lead us through the door of our own hearts to a better understanding, and ultimate embracing, of one another.

Carla

I knew the moment Carla first walked through the doors of The Children's Ark that my work with her would be a challenge. She was loud, cocky, dismissing, and what we had come to refer to as "esteem sensitive."[4] I knew of course that the bluster was all defense, but my ability to see past the fear and to warm to her was limited. And her baby, Kelsey, was a screamer. Some parents and children leapt into my heart immediately and with very little effort. Caring about them came easily. With others, like Carla and Kelsey, just staying therapeutically engaged sometimes seemed an impossible task.

Though cynical and resistant, Carla was also determined and stubborn. She had already lost three children to the system and had a significant history of drug abuse. These facts alone were predictive of a poor prognosis. Her resolve was impressive, however, and so we moved cautiously forward. As the months passed, it became clear that—whatever the outcome—she would see it through. Very slowly she softened, and the bond with her daughter grew. Although she had very little formal schooling, Carla proved to be very bright and interested in the educational information. Through persistence and perseverance, she was also able to embrace the therapeutic process enough to transform her understanding of her own history into empathy for her daughter's experience. And she stayed clean and sober. At the end of nine months, as her permanency planning hearing approached, we made the decision to recommend returning custody.

As the only available staff member that day, I accompanied Carla to the hearing. The atmosphere in the courtroom was festive as the judge granted our recommendation that Kelsey be returned home, a clear cause for celebration. Having never really warmed to Carla, however, I remained indifferent, a bit skeptical, and even apprehensive.

As we returned to my car at the end of the afternoon, I noticed that Carla seemed depressed when I expected her to be elated. Once we were settled in the car, I turned to her and was stunned to see a tear trickling down her cheek. "What's wrong?" I asked. "I didn't expect that," she answered. Carla then told me that sitting in the courtroom had been both women who had adopted her other children. She went on with heartfelt emotion to acknowledge how the joy of this day would always be diminished by her deep grief and profound remorse over the cost to her children—all of her children—of her addiction.

In that moment I was aware of touching into my own grief as I contemplated all the ways I had failed my own children. I was further aware of a profound shift in my feelings for Carla. In that instant my heart opened to her. I was filled with compassion and affection. Carla's ability to empathize and resonate with her children's experiences and her willingness to expose that vulnerability to me allowed me to open to my own pain and created a powerful affective bond between us. I learned that day that the road to true compassion comes—in the words of Zen teacher and author Ezra Bayda—"from the realization of our shared pain" (2002, p.138). Until we understand as a society that we are all responsible for each other, that we are all in this together, promoting and effecting change and healing in families at risk will remain a difficult, costly, and elusive endeavor.

It is easy in this work to feel overwhelmed, discouraged, and hopeless. The odds are seldom favorable; the obstacles to overcome seemingly endless. To watch just one young parent like Carla break out of generational patterns, however, and step down her own path to success makes the struggle worthwhile.[5] As the Star Thrower observed when asked how it could matter for him to keep throwing stranded starfish back into the sea when there were so many, and he couldn't possibly save them all…it matters to this one.[6]

Research and theory: from science to practice and policy

In the introduction to her book *To the End of June: The Intimate Life of American Foster Care*, journalist Cris Beam (2014) writes:

> More than a million adults are directly or indirectly employed to ensure their [foster children's] well-being, and $15 to $20 billion a year are poured into overseeing their health and management. And yet nobody—not the kids, not the foster or biological parents, not the social workers, the administrators, the politicians, the policy experts—think the system is working. (p. xii)

Pre-dating Cris Beam's provocative account of American foster care, Columbia University social work professor Jane Waldfogel (2000) declared the United States' Child Protective Services (CPS) a system "in crisis" and "in urgent need of reform" (p.43). Similar appeals for reform have been made in other countries, including the UK, Canada, Switzerland, and Australia.[7] In fact, a bold agenda for reform—one grounded in relationships, families, and communities—was recently proposed by the president of the Australian Association of Social Workers, Bob Lonne, and his colleagues.[8] Common to these appeals for reform are several themes that are remarkably consonant with the philosophy of The Children's Ark.

First and foremost is the need to reimagine systems that are truly child-centered: in the words of London School of Economics professor Eileen Munro (2011), "to reform the child protection system from being over-bureaucratized and concerned with compliance to one that keeps the focus on children" (p.5). Other key themes include directing resources toward early, comprehensive support and intervention before children's safety is compromised and tailoring intervention to the needs of individual families. According to Waldfogel (2000), "If CPS [Child Protective Services] continues to respond to families with a one-size-fits-all approach, then CPS will continue to provide an inappropriate response to many of the families coming to its attention" (p.47). Perhaps most resonant with the philosophy of The Children's Ark is something that Trevor Spratt, Director of the Children's Research Centre at Trinity College, Dublin, and his colleagues referred to as "building a relational heart" (Spratt et al. 2014, p.1521), a concept that highlights the importance of attending to the relationships at every intersection within child protection systems.

Underpinning all recommendations for child protection reform is the widespread agreement that policy development and service provision be informed by knowledge of the latest research and theory—evidence-based "best practices." Too often reform is driven by ideology rather than evidence and is often reactive and punitive rather than proactive and empowering. Research stemming from multiple perspectives including attachment theory, developmental neuroscience, and trauma- and resilience-informed intervention frameworks offers ample evidence from which to guide improvements to child protection systems. As exemplified by The Children's Ark, a child-focused and relationship-based approach is at the center of the following ideas.

Recognizing the costs of separation

Children have an essential need to be connected to their caregivers, and they develop profound attachments even to abusive or addicted or otherwise incapacitated caregivers; this attachment is primal— built into our species to help ensure our survival. Mindful of the costs of separation, we argue that removing children from their families should be undertaken only when leaving them is worse than the trauma of separation and loss, followed—too often—by an uncertain future in foster care. Instead, can we imagine reorienting our approach so that we provide comprehensive support to families at risk *before* children's safety is compromised? As Lonne and colleagues argue:

> One major change required is to support rather than monitor families... It would appear that many of these children and families are on the radar of child protective services, but rather than receiving the assistance to reduce the impact of the stresses they are experiencing, they are "monitored" until the threshold for removal is reached. (Lonne *et al.* 2009, p.107)

To be serious about supporting families at risk requires that we recognize the illusory nature of "quick fixes," particularly for families impacted by generations of poverty, addiction, mental illness, maltreatment, and so forth.[9] Although initially resource-intensive, providing comprehensive support will be far less expensive in the long run, both in terms of resources and the emotional and relational consequences of separation and loss.[10]

When children must be removed from the custody of their parents, they should be included in comprehensive treatment with their parents as long as reunification remains the goal. Limited visitation, characteristic of many foster care systems, is often only confusing, heart-wrenching, and likely to be further disorganizing for infants and young children. Programs in which parents can reside with their children, as The Children's Ark was initially designed, or day treatment programs in which parents come together with their children for a substantial and predictable period of time each week, would help to maintain and enhance the developing relationship, so that the lack of a bond does not become a barrier to reunification.

Sometimes it is in the best interests of children for their birth parents to relinquish custody (or have their parental rights terminated). Among the benefits of the intensive approach taken by The Children's Ark was that parents tended to either engage in and commit to the significant work that would allow them to nurture their children safely or—fairly quickly—recognize their inability to do so. Although the voluntary relinquishment of custody was not initially identified as a positive outcome, it came to be regarded as one. With the support of the staff at the Ark, parents could relinquish with dignity and respect, knowing that they were acting in their children's best interests and allowing their children to move to permanent placements without further delay. Often these permanent placements allowed birth parents to maintain relationships with their children.

Even when it is in children's best interests to find permanency without their birth parents, it is essential to recognize the emotional impact of their loss and to provide them with the support they need to move toward understanding and resolution. Robbie Gilligan (2006), from the Children's Research Center, Trinity College, Dublin, powerfully captured the nature of this loss for children in care:

> Many children in care may never be the same—following the enormity of their loss. They may have to learn to endure the *ongoingness of withoutness*, to quote the memorable phrase of a woman writing about coping with life after the death of her 11-year-old son (Vincent 1998). Life may never be the same after a grievous loss. And we must remember that the loss of parents who are still alive may actually be harder to accept or come to terms with than the more logical and legitimate loss of parents through death (Eagle 1994). (Gilligan 2014, p.18)

Even infants who are pre-verbal or young children who have limited verbal abilities need their new caregivers to help them make meaning of the emotions, reactions, questions, and so forth that will inevitably arise. Rachel (Chapter 2) was placed into a nurturing adoptive home just before she turned three. She later said to Janet, "People give me away." Three-year-old Ryan (Chapter 8) believed that he had done something wrong the night the police came and took him away from his parents. Beliefs like those are too heavy for children to carry alone and, if not resolved, create devastating templates on which ongoing development builds.

Creating secure and stable placements

If there is one message that we can draw from attachment theory and from the resilience research, it is the essential need to create stable placements with nurturing caregivers when children must be removed from their homes. As described in Chapter 7, infants and young children do not have the concept of temporary. They only know what they experience, and if what they experience is a series of moves—a series of separations and losses—how are they to learn to trust relationships going forward? How are they to develop the feeling that they matter, that they have worth if no one will claim them? The research evidence is clear: not only does moving from one foster care home to another seriously undermine the development of secure attachment but also it misses the opportunity for a child to experience a nurturing, stable relationship as a substitute for parental care. As described in Chapter 9, the most significant predictor of resilience for children from maltreating or disrupted families is the presence of another caring adult in the child's life. Isaac (Chapter 9) made a grievous mistake for which he is in prison. His ongoing relationship with his foster parents, who visit him regularly, is helping to sustain him and may assist him in choosing a new path when he is released.

To create more stable and secure placements we need to reconsider the role and status of foster parents. Could we imagine working with foster parents as important, committed, and even long-term partners to at-risk families where everyone is focused on the best interests of the child? Investing in foster parents as valuable members of a team may help them to more fully commit to the children in their care, increasing children's sense of security and connection.[11] Janet modeled this approach as a foster parent, herself, and engaged foster parents as partners while she was the director of The Children's Ark. More intensive and focused training for foster parents about the relational needs and behavioral challenges of the children in their care is especially critical, and foster parents need ongoing support. Transitions are likely to be pivotal periods; particularly important is to help foster parents better understand the history, behavior, and needs of a new child in their care as well as cope with the losses of any previous foster children.[12] Promising training and support models from an attachment theory perspective include the Circle of Security intervention (Powell and colleagues), Attachment and Biobehavioral Catch-Up (Dozier and colleagues), The Early Intervention Foster Care Program (Fisher and colleagues), the New Orleans Intervention (Zeanah and Larrieu), and the Bucharest Early Intervention Project (Smyke, Zeanah, and colleagues).[13]

To remain available to the needs of the families in their caseloads, child protection professionals need support too. Social service professionals are chronically overwhelmed with caseloads they cannot manage; emotional exhaustion, burnout, role conflict, and challenges in work–life balance are among the consequences for those dedicated to this profession.[14] Raising the status of this professional role, creating attractive workforce policies, and providing comprehensive emotional support may attract talented people to the field and help sustain them in their difficult work. University of Nottingham social work professor Harry Ferguson communicates the importance of support for those on the front lines:

> The extent to which social workers are able to delve into the depths to protect children and explore the deeper reaches and inner lives of service users...is directly related to how secure and contained they feel... They can only really take risks if they feel they will be emotionally held and supported on returning to the office, that their feelings and struggles will be listened to. Workers' state of mind and the quality of attention they can

give to children is directly related to the quality of support, care and attention they themselves receive from supervision, managers and peers. (Ferguson 2011, p.205)

More broadly, Munro (2011) recommends moving away from a "command-and-control culture" that encourages compliance to one that supports learning and adaptation (pp.106–107), and Lonne and colleagues (2009) urge "a return to work that is relationship-based rather than procedurally dominated and 'managed'" (p.108). The staff at The Children's Ark, all of whom were highly respected and valued as part of the intervention team, showed very low turn-over. The work was exhausting, but staff members were held in relationship just as were the clients.

Building community

The Children's Ark created community; however, as Janet described, many parents struggled when they returned to their challenging environments, isolated from healthy support. Strengthening whole communities, then, becomes essential; "Children thrive where communities (rather than child protection teams) flourish" (Lonne *et al.* 2009, p.112). Supporting communities, particularly those that are in poverty, requires that we confront something that Halpern (as cited in Kemp *et al.* 2014, p.54) noted as a "chronic ambivalence" toward impoverished families, who are overwhelmingly representative of the families involved in child protection systems worldwide. Lonne and colleagues (2009) advocate for assistance that comes from "people being part of the fabric of neighborhood and community that sustains their children and their families and in so doing, builds communities, social capital, and civil societies that in turn grow their own capacity to care for children" (p.112). For models of community-based initiatives, Lonne and colleagues point to the work of Joan Lombardi, international expert on child development and social policy and author of *Time to Care:*

Redesigning Child Care to Promote Education, Support Families, and Build Communities.

Schools can be community hubs, offering the prospect of a safe haven for children and resources for their families. Yet many children in foster care experience multiple changes in schools as they are moved from one foster placement to another, sometimes within the same year and even when they are moving within the same or contiguous districts.[15] Such disruptions not only compromise a child's educational progress but also ignore the possibilities for a sense of connection that may be created by caring, continuous relationships with teachers and other school personnel. Kristin Kelly and her colleagues (Kelly, McNaught, and Stotland 2014) at the Law Legal Center for Foster Care and Education articulate several education-related goals for foster children including that they are entitled to remain at their same school whenever possible. Social work professor Angelique Day and her colleagues (2014) advocate for comprehensive training, enhanced collaboration, and increased communication so that school personnel and child welfare professionals more effectively work together to support the unique needs of foster children.[16] High-quality early child care and education may offer particular benefits to infants and toddlers in the child welfare system, particularly when they can remain in the same program for a sustained period of time.[17]

Innovative, community-based projects can also induce change. "One child. One therapist. For as long as it takes," is the model developed by the Children's Psychotherapy Project, which recognized that "the single most important factor in the lives of children and youth in foster care is a stable and lasting relationship with a caring adult" (Heineman 2006, p.11). This project, conceived in San Francisco but now in operation all over the world, provides a continuous therapeutic relationship (same therapist, working pro bono) for children in foster care, many of whom have experienced multiple placements and an ever-changing group of service providers, only compounding attachment-related and mental health problems.

A wider view of reform

The nature of support provided for families caught up in child protection systems is undoubtedly influenced by the personal perspectives of the professionals working within those systems as well as broader, societal ideologies. For example, researchers Jesse Russell and Stephanie Macgill (2015) found that states with less diverse populations and states with more individualistic rather than collectivistic orientations more frequently remove children. Further, sociologist Frank Edwards (2016) discovered that states with "extensive and punitive criminal justice systems," as compared to states with "broad and generous welfare programs," are more likely to remove children, and those children are more likely to be placed in institutional care (p.575). In his words, "Regimes structure the ideological frameworks and schemas that policymakers, bureaucrats, and the public use to narrate the causes of social problems and orient their attitudes toward particular styles of intervention or governance" (p.578). Further, numerous researchers have reported that minority families are disproportionately represented within social welfare systems, raising issues ranging from insensitivity to diverse social and cultural structures to bias and discrimination.

It will take a collective effort to reshape social policy and push forward changes in child welfare practice to heal broken systems. Lonne and colleagues (2009) contend that such a reorientation toward substantial change is no less formidable than "continuing to prop up the now vast, cumbersome and unworkable infrastructure" that many countries have built around "forensic child protection services that are spending most of their time on controlling poor families" (p.113). Their book, *Reforming Child Protection*, offers a framework for broader, systemic change. In a comprehensive analysis of child protection systems globally, researchers Neil

Gilbert and colleagues described two primary approaches to child welfare: the child protection orientation and the family services orientation. Recognizing that neither approach reflected growing trends in child protection, they identified "the emergence of an alternative approach," which they called "child-focused" (Gilbert, Parton, and Skivenes 2011, p.252). The momentum toward more child-centered systems may be building.

In our view, moving custodial decisions out of the judicial system into mediational arenas will help all of us keep the focus on the best interests of children. Janet's words are worth repeating here:

> [Child protection] is not a process that should be either adversarial or punitive. It should not be about winning or losing but about resolving. It should not be about punishing but about helping. The judicial system by its very nature is adversarial, which in a child protection action just increases the barriers to solutions. Although we profess to be about reconciling families, putting solutions in the hands of an adversarial system simply pits party against party and increases discord. Instead all parties should be encouraged to work together, to negotiate, and to compromise.

Being in relationship

As we continue to advocate for systemic change, there are also a number of things we can do in our daily work with at-risk children and families to make the child protection system kinder, more compassionate, and ultimately more effective. Spratt and his colleagues (2014) referred to "building a relational heart," our Circle of Security colleagues developed the concept of "being with" (Powell *et al.* 2014), and we use the term "being in relationship." Common to all of these perspectives is the central human need for connection: the need to feel seen, heard, understood, held, and valued. Whether in relationships between parents (birth and foster) and their children, between families and social service professionals, or between professionals and their colleagues and supervisors, we all long for connection. When connection is disrupted, broken, or lost, we grieve. When it is supported, nurtured, and enhanced, we flourish. Keeping a relationship-based way of proceeding at the center of our work with vulnerable children and families may not solve all that ails child protection systems but will—at the very least—move us in the right direction.

A Special Place

There is a place a special place.
It's where I found my poker face.
All my life people would tell me what I couldn't believe.
Because of this program I can achieve.
I went to Circle of Security one day.
I saw that face on the screen I saw my
Mother's cold stare in me.
I saw my daughter's distress I wanted to learn and you
helped me to see.
So cold and scary I will never forget.
In that room you supported me as I went through feeling it.
I thought holding in my feelings was being strong.
Now I sing a very different very special song.
Because it was that day I grew, I grew, because of you.
And because I chose to.
I saw the confusion in my baby's eyes.
You were there to guide me out of my masked disguise.
You see when I showed that poker face she knew.
She acted as if she didn't know what to do.
12 month old sharing my face so cold,
I wasn't present and she could feel it.
She wouldn't go far from where I would sit.
Her circles were short she wouldn't stay out long.
Wanting up no down I saw for the first time

what was I doing wrong.
I knew I had to work hard to shine through that mask.
You stood by me and helped me through
I didn't have to ask.
You shared it in a gentle way.
I knew you cared when I shared my feelings that day.
I felt safe something I haven't known that well.
You reached out to catch me when I fell.
You cared about my child and believed in what you do.
You desire your truth I could see it shining through.
You spoke so kind in a way that is new.
I used to dream of the kindness and respect I got from you.
This kind of kindness I never knew.
I wasn't treated like someone less than anyone.
When I could see the truth this is when God's victory won.
Then I chose to be more real.
Choosing not to run from how I feel.
Because of you I am real today.
Because of you my child is with me today.
Other services not the same.
You deserve a special name. You gave me
    the tools I needed I am free.
Because of your program you showed
    me truth I will always see.
Not the kind that will fade away.
The classes, the films, individuals the kind of
    information that doesn't just go away.

To The Children's Ark.

> *Special thanks from,*
> *Tonia Vansant (Ark mom)*

NOTES

Preface

1. The Circle of Security (COS), now an internationally recognized attachment-based intervention, was designed in close proximity to The Children's Ark by our colleagues Bert Powell, Glen Cooper, Kent Hoffman, and Bob Marvin (Cooper et al. 2005; Powell et al. 2014). Its language and philosophy were foundational to the comprehensive intervention developed at The Children's Ark.

2. We obtained consents from most of the families whose stories we share: for the extended case presentations in Parts 1 and 2 and for many of the shorter examples in Part 2. When it was not possible to obtain consent (e.g., parent was deceased or unable to be located), we substantially modified any potentially identifying details, or we blended cases. Additionally, all names of family members and children were changed to further protect their identity and privacy. Whenever possible, Janet invited families to read their stories to ensure that we had captured an authentic representation of their experience and that they were comfortable with the information shared. Janet's ability to engage with the families in this way—even when the cases were difficult—is further testimony to the power of compassion, connection, and truth-telling.

3. Cozolino (2014); Perry et al. (1995); Perry and Szalavitz (2006); Siegel (2010).

4. Powell et al. (2014); Sroufe et al. (2005).

Chapter 1

1. I just recently visited with Laura to obtain her consent for this story. She is clearly the glue that holds the entire family together. She still has one child at home as well as an adult child and a grandchild currently living with her. She visits Rickie in prison once a month. As we talked about this chapter, I was impressed with her insights and her compassion. I truly admire her determination to stay present for all her children through both their successes and their failures.

2. Family systems theorists have long argued that family problems, including maltreatment, are relational and that treatment must focus on the relationships within the family system rather than on individual family members to be effective (Bowen 1978; Minuchin 1974). These propositions have been reinforced within the more recently emerging field of developmental psychopathology as well as

by research stemming from both perspectives (Cicchetti and Howes 1991; Howes *et al.* 2000; Macfie *et al.* 2005; Sroufe 2016; see also Hinde and Stevenson-Hinde 1988 and Sameroff and Emde 1989).

3. Granat *et al.* (2016); Hayes, Goodman, and Carlson (2013); Martins and Gaffan (2000).

4. See psychologist Robert Karen's 1998 book, *Becoming Attached: First Relationships and How They Shape Our Capacities to Love* for an illuminating account of the routine nature of separation and its impact on infants and young children.

5. Bowlby (1982, first published 1969; 1988).

6. Bowlby (1982, first published 1969); Cassidy (2016); Marvin, Britner and Russell (2016).

7. Ainsworth *et al.* (1978). See also Fearon and Belsky (2016).

8. As part of their pioneering research, Ainsworth and her colleagues (1978) completed numerous hours of home observations over the infants' first year of life. They initially created the SSP as a way to validate the home observations. Over the past several decades, many other researchers have done similar observations, adding more detail to our understanding of what predicts security and what predicts insecurity. See Fearon and Belsky (2016) for a review. See also Isabella (1993) and Isabella and Belsky (1991).

9. Main and Solomon (1986, 1990).

10. Bowlby (1982, first published 1969). A number of empirical studies have provided evidence in support of the internal working model construct (e.g. Beebe *et al.* 2010; Beebe *et al.* 2012a; Beebe *et al.* 2012b; Johnson, Dweck and Chen 2007). See Bretherton and Munholland (2008) for a comprehensive review.

11. Sroufe *et al.* (2005); Weinfield *et al.* (2008).

12. The term "disorganized" has become standard short-hand for "disorganized/ disoriented," the original description of this attachment classification; however, "disoriented" remains an important part of how we think about this classification (Main, personal communication).

13. Lyons-Ruth and Jacobvitz (2008, 2016); Solomon and George (1999b, 2011b).

14. Bowlby (1982, first published 1969).

Chapter 2

1. Rachel's story was originally published in 2006 in *Zero to Three* (Mann and Kretchmar 2006). We are grateful to Zero to Three for allowing us to reproduce her story here.

2. The concept of "repair" comes from the seminal work of psychologist Ed Tronick and his colleagues who observed and identified disruptions in the coordination of maternal–infant interactions and the subsequent repair of those disruptions (Gianino and Tronick 1988; Tronick 1989). The concepts of relational "rupture and repair" are now used in a wide range of therapeutic contexts (see Powell *et al.* 2014, pp.292–293).

3. Our use of "seen, heard, and understood" (or its variations, e.g. "seen, heard, understood, and held") was influenced by the work of psychotherapist Diana Fosha (Fosha 2000).

4. Understanding problem behavior as the expression of genuine need was inspired by our work with the COS intervention (Powell *et al.* 2014).

5. The concept of "good enough"—usually in reference to parenting—can be traced to British psychoanalyst, Donald Winnicott (as cited in Choate and Engstrom 2014).

6. This articulation of "miscue" is taken directly from the COS language and philosophy (Powell *et al.* 2014).

7. Powell *et al.* (2014, p.38).

8. Multiple experiences of rupture and repair are characteristic of normal interactions and are believed to support the development of relational competence, intimacy, resilience, and so forth (Gianino and Tronick 1988; Tronick 1989).

9. 'State of mind,' as used here, is a concept derived from the literature on adult attachment (see Hesse 2016).

10. Particularly important and provocative research examining the development of internal working models is that of Beatrice Beebe, from the New York State Psychiatric Institute, and her colleagues. Using micro-analytic observational techniques, Beebe and her colleagues identified communication patterns between mothers and their *four-month-old* infants that predicted disorganized (D) attachment at 12 months. As they describe, "the central feature of future D dyads is intrapersonal and interpersonal discordance or conflict, when infants are intensely distressed" (Beebe *et al.* 2010, p.109). On the basis of their findings, they hypothesize that the future D infant's developing working model is characterized by "not being sensed and known by the mother, and confusion in sensing and knowing himself, especially at moments of distress. Thus the emerging internal working model of future D infants includes confusion about their own basic emotional organization, their mothers' emotional organization, and their mothers' response to their distress, setting a trajectory in development which may disturb the fundamental integration of the person" (p.119). See also Beebe *et al.* (2012a); Beebe *et al.* (2012b).

11. See Lyons-Ruth and Jacobvitz (2008, 2016) for a review of disorganized/disoriented attachment. See DeOliveira *et al.* (2004) for a provocative discussion of the relationship between emotion socialization and regulation and disorganized attachment.

12. Research has consistently shown that children with secure attachment histories do better with their peers (e.g. more likely to be accepted and less likely to be rejected) than do children with insecure attachments. However, there is less research exploring specific peer relationship dynamics among children with various insecure attachment histories and very little research on the peer relationships of children with disorganized attachments (Kerns and Brumariu 2016). Researchers Deborah Jacobvitz and Nancy Hazen (1999) observed three young children, classified as disorganized during infancy, multiple times with peers and witnessed a range of odd, troubling behavior. Although their research needs replication and extension with larger samples, it is likely that children

with disorganized attachment histories will struggle in multiple relationships, including those with peers. Jacobvitz and Hazen note that future research should look beyond traditional measures of peer aggression and social withdrawal to include odd, emotionally disconnected, and out-of-sync behavior.

13. Crittenden (2006); Liotti (2011).

14. One of the hallmarks of disorganized relationship dynamics by early childhood is role-reversal. While children take on a controlling role in the relationships, their caregivers abdicate their 'executive' control, identified by Solomon and George as 'caregiving helplessness' (2011a, p.27).

15. Moss *et al.* (2011); Moss, Cyr and Dubois-Comtois (2004).

16. Jacobvitz and Hazen (1999); see also Lyons-Ruth and Jacobvitz (2016). Moss *et al.* (2004) found that by age six, two-thirds of their sample adopted a controlling strategy. See Moss *et al.* (2011) for other factors related to disorganized sub-groups.

17. Biehal (2014).

Chapter 3

1. Barbara and Nathan's account was originally published in 2008 in *Zero to Three* (Mann *et al.* 2008). We are grateful to Zero to Three for allowing us to reproduce their story here.

2. Powell *et al.* (2014); Siegel and Hartzell (2014).

3. A related study undertaken by Canadian researchers, Sophia Hébert and her colleagues, found that empowerment and agency help with the psychological adjustment that accompanies changes in placement. Hébert, Lanctôt and Turcotte (2016) interviewed young women with a history of foster care placements. They reported that the psychological shifts these young women experienced during placement transitions were related to their own sense of agency, or control, during transitions.

4. Eagle (1993); Kenrick (2000); Rock *et al.* (2015). See also D'Andrade and James (2014).

Chapter 4

1. Perry (2009).

2. Cozolino (2014); Perry and Pollard (1998); see also Coan (2016).

3. Prenatal alcohol exposure causes cell death, resulting in a decrease in brain cells—neurons—by up to one-third in affected areas. Alcohol exposure also interferes with the normal migration of neurons, leading to malformations in brain structure, and disrupts their potential connections, resulting in abnormal communication between brain cells (Deming and McCabe 2010). See also Curley and Champagne (2016).

4. Glaser (2000).

5. Cozolino (2014); Perry (2009); Perry *et al.* (1995).

6. Research has established that mirror neurons are involved in observing voluntary action. Less is known about their contributions to various forms of social cognition, such as empathy (Baird, Scheffer, and Wilson 2011). However, research indicates that mirror neurons are at least generally involved in "emotional interpersonal cognition" (Schulte-Rüther *et al.* 2007, p.1354).

7. Perry (2009).

8. Perry (2009); Perry *et al.* (1995); Perry and Szalavitz (2006). See also Gunnar and Quevedo (2007).

9. Perry (2009); Perry *et al.* (1995).

10. Perry and Szalavitz (2006).

11. In reviewing this chapter with Hannah I was struck by her ability to reflect on her experience and own her regrets while holding compassion for the apparent failings of others, and to turn insight into aspiration for growth. Her life continues to offer her many challenges, but I was encouraged by her willingness to hold the past gently.

12. Bowlby (1973, 1980).

13. The caring presence of another is one of the most significant predictors of resilience (Masten 2014).

14. On the occasion of Ashley's 24th birthday I was reminded yet again of what a gift her adoptive family offers her in reading the following posting on Facebook by her mother: "My baby girl is turning 24. Does that mean my heart is supposed to let her go into the wild and scary world? Of my three kiddos she is the most spiritual, frustrating, appreciative, challenging, loving, infuriating and kind to all mankind. What would I do without her in our lives? We lived life before she came to us, not knowing how significantly she would change my spirit and passion for life. Happy birthday my sweet but challenging 24-year-old young lady."

Chapter 5

1. Our use of "holds in heart and mind" was influenced by the work of psychotherapist Diana Fosha (Fosha 2000).

2. Disabled World (2013); National Council on Disability (2008); United Cerebral Palsy and Children's Rights (2006).

3. National Council on Disability (2008); United Cerebral Palsy and Children's Rights (2006).

4. National Council on Disability (2008).

5. National Council on Disability (2008); United Cerebral Palsy and Children's Rights (2006).

6. Baker (2013); National Autism Center (2015).

Chapter 6

1. Desirae's story was originally published in 2011 in *Zero to Three* (Mann *et al.* 2011). We are grateful to Zero to Three for allowing us to reproduce her story here.

2. The lessons reflect my thinking and experience but are certainly influenced by my immersion in the Circle of Security language and philosophy as well as my experience with Sandra Powell, Clinical Director at The Children's Ark.

3. The concept of 'holding environment' comes from the work of Winnicott (as cited in Powell *et al.* 2014).

4. A meta-analysis published in 1995 by researcher Marinus Van IJzendoorn demonstrated that the caregiver's state of mind as identified using the Adult Attachment Interview strongly predicted the infant's attachment strategy in the next generation. However, caregiver responsiveness (identified through observed behavior) did not fully account for this intergenerational transmission, raising questions about a "transmission gap." Verhage *et al.* (2016) recently revisited the "transmission gap" and concluded that "intergenerational transmission may depend on multiple pathways besides caregiver sensitivity and on multiple levels besides the behavioral level (e.g., the cognitive level)" (p.358). Indeed, researcher Elizabeth Meins and her colleagues found that maternal mind-mindedness (a mother's ability to accurately read and comment on her infant's mental states) was a strong predictor of infant attachment security (Meins *et al.* 2001).

5. Aronoff (2015); Foster, Beadnell and Pecora (2015).

Chapter 7

1. Implicit memory is enabled by early-developing brain structures. These parts of the brain do not require higher-level "conscious" processing or even conscious awareness to encode memory and include behavioral, emotional, and perceptual experiences. According to child psychiatrist Dan Siegel (2012), "By a child's first birthday,…repeated patterns of implicit learning are deeply encoded in the brain" (p.55).

2. University of Washington researcher John Gottman identified different patterns in parents' responses to their children's emotional states and how these patterns affected children's development. The pattern that led to the best outcomes was one Gottman called "emotion coaching." Emotion coaches get involved with their children's feelings, helping children to process and regulate their emotions without ignoring, objecting to, or punishing negative emotion (e.g. anger, sadness, fear): "They use emotional moments as opportunities for teaching their kids important life lessons and building closer relationships" (Gottman 1997, p.21). See also Lacher *et al.* (2012) on the power of narrative to help children move toward resolution of trauma.

3. Sroufe (2016); Sroufe *et al.* (2005).

4. Bernard and Dozier (2011); Dozier *et al.* (2007); Dozier and Lindhiem (2006).

5. Bates and Dozier (2002); Dozier *et al.* (2001); see also Dozier and Rutter (2016).

Chapter 8

1. The elements important to the creation of a holding environment essential to effective intervention reflect my thinking and experience but are certainly influenced by my immersion in the Circle of Security language and philosophy as well as my experience with Sandra Powell, Clinical Director at The Children's Ark.

2. The language 'clarity and kindness' comes from my work with Zen teacher Ezra Bayda.

3. See Harvey and Henderson (2014) for a discussion of reflective supervision for child protection practitioners.

4. My thinking about the process of attunement, rupture, and repair was influenced by the work of psychotherapist Diana Fosha (Fosha 2009).

5. These presumptions are taken directly from the Circle of Security intervention (Powell *et al.* 2014). We have presented only a summary here.

6. Masterson, as cited in Powell *et al.* 2014.

7. Jonathan and Heidi have had a second daughter and have moved out of the area. Both are employed. Jonathan has dedicated his time and energy to working with at-risk families entering the child protection system in an effort to give back in gratitude for his own transformation—work he has to do pro bono because his record prevents him from paid employment in this area. They stay in touch.

8. My thinking about reflective functioning was influenced by Siegel (2010). See also Steele and Steele (2008) for a review of the "reflective functioning" construct.

9. Anna's interactions with her infant, Kendra, illustrate researcher Karlen Lyons-Ruth's concept of the hostile-helpless caregiving system in action, particularly the "helpless-fearful" stance (see Chapter 6). Lyons-Ruth and her colleagues found that this caregiving dynamic predicted disorganized attachment in the next generation. Interestingly, the "helpless-fearful" stance was predicted by sexual abuse in the mother's history whereas the "hostile/self-referential" stance was predicted by physical abuse (see Lyons-Ruth, Bronfman, and Atwood 1999; Lyons-Ruth and Spielman 2004).

10. Although not quoting him directly, I wish to acknowledge the influence of my time, interactions, and conversations with Zen teacher, Ezra Bayda, on my thinking about the concepts of 'refraining' and 'reframing.'

11. See Lieberman (2004); Lieberman and Van Horn (2011).

12. See also Fonagy *et al.* (1991).

Chapter 9

1. The research literature on resilience is now quite broad, and yet capturing it in practice can feel elusive. University of Minnesota researcher Ann Masten, who has dedicated her professional life to the study of resilience, described "four waves" of resilience research over the past four decades. The first wave focused on describing resilience and its related concepts. Later waves tested models of process and intervention. As part of the fourth wave, she calls for "a new

synthesis…to blaze a trail for translational resilience research that accelerates simultaneously the theoretical and practical knowledge on resilience" (Masten 2011, p.503)—a wave that combines research and theory with intervention in mutually informative ways. As she writes, "Children suffering now or threatened with imminent harm cannot wait for definitive science and experimental evidence on what works best for every child and situation" (p.501).

2. My thinking about "surrender" was influenced by my work with Zen teacher, Ezra Bayda.

3. I located and visited with Carrie in anticipation of the publication of this book. She is happily married, employed, and raising Sean, a subsequently born child, and a step child. The family recently bought and moved into their first home. Carrie reports that Sean's dad is also doing well and visits as he can.

4. Just as children need nurturance and connection, they also need their parents to be "in charge." A role-reversed dynamic, in which parents relinquish control to their children, is predictive of disorganized attachment (see Chapter 2). Our Circle of Security colleagues teach parents the following: "Always be: bigger, stronger, wiser, and kind. Whenever possible: follow my child's need. Whenever necessary: take charge" (Powell *et al.* 2014, p.282).

5. A total of 119 children, representing 108 families, were served through The Children's Ark. Of those, approximately one-third regained custody, about one-third relinquished voluntarily, and about one-third sought other services within the system or had their parental rights terminated.

6. My colleague —clinical psychologist Nancy Worsham —and I (MKH) engaged in a qualitative study of The Children's Ark through some of its residential years. We followed a total of eight mothers, some of whom are discussed in this book. In an extensive analysis of two of the eight mothers, we documented ongoing growth in their relationship with their child, in their resolution of past trauma, and in their sense of self (see Kretchmar, Worsham, and Swenson 2005 and Worsham *et al.* 2009).

7. Researchers Koren-Karie, Oppenheim, and Getzler-Yosef (2008) found that mothers sexually abused as children who were more resolved about their past trauma showed more sensitive guidance with their children. Their children, in turn, were more cooperative, and the mother–child co-narratives about emotional events were more coherent. They conclude, "A higher level of resolution…may act as a buffer between trauma and parenting, helping mothers separate the present context from past experiences" (p.477).

Chapter 10

1. "Narratives organize and shape our experience—change the story, change the mind" (Lacher *et al.* 2012, p.210). Based on research suggesting that narrative is vital to integration of experience and sense of self, psychologists at the Family Attachment and Counseling Center in Minnesota, USA, have developed a promising approach to changing traumatized children's narratives through story-telling. In their words, "Children deprived of a nurturing, attuned relationship with a caregiver tend not only to construct a chaotic life narrative but also form

mistaken, destructive conclusions about personal value and the meaning of experiences. Fortunately, children also possess the ability to embrace an alternate or the deserved ideal, and construct new narratives" (Lacher *et al.* 2012, p.39).

2. Sroufe (2016); see also Perry and Szalavitz (2006).

3. Once again, I want to acknowledge the impact of the Circle of Security as well as Sandra Powell on my language and thinking.

4. "Esteem sensitive" is a concept developed by our Circle of Security colleagues: "Esteem sensitivity involves the need to be seen as special, while always struggling with the fear of being exposed as imperfect and disappointing" (Powell *et al.* 2014, p.197). According to Powell *et al.* this sensitivity often develops when a person was raised in an environment where one's self-worth was based on accomplishment: "When self-esteem is based primarily on performance, rather than on a secure base of mutual respect, it tends to be fragile" (p.197).

5. Carla eventually moved out of the clean and sober house with her daughter and into her own apartment. She has maintained a long-term relationship with a man who is clearly devoted to both her and her daughter. After completing her high school equivalency and obtaining a two-year degree, Carla transferred to a local university where she graduated with a bachelor's degree and is currently enrolled in a master's program. Carla has forged relationships with all of her children and their families, and they visit her regularly. I meet and share a meal with Carla about once a month and continue to stand in awe of her strength, wisdom, and caring for all of humankind.

6. Eiseley (1978).

7. Based on a comprehensive analysis of their child protection system, Australia, in 2009, created a national framework to guide child protection efforts. In 2010, the United Kingdom's Secretary of State for Education commissioned a full review of England's child protection system, led by London School of Economics professor Eileen Munro. Additionally, in 2014, Trevor Spratt, Director of the Children's Research Centre at Trinity College Dublin, and his colleagues provided recommendations to redesign the Swiss child protection system based on results from a commissioned study that compared child protection policies across five nations.

8. Lonne *et al.* (2009) take issue with recent changes to many child protection systems, which—in their words—have placed "ever greater emphasis upon introducing complex systems, intricate procedures, risk assessments, relentless monitoring, and a preoccupation with the management of risk" (p.99). In response, Lonne and colleagues propose a "radical rethinking" of child protection and recommend fundamental revisions of policies and practice characterized by several principles, including "a clear and unwavering focus on positive outcomes for children and families as the central goal of a dynamic system that promotes the well-being of children and their parents, families, and communities…a child-centered, family-focused, culturally respectful framework for intervention… ethical, value-driven and relationship-based practice that is grounded in, and facilitative of, neighborhood- and community-based social care systems" (p.100).

9. One review of family support programs concluded that the only support programs that showed success in preventing child maltreatment and reducing

out-of-home placements were those that had "high levels of contact with families and made a variety of supports available." Programs that focused on particular issues (e.g. parent training) with limited contact with families did not "produce encouraging benefits if participants were confronting multiple stressors in their lives" (Cameron and Vanderwoerd 1997, p.215).

10. The costs of running a comprehensive intervention program for vulnerable families are substantial. The Children's Ark was supported through traditional public child welfare funding but also through grants and private donations. In fact, Paul Mann, the Ark's Financial Director, initially raised about 70 percent of the funding through grants and private donations. However, toward the end of the program the state provided about 70 percent of the funding because they recognized the value of the program. Additionally, Paul and Janet Mann did not draw salaries, and many of the treatment professionals provided services pro bono. However, it is our view that we can pay now or *pay more later* both in terms of human suffering and real dollars. Smyke and Breidenstine (2009) provided the following summary: "The cost, in human lives and in government resources, involved in managing the dysregulated, out-of-control behavior of a maltreated adolescent whose needs have never been properly addressed is much greater than that of intervening in the life of the infant or toddler in foster care" (p.512). Further, a recent study found that the total (i.e. lifetime) estimated financial costs related to *just one year* of confirmed cases of child maltreatment (physical abuse, sexual abuse, psychological abuse, and neglect) is approximately $124 billion (Fang *et al.* 2012).

11. Dozier *et al.* (2007); Dozier and Lindhiem (2006).

12. Smyke and Breidenstine (2009).

13. Dozier, Lindhiem, and Ackerman (2005); Fisher, Burraston, and Pears (2005); Powell *et al.* (2014); Zeanah and Larrieu (1998); Smyke *et al.* (2009).

14. Studying job stress among social workers in the Nordic countries, Blomberg *et al.* (2015) found that social workers, particularly those with limited experience, were often burdened with extensive caseloads. Further, in a recent study of human service workers in Central California, USA, researchers found that caseload size was the biggest predictor of job burnout (Madhavappallil, Kohli, and Choi 2014). Lizano and Mor Barak (2015) explored social worker burnout, finding that job demands (e.g. role ambiguity, work–family conflict) were predictive of burnout and that higher levels of emotional exhaustion were negatively related to job satisfaction. They also discovered that supervisor support buffered against burnout. Finally, Lizano *et al.* (2014) determined that work–family conflict was related to increased job burnout and negatively related to worker well-being. They suggest that practices and policies should be designed to improve work–family conflict such as flexible work schedules and opportunities to telecommute.

15. Pears *et al.* (2015) found that children in foster care were approximately 4.5 times more likely to move schools than comparison children not in foster care. Further, being in foster care negatively impacted early learning skills in kindergarten and academic and socioemotional competence in grades 3–5. Catherine Zorc, from the Children's Hospital of Philadelphia, and her colleagues (2013) reported that school absenteeism among 5–8-year-old children in foster care increased as school stability decreased.

16. In a study of 249 school personnel and social workers, Day *et al.* (2014) found that nearly half of the school personnel reported that they were not aware of the foster children on their caseloads within their schools. Only about 5 percent of school personnel reported weekly or monthly communication with the child's caseworker. Day *et al.* recommended increased training for school personnel as well as more communication and collaboration between schools and community agencies.

17. McCrae *et al.* (2016).

REFERENCES

Ainsworth, M.D.S., Blehar, M.C., Waters, E., and Wall, S. (1978) *Patterns of Attachment: A Psychological Study of the Strange Situation.* Hillsdale, NJ: Erlbaum.

Aronoff, M. (2015) 'Intergenerational continuity in foster care involvement.' *Dissertation Abstracts International: Section B: The Sciences and Engineering, 75,* 10.

Baird, A.D., Scheffer, I.E., and Wilson, S.J. (2011) 'Mirror neuron system involvement in empathy: A critical look at the evidence.' *Social Neuroscience, 6,* 4, 327–335.

Baker, J. (2013) 'Key Components of Social Skills Training.' In A. Bondy and M.J. Weiss (eds) *Teaching Social Skills to People with Autism: Best Practices in Individualizing Interventions.* Bethesda, MD: Woodbine House, Inc.

Bates, B.C. and Dozier, M. (2002) 'The importance of maternal state of mind regarding attachment and infant age at placement to foster mothers' representations of their foster infants.' *Infant Mental Health Journal, 23,* 4, 417–431.

Bayda, E. (2002) *Being Zen: Bringing Meditation to Life.* Boston, MA: Shambhala Publications, Inc.

Beam, C. (2014) *To the End of June: The Intimate Life of American Foster Care.* New York: Mariner Books.

Beebe, B., Jaffe, J., Markese, S., Buck, K. *et al.* (2010) 'The origins of 12-month attachment: A microanalysis of 4-month mother–infant interaction.' *Attachment and Human Development, 12,* 1–2, 3–141.

Beebe, B., Lachmann, F.M., Markese, S., and Bahrick, L. (2012a) 'On the origins of disorganized attachment and internal working models: Paper I. A dyadic systems approach.' *Psychoanalytic Dialogues, 22,* 2, 253–272.

Beebe, B., Lachmann, F.M., Markese, S, Buck, K.A. *et al.* (2012b) 'On the origins of disorganized attachment and internal working models: Paper II. An empirical microanalysis of 4-month mother–infant interaction.' *Psychoanalytic Dialogues, 22,* 3, 352–374.

Berg, E. (2006) *We Are All Welcome Here.* New York: Random House.

Bernard, K., and Dozier, M. (2011) 'This is my baby: Foster parents' feelings of commitment and displays of delight.' *Infant Mental Health Journal, 32,* 2, 251–262.

Biehal, N. (2014) 'Maltreatment in foster care: A review of the evidence.' *Child Abuse Review, 23,* 1, 48–60.

Blomberg, H., Kallio, J., Kroll, C., and Saarinen, A. (2015) 'Job stress among social workers: Determinants and attitude effects in the Nordic countries.' *British Journal of Social Work, 45,* 7, 2089–2105.

Bowen, M. (1978) *Family Therapy in Clinical Practice.* New York: Aronson.

Bowlby, J. (1982, first published 1969) *Attachment and Loss: Vol. 1 Attachment.* New York: Basic Books.

Bowlby, J. (1973) *Attachment and Loss: Vol. 2 Separation.* New York: Basic Books.

Bowlby, J. (1980) *Attachment and Loss: Vol. 3 Loss.* New York: Basic Books.

Bowlby, J. (1988) *A Secure Base: Parent–Child Attachment and Healthy Human Development.* New York: Basic Books.

Boyle, G. (2010) *Tattoos on the Heart: The Power of Boundless Compassion.* New York: Free Press.

Brach, T. (2003) *Radical Acceptance: Embracing Your Life with the Heart of a Buddha.* New York: Random House.

Bretherton, I. and Munholland, K.A. (2008) 'Internal Working Models in Attachment Relationships: Elaborating a Central Construct in Attachment Theory.' In J. Cassidy and P. Shaver (eds) *Handbook of Attachment: Theory, Research, and Clinical Applications* (2nd ed). New York: Guilford.

Brooks, D. (2011) *The Social Animal: The Hidden Sources of Love, Character, and Achievement.* New York: Random House.

Cameron, G. and Vanderwoerd, J. (1997) *Protecting Children and Supporting Families: Promising Programs and Organizational Realities.* New York: Aldine de Gruyter.

Cassidy, J. (2016) 'The Nature of the Child's Ties.' In J. Cassidy and P. Shaver (eds) *Handbook of Attachment: Theory, Research, and Clinical Applications* (3rd ed). New York: Guilford.

Choate, P.W. and Engstrom, S. (2014) 'The "good enough" parent: Implications for child protection.' *Child Care in Practice, 20,* 4, 368–382.

Chodron, P. (1997) *When Things Fall Apart.* Boston, MA: Shambhala Publications, Inc.

Cicchetti, D. and Howes, P.W. (1991) 'Developmental psychopathology in the context of the family: Illustrations from the study of child maltreatment.' *Canadian Journal of Behavioural Science, 23,* 3, 257–281.

Coan, J.A. (2016) 'Toward a Neuroscience of Attachment.' In J. Cassidy and P. Shaver (eds) *Handbook of Attachment: Theory, Research, and Clinical Applications* (3rd ed). New York: Guilford.

Colin, V. (1996) *Human Attachment.* New York: McGraw Hill.

Cooper, G., Hoffman, K., Powell, B., and Marvin, R. (2005) 'The Circle of Security Intervention: Differential Diagnosis and Differential Treatment.' In L.J. Berlin, Y. Ziv, L. Amaya-Jackson, and M.T. Greenberg (eds) *Enhancing Early Attachment: Theory, Research, Interventions, and Policy.* New York: Guilford.

Cozolino, L. (2010) *The Neuroscience of Psychotherapy: Healing the Social Brain* (2nd ed). New York: W.W. Norton and Company, Inc.

Cozolino, L. (2014) *The Neuroscience of Human Relationships: Attachment and the Developing Social Brain* (2nd ed). New York: W.W. Norton and Company.

Crittenden, P. (2006) 'A dynamic-maturational model of attachment.' *Australian and New Zealand Journal of Family Therapy, 27*, 2, 105–115.

Curley, J.P. and Champagne, F.A. (2016) 'Influence of maternal care on the developing brain: Mechanisms, temporal dynamics, and sensitive periods.' *Frontiers in Neuroendocrinology, 40*, 52–66.

D'Andrade, A.C. and James, S. (2014) 'Placement Stability.' In G.P. Mallon and P.M. Hess (eds) *Child Welfare for the 21st Century: A Handbook of Practices, Policies and Programs* (2nd ed). New York: Columbia University Press.

Day, A.G., Somers, C., Darden, J.S., and Yoon, J. (2014) 'Using cross-system communication to promote educational well-being of foster children: Recommendations for a national research, practice, and policy agenda.' *Children & Schools, 31*, 1, 54–62.

Deming, E.J. and McCabe, P.C. (2010) 'Prenatal Alcohol Exposure: Biological and Behavioral Outcomes.' In P.C. McCabe and S.R. Shaw (eds) *Genetic and Acquired Disorders: Current Topics and Interventions for Educators.* Thousand Oaks, CA: Corwin Press.

DeOliveira, C., Bailey, H.N., Moran, G., and Pederson, D.R. (2004) 'Emotion socialization as a framework for understanding the development of disorganized attachment.' *Social Development, 13*, 3, 437–467.

Disabled World (2013) *Children with Disabilities and Foster Care.* Accessed on November 25, 2016 at www.disabled-world.com/disability/children/foster.php.

Dozier, M., Grasso, D., Lindhiem, O., and Lewis, E. (2007) 'The Role of Caregiver Commitment in Foster Care: Insights from the "This Is My Baby" Interview.' In D. Oppenheim and D.F. Goldsmith (eds) *Attachment Theory in Clinical Work with Children: Bridging the Gap between Research and Practice.* New York: Guilford.

Dozier, M. and Lindhiem, O. (2006) 'This is my child: Differences among foster parents in commitment to their young children.' *Child Maltreatment, 11*, 4, 338–345.

Dozier, M., Lindhiem, O., and Ackerman, J.P. (2005) 'Attachment and Biobehavioral Catch-up: An Intervention Targeting Empirically Identified Needs of Foster Infants.' In L.J. Berlin, Y. Ziv, L. Amaya-Jackson, and M.T. Greenberg (eds) *Enhancing Early Attachments: Theory, Research, Intervention, and Policy.* New York: Guilford Press.

Dozier, M. and Rutter, M. (2016) 'Challenges to the development of attachment relationships faced by young children in foster and adoptive care.' In J. Cassidy and P.R. Shaver (eds) *Handbook of Attachment: Theory, Research and Clinical Applications* (3rd ed). New York: The Guilford Press.

Dozier, M., Stovall, C., Albus, K., and Bates, B. (2001) 'Attachment for infants in foster care: The role of caregiver state of mind.' *Child Development, 72*, 5, 1467–1477.

Dozier, M., Zeanah, C.H., Jr., and Bernard, K. (2013) 'Infants and toddlers in foster care.' *Child Development Perspectives, 7*, 3, 166–171.

Duckworth, A. (2016) *Grit: The Power of Passion and Perseverance.* New York: Scribner.

Eagle, R.S. (1993) '"Airplanes crash, spaceships stay in orbit": The separation experience of a child "in care."' *Journal of Psychotherapy Practice and Research, 2*, 4, 318–334.

Edwards, F. (2016) 'Saving children, controlling families: Punishment, redistribution, and child protection.' *American Sociological Review, 81*, 3, 575–595.

Eiseley, L. (1978) *The Star Thrower.* New York: Random House.

Ellermann, C.R. (2007) 'Influences on the mental health of children placed in foster care.' *Family & Community Health: The Journal of Health Promotion & Maintenance, 30,* 2S, S23–S32.

Epstein, M. (2013) *The Trauma of Everyday Life.* New York: Penguin Random House.

EveryChild, Inc. (n.d.) 'About Us.' Accessed on November 25, 2016 at http://everychildtexas.org/AboutUs.html.

Fang, X., Brown, D.S., Florence, C.S., and Mercy, J. (2012) 'The economic burden of child maltreatment in the United States and implications for prevention.' *Child Abuse & Neglect, 36,* 2, 156–165.

Fearon, R.M.P. and Belsky, J. (2016) 'Precursors to Attachment Security.' In J. Cassidy and P. Shaver (eds) *Handbook of Attachment: Theory, Research, and Clinical Applications* (3rd ed). New York: Guilford.

Ferguson, H. (2011) *Child Protection Practice.* New York: Palgrave McMillan.

Fisher, P.A., Burraston, B., and Pears, K.C. (2005) 'The early intervention foster care program: Permanent placement outcomes from a randomized trial.' *Child Maltreatment, 10,* 1, 61–71.

Fonagy, P., Steele, M., Steele, H., Moran, G.S., and Higgitt, A.C. (1991) 'The capacity for understanding mental states: The reflective self in parent and child and its significance for security of attachment.' *Infant Mental Health Journal, 12,* 3, 201–218.

Fosha, D. (2000) *The Transforming Power of Affect: A Model for Accelerated Change.* New York: Basic Books.

Fosha, D. (2009) 'Emotion and Recognition at Work: Energy, Vitality, Pleasure, Truth, Desire, and the Emergent Phenomenology of Transformational Experience.' In D. Fosha, D.J. Siegel, and M. Solomon (eds) *The Healing Power of Emotion: Affective Neuroscience, Development and Clinical Practice.* New York: W.W. Norton and Company, Inc.

Foster, L.J.J., Beadnell, B., and Pecora, P.J. (2015) 'Intergenerational pathways leading to foster care placement of foster care alumni's children.' *Child and Family Social Work, 20,* 1, 72–82.

Fraiberg, S., Adelson, E., and Shapiro, V. (1975) 'Ghosts in the nursery: A psychoanalytic approach to the problem of impaired infant–mother relationships.' *Journal of the America Academy of Child Psychiatry, 14,* 3, 387–421.

Gianino, A. and Tronick, E.Z. (1988) 'The Mutual Regulation Model: The Infant's Self and Interactive Regulation. Coping and Defense Capacities.' In T. Field, P. McCabe, and N. Schneiderman (eds) *Stress and Coping.* Hillsdale, NJ: Lawrence Erlbaum.

Gilbert, N., Parton, N. and Skivenes, M. (eds) (2011) *Child Protection Systems: International Trends and Orientations.* Oxford: Oxford University Press.

Gilligan, R. (2006) 'Promoting Resilience and Permanence in Child Welfare.' In R.J. Flynn, P.M. Dudding, and J.G. Barber (eds) *Promoting Resilience in Child Welfare.* Ottawa, Ontario: University of Ottowa Press.

Glaser, D. (2000) 'Child abuse and neglect and the brain—A review.' *Journal of Child Psychology and Psychiatry, 41,* 1, 97–116.

Gottman, J. (1997) *Raising an Emotionally Intelligent Child: The Heart of Parenting.* New York: Simon & Schuster.

Granat, A., Gadassi, R., Gilboa-Schechtman, E., and Feldman, R. (2016) 'Maternal depression and anxiety, social synchrony, and infant regulation of negative and positive emotions.' *Emotion, 17,* 1, 11–27.

Gunnar, M. and Quevedo, K. (2007) 'The neurobiology of stress and development.' *Annual Review of Psychology, 58,* 145–173.

Harvey, A. and Henderson, F. (2014) 'Reflective supervision for child protection practice—Reading beneath the surface.' *Journal of Social Work Practice, 28,* 3, 343–356.

Hayes, L.J., Goodman, S.H. and Carlson, E. (2013) 'Maternal antenatal depression and infant disorganized attachment at 12 months.' *Attachment and Human Development, 15,* 2, 133–153.

Hébert, S.T., Lanctôt, N., and Turcotte, M. (2016) 'I didn't want to be moved there': Young women remembering their perceived sense of agency in the context of placement instability. *Children and Youth Services Review, 70,* 229–237.

Heineman, T.V. (2006) 'The Children's Psychotherapy Project: One Child. One Therapist. For as Long as It Takes.' In T.V. Heineman and D. Ehrensaft (eds) *Building a Home Within: Meeting the Emotional Needs of Children and Youth in Foster Care.* Baltimore,MD: Paul H. Brooks Publishing Co.

Hesse, E. (2016) 'The Adult Attachment Interview: Protocol, Method of Analysis, and Selected Empirical Studies.' In J. Cassidy and P.R. Shaver (eds) *The Handbook of Attachment: Theory, Research and Clinical Applications* (3rd ed). New York: The Guilford Press.

Hesse, E. and Main, M. (1999) 'Second-generation effects of unresolved trauma in nonmaltreating parents: Dissociated, frightened, and threatening parental behavior.' *Psychoanalytic Inquiry, 19,* 4, 481–540.

Hinde, R.A. and Stevenson-Hinde, J. (eds) (1988) *Relationships Within Families: Mutual Influences.* Oxford: Oxford University Press.

Hindle, D. and Shulman, G. (2008) 'Introduction.' In D. Hindle and G. Shulman (eds) *The Emotional Experience of Adoption: A Psychoanalytic Perspective.* New York: Routledge.

Howes, P.W., Cicchetti, D., Toth, S.L., and Rogosch, F.A. (2000) 'Affective, organizational, and relational characteristics of maltreating families: A systems perspective.' *Journal of Family Therapy, 14,* 1, 95–110.

Isabella, R.A. (1993) 'Origins of attachment: Maternal interactive behavior across the first year.' *Child Development, 64,* 2, 605–621.

Isabella, R.A. and Belsky, J. (1991) 'Interactional synchrony and the origins of infant–mother attachment: A replication study.' *Child Development, 62,* 2, 373–384.

Jacobvitz, D. and Hazen, N. (1999) 'Developmental Pathways from Infant Disorganization to Childhood Peer Relationships.' In J. Solomon and C. George (eds) *Attachment Disorganization.* New York: The Guilford Press.

Johnson, S.C., Dweck, C.S., and Chen, F.S. (2007) 'Evidence for infants' internal working models of attachment.' *Psychological Science, 18,* 6, 501–502.

Karen, R. (1998) *Becoming Attached: First Relationships and How They Shape Our Capacity to Love*. New York: Oxford University Press.

Kelly, K., McNaught, K. and Stotland, J. (2014) 'Educational Issues for Children and Youth.' In G.P. Mallon and P.M. Hess (eds) *Child Welfare for the 21st Century: A Handbook of Practices, Policies and Programs* (2nd ed). New York: Columbia University Press.

Kemp, S.P., Burke, T.K., Allen-Eckard, K., Becker, M.F. and Ackroyd, A. (2014) 'Family Support Services.' In G.P. Mallon and P.M. Hess (eds) *Child Welfare for the 21st Century: A Handbook of Practices, Policies and Programs* (2nd ed). New York: Columbia University Press.

Kenrick, J. (2000) '"Be a kid": The traumatic impact of repeated separations on children who are fostered and adopted.' *Journal of Child Psychotherapy, 26*, 3, 393–412.

Kerns, K.A. and Brumariu, L.E. (2016) 'Attachment in Middle Childhood.' In J. Cassidy and P. Shaver (eds) *Handbook of Attachment: Theory, Research, and Clinical Applications* (3rd ed). New York: Guilford.

Koren-Karie, N., Oppenheim, D. and Getzler-Yosef, R. (2008) 'Shaping children's internal working models through mother–child dialogues: The importance of resolving past maternal trauma.' *Attachment and Human Development, 10*, 4, 465–483.

Kretchmar, M.D., Worsham, N.L., and Swenson, N. (2005) 'Anna's story: A qualitative analysis of an at-risk mother's experience in an alternative foster care.' *Attachment and Human Development, 7*, 1, 31–49.

Lacher, D.B., Nichols, T., Nichols, M. and May, J.C. (2012) *Connecting with Kids through Stories: Using Attachment Narrative to Facilitate Attachment in Adopted Children*. Philadelphia, PA: Jessica Kingsley Publishers.

Lieberman, A.F. (2004) 'Child–Parent Psychotherapy: A Relationship-Based Approach to the Treatment of Mental Health Disorders in Infancy and Early Childhood.' In A.J. Sameroff, S.C. McDonough, and K.L. Rosenblum (eds) *Treating Parent–Infant Relationship Problems*. New York: Guilford Press.

Lieberman, A.F., Padron, E., Van Horn, P., and Harris, W.W. (2005) 'Angels in the nursery: The intergenerational transmission of benevolent parental influences.' *Infant Mental Health Journal, 26*, 6, 504–520.

Lieberman, A.F. and Van Horn, P. (2011) *Psychotherapy with Infants and Young Children: Repairing the Effects of Stress and Trauma in Early Attachment*. New York: The Guilford Press.

Liotti, G. (2011) 'Attachment Disorganization and the Clinical Dialogue: Themes and Variations.' In J. Solomon and C. George (eds) *Disorganized Attachment and Caregiving*. New York: The Guilford Press.

Lizano, E.L., Hsiao, H.Y., Mor Barak, M., and Casper, L.M. (2014) 'Support in the workplace: Buffering the deleterious effects of work–family conflict on child welfare workers' well-being and job burnout.' *Journal of Social Service Research, 40*, 2, 178–188.

Lizano, E.L. and Mor Barak, M. (2015) 'Job burnout and affective wellbeing: A longitudinal study of burnout and job satisfaction among public child welfare workers.' *Children and Youth Services Review, 55*, 18–28.

Lombardi, J. (2002) *Time to Care: Redesigning Child Care to Promote Education, Support Families, and Build Communities.* Philadelphia, PA: Temple University Press.

Lonne, B., Parton, N., Thomson, J., and Harries, M. (2009) *Reforming Child Protection.* New York: Routledge.

Lyons-Ruth, K., Bronfman, E., and Atwood, G. (1999) 'A relational-diathesis model of hostile-helpless states of mind: Expressions in mother–infant interaction.' In J. Solomon and C. George (eds) *Attachment Disorganization.* New York: Guilford.

Lyons-Ruth, K. and Jacobvitz, D. (2008) 'Attachment Disorganization: Genetic Factors, Parenting Contexts, and Developmental Transformation from Infancy to Adulthood.' In J. Cassidy and P.R. Shaver (eds) *Handbook of Attachment: Theory, Research and Clinical Applications* (2nd ed). New York: The Guilford Press.

Lyons-Ruth, K. and Jacobvitz, D. (2016) 'Attachment Disorganization from Infancy to Adulthood: Neurobiological Correlates, Parenting Contexts, and Pathways to Disorder.' In J. Cassidy and P. Shaver (eds) *Handbook of Attachment: Theory, Research, and Clinical Applications* (3rd ed). New York: Guilford.

Lyons-Ruth, K. and Spielman, E. (2004) 'Disorganized infant attachment strategies and helpless-fearful profiles of parenting: Integrating attachment research with clinical intervention.' *Infant Mental Health Journal, 25,* 4, 318–335.

Macfie, J., McElwain, N.L., Houts, R.M., and Cox, M.J. (2005) 'Intergenerational transmission of role reversal between parent and child: Dyadic and family systems internal working models.' *Attachment and Human Development, 7,* 1, 51–65.

Madhavappallil, T., Kohli, V., and Choi, J. (2014) 'Correlates of job burnout among human services workers: Implications for workforce retention.' *Journal of Sociology and Social Welfare, 41,* 4, 69–90.

Maier, S.F. and Seligman, M.E.P. (2016) 'Learned helplessness at fifty: Insight from neuroscience.' *Psychological Review, 123,* 4, 349–367.

Main, M. and Solomon, J. (1986) 'Discovery of a New, Insecure-Disorganized/ Disoriented Attachment Pattern.' In T.B. Brazelton and M.W. Yogman (eds) *Affective Development in Infancy.* Norwood, NJ: Ablex.

Main, M. and Solomon, J. (1990) 'Procedures for Identifying Infants as Disorganized/ Disoriented during the Ainsworth Strange Situation.' In M.T. Greenberg, D. Cicchetti, and E.M. Cummings (eds) *Attachment in the Preschool Years: Theory, Research, and Intervention.* Chicago, IL: University of Chicago Press.

Mann, J.C. and Kretchmar, M.D. (2006) 'A disorganized toddler in foster care: Healing and change from an attachment theory perspective.' *Zero to Three, 26,* 5, 29–36.

Mann, J.C., Kretchmar, M.D. and Worsham, N.L. (2008) 'Critical issues in foster care: Lessons The Children's Ark learned from Barbara and Nathan.' *Zero to Three, 28,* 6, 41–46.

Mann, J.C., Kretchmar, M.D., and Worsham, N.L. (2011) 'Being in relationship: Paradoxical truths and opportunities for change in foster care.' *Zero to Three, 31,* 3, 11–16.

Martins, C. and Gaffan, E. (2000) 'Effects of early maternal depression on patterns of infant–mother attachment: A meta-analytic investigation.' *Journal of Child Psychology and Psychiatry, 41,* 6, 737–746.

Marvin, R.S., Britner, P.A. and Russell, B.S. (2016) 'Normative Development: The Ontogeny of Attachment in Childhood.' In J. Cassidy and P. Shaver (eds) *Handbook of Attachment: Theory, Research, and Clinical Applications* (3rd ed). New York: Guilford.

Masten, A.S. (2011) 'Resilience in children threatened by extreme adversity: Frameworks for research, practice, and translational synergy.' *Development and Psychopathology, 23,* 2, 493–506.

Masten, A.S. (2014) *Ordinary Magic: Resilience in Development.* New York: Guilford.

McCrae, J.S., Brown, S.M., Yang, J., and Groneman, S. (2016) 'Enhancing early childhood outcomes: Connecting child welfare and Head Start.' *Early Child Development and Care, 186,* 7, 1110–1125.

Meins, E., Fernyhough, C., Fradley, E., and Tuckey, M. (2001) 'Rethinking maternal sensitivity: Mothers' comments on infants' mental processes predict security of attachment at 12 months.' *Journal of Child Clinical Psychiatry, 42,* 5, 637–648.

Minuchin, S. (1974) *Families and Family Therapy.* Cambridge,MA: Harvard University Press.

Moss, E., Bureau, J., St. Laurent, D., and Tarabulsy, G.M. (2011) 'Understanding Disorganized Attachment at Preschool and School Age: Examining Divergent Pathways of Disorganized and Controlling Children. In J. Solomon and C. George (eds) *Disorganized Attachment and Caregiving.* New York: The Guilford Press.

Moss, E., Cyr, C., and Dubois-Comtois, K. (2004) 'Attachment at early school age and developmental risk: Examining family contexts and behavior problems of controlling-caregiving, controlling-punitive, and behaviorally disorganized children.' *Developmental Psychology, 40,* 4, 519–532.

Munro, E. (2011) *The Munro Review of Child Protection: Final Report. A Child-Centred System.* London: Crown Copyright. Accessed on February 15, 2017 at https://www.gov.uk/government/uploads/system/uploads/attachment_data/file/175391/Munro-Review.pdf.

National Autism Center (2015) *Findings and Conclusions: National Standards Project, Phase 2.* Randolph, MA: Author.

National Council on Disability (2008) *Youth with Disabilities in the Foster Care System: Barriers to Success and Proposed Policy Solutions.* Accessed on November 25, 2016 at www.aypf.org/publications/documents/ncd96_FosterYouth_w_cover.pdf.

Pears, K.C., Kim, H.K., Buchanan, R., and Fisher, P.A. (2015) 'Adverse consequences of school mobility for children in foster care: A prospective longitudinal study.' *Child Development, 86,* 4, 1210–1226.

Perry, B.D. (2009) 'Examining child maltreatment through a neurodevelopmental lens: Clinical applications of the neurosequential model of therapeutics.' *Journal of Loss and Trauma, 14,* 4, 240–255.

Perry, B.D. and Pollard, R.A. (1998) 'Homeostasis, stress, trauma, and adaptation: A neurodevelopmental view of childhood trauma.' *Child and Adolescent Psychiatric Clinics of North America, 7,* 1, 33–51.

Perry, B.D., Pollard R.A., Blakley, T.L., Baker, W.L., and Vigilante, D. (1995) 'Childhood trauma, the neurobiology of adaptation, and "use dependent" development of the brain: How "states" become "traits."' *Infant Mental Health Journal*, 16, 4, 271–291.

Perry, B.D. and Szalavitz, M. (2006) *The Boy Who Was Raised as a Dog and Other Stories from a Child Psychiatrist's Notebook: What Traumatized Children Can Teach Us about Loss, Love, and Healing.* New York: Basic Books.

Powell, B., Cooper, G., Hoffman, K., and Marvin, B. (2014) *The Circle of Security Intervention: Enhancing Attachment in Early Parent–Child Relationships.* New York: The Guilford Press.

Richo, D. (2008) *When the Past Is Present: Healing the Emotional Wounds that Sabotage Our Relationships.* Boston, MA: Shambhala Publications, Inc.

Rock, S., Michelson, D., Thomson, S., and Day, C. (2015) 'Understanding foster placement instability for looked after children: A systematic review and narrative synthesis of quantitative and qualitative evidence.' *British Journal of Social Work*, 45, 1, 177–203.

Rosenau, N. (2005/06) 'Supporting family life for children with disabilities: What we know and don't know.' In Gaylord, V., LaLiberte, T., Lightfoot, E., and Hewitt, A. (eds) *Impact: Feature Issue on Children with Disabilities in the Child Welfare System, 19*, 1. [Minneapolis: University of Minnesota, Institute on Community Integration.]

Russell, J. and Macgill, S. (2015) 'Demographics, policy, and foster care rates: A predictive analytics approach.' *Children and Youth Services Review, 58*, 118–126.

Sameroff, A.J. and Emde, R.N. (1989) *Relationship Disturbances in Early Childhood.* New York: Basic Books.

Schulte-Rüther, M., Markowitsch, H.J., Fink, G.R., and Piefke, M. (2007) 'Mirror neurons and theory of mind mechanisms involved in face-to-face interactions: A functional magnetic resonance imaging approach to empathy.' *Journal of Cognitive Neuroscience, 19*, 8, 1354–1372.

Siegel, D.J. (2010) *Mindsight: The New Science of Personal Transformation.* New York: Random House.

Siegel, D.J. (2012) *The Developing Mind: How Relationships and the Brain Interact to Shape Who We Are* (2nd ed). New York: The Guilford Press.

Siegel, D.J. and Hartzell, M. (2014) *Parenting from the Inside Out: How a Deeper Self-Understanding Can Help You Raise Children Who Thrive.* New York: Penguin Putnam, Inc.

Slade, A. (2005) 'Parental reflective functioning: An introduction.' *Attachment and Human Development, 7*, 1, 269–281.

Slade, A. (2014) 'Imagining fear: Attachment, threat, and psychic experience.' *Psychoanalytic Dialogues, 24*, 3, 253--266.

Smyke, A.T. and Breidenstine, A.S. (2009) 'Foster Care in Early Childhood.' In C.H. Zeanah, Jr. (ed) *The Handbook of Infant Mental Health, Third Edition.* New York: Guilford.

Smyke, A.T., Zeanah, C.H., Jr., Fox, N.A., and Nelson, C.A. (2009) 'A new model of foster care for young children: The Bucharest Early Intervention Project.' *Child and Adolescent Psychiatric Clinics of North America, 18*, 3, 721–734.

Solomon, J. and George, C. (1999a) 'The Place of Disorganization in Attachment Theory: Linking Classic Observations with Contemporary Findings.' In J. Solomon and C. George (eds) *Attachment Disorganization*. New York: The Guilford Press.

Solomon, J. and George, C. (eds) (1999b) *Attachment Disorganization*. New York: The Guilford Press.

Solomon, J. and George, C. (2011a) 'Disorganization of Maternal Caregiving across Two Generations: Origins of Caregiver Helplessness.' In J. Solomon and C. George (eds) *Disorganized Attachment and Caregiving*. New York: The Guilford Press.

Solomon, J. and George, C. (eds) (2011b) *Disorganized Attachment and Caregiving*. New York: The Guilford Press.

Spratt, T., Nett, J., Bromfield, L., Hietamaki, J., Kindler, H., and Ponnert, L. (2014) 'Child protection in Europe: Development of an international cross-comparion model to inform national policies and practices.' *British Journal of Social Work, 45,* 5, 1508–1525.

Sroufe, L.A. (2016) 'The Place of Attachment in Development.' In J. Cassidy and P. Shaver (eds) *Handbook of Attachment: Theory, Research, and Clinical Applications* (3rd ed). New York: Guilford.

Sroufe, L.A., Egeland, B., Carlson, E.A., and Collins, W.A. (2005) *The Development of the Person: The Minnesota Study of Risk and Adaptation from Birth to Adulthood*. New York: Guilford.

Steele, H. and Steele, M. (2008) 'On the Origins of Reflective Functioning.' In F. Busch (ed) *Mentalization: Theoretical Considerations, Research Findings, and Clinical Implications*. New York: Analytic Press.

Tronick, E.Z. (1989) 'Emotions and emotional communication in infants.' *American Psychologist, 44,* 2, 112–119.

United Cerebral Palsy and Children's Rights (2006) *Forgotten Children: A Case for Action for Children and Youth with Disabilities in Foster Care*. Accessed on November 25, 2016 at www.childrensrights.org/wp-content/uploads/2008/06/forgotten_children_children_with_disabilities_in_foster_care_2006.pdf.

Van IJzendoorn, M.H. (1995) 'Adult attachment representations, parental responsiveness, and infant attachment: A meta-analysis on the predictive validity of the Adult Attachment Interview.' *Psychological Bulletin, 117,* 3, 387–403.

Verhage, M.L., Schuengel, C., Madigan, S., Fearon, R.M.P. *et al.* (2016) 'Narrowing the transmission gap: A synthesis of three decades of research on intergenerational transmission of attachment.' *Psychological Bulletin, 142,* 4, 337–366.

Waldfogel, J. (2000) 'Reforming child protective services.' *Child Welfare: Journal of Policy, Practice, and Program, 79,* 1, 43–57.

Weinfield, N.S., Sroufe, L.A., Egeland, B., and Carlson, E. (2008) 'Individual Differences in Infant–Caregiver Attachment: Conceptual and Empirical Aspects of Security.' In J. Cassidy and P.R. Shaver (eds) *Handbook of Attachment: Theory, Research, and Clinical Applications* (2nd ed). New York: Guilford.

Worsham, N.L., Kretchmar, M.D., Swenson, N., and Goodvin, R. (2009) 'At-risk mothers' parenting capacity: An attachment theory and epistemological analysis.' *Clinical Child Psychology and Psychiatry, 14,* 1, 25–41.

Yalom, I. (1999) *Momma and the Meaning of Life: Tales of Psychotherapy.* New York: Basic Books, Inc.

Zeanah, C.H., Jr. (2014) 'Foreword.' In B. Powell, G. Cooper, K. Hoffman, and B. Marvin, *The Circle of Security Intervention: Enhancing Attachment in Early Parent–Child Relationships.* New York: The Guilford Press.

Zeanah, C.H., Jr. and Larrieu, J.A. (1998) Intensive intervention for maltreated infants and toddlers in foster care. *Child and Adolescent Psychiatric Clinics of North America, 7,* 2, 357–371.

Zeanah, C.H., Jr., Shauffer, C., and Dozier, M. (2011) 'Foster care for young children: Why it must be developmentally informed.' *Journal of the American Academy of Child & Adolescent Psychiatry, 50,* 12, 1199–1201.

Zorc, C.S., O'Reilly, A.L.R., Matone, M., Long, J., Watts, C., and Rubin, D. (2013) 'The relationship of placement experience to school absenteeism and changing schools in young, school-aged children in foster care.' *Children and Youth Services Review, 35,* 5, 826–833.

FURTHER READING

Beam, C. (2014) *To the End of June: The Intimate Life of American Foster Care*. New York: Mariner Books.

Boyle, G. (2010) *Tattoos on the Heart: The Power of Boundless Compassion*. New York: Free Press.

Brooks, D. (2011) *The Social Animal: The Hidden Sources of Love, Character, and Achievement*. New York: Random House.

Cozolino, L. (2014) *The Neuroscience of Human Relationships: Attachment and the Developing Social Brain* (2nd ed). New York: W.W. Norton and Company.

Ferguson, H. (2011) *Child Protection Practice*. New York: Palgrave McMillan.

Flynn, R.J., Dudding, P.M., and Barber, J.G. (eds) *Promoting Resilience in Child Welfare*. Ottowa, Ontario: University of Ottowa Press.

Heineman, T.V. and Ehrensaft, D. (eds) *Building a Home Within: Meeting the Emotional Needs of Children and Youth in Foster Care*. Baltimore, MD: Paul H. Brooks Publishing Co.

Hoffman, K., Cooper, G, Powell, B. and Benton, C.M. (2017) *Raising a Secure Child: How Circle of Security Parenting Can Help You Nurture Your Child's Attachment, Emotional Resilience, and Freedom to Explore*. New York: The Guilford Press.

Karen, R. (1998) *Becoming Attached: First Relationships and How They Shape Our Capacity to Love*. New York: Oxford University Press.

Lacher, D.B., Nichols, T., Nichols, M., and May, J.C. (2012) *Connecting with Kids through Stories: Using Attachment Narrative to Facilitate Attachment in Adopted Children*. Philadelphia, PA: Jessica Kingsley Publishers.

Lonne, B., Parton, N., Thomson, J., and Harries, M. (2009) *Reforming Child Protection*. New York: Routledge.

Mallon, G.P. and Hess, P.M. (eds) (2014) *Child Welfare for the 21st Century: A Handbook of Practices, Policies and Programs* (2nd ed). New York: Columbia University Press.

Masten, A.S. (2014) *Ordinary Magic: Resilience in Development*. New York: Guilford.

Perry, B.D. and Szalavitz, M. (2006) *The Boy Who Was Raised as a Dog and Other Stories from a Child Psychiatrist's Notebook: What Traumatized Children Can Teach Us about Loss, Love, and Healing*. New York: Basic Books.

Powell, B., Cooper, G., Hoffman, K., and Marvin, B. (2014) *The Circle of Security Intervention: Enhancing Attachment in Early Parent–Child Relationships.* New York: The Guilford Press.

Siegel, D.J. (2012) *The Developing Mind: How Relationships and the Brain Interact to Shape Who We Are* (2nd ed). New York: The Guilford Press.

Siegel, D.J. and Hartzell, M. (2014) *Parenting from the Inside Out: How a Deeper Self-Understanding Can Help You Raise Children Who Thrive.* New York: Penguin Putnam, Inc.

Sroufe, L.A., Egeland, B., Carlson, E.A., and Collins, W.A. (2005) *The Development of the Person: The Minnesota Study of Risk and Adaptation from Birth to Adulthood.* New York: Guilford.

SUBJECT INDEX

adoptions
    Ashley's experience 82–4, 88–9
    Hannah's experience 82–3, 84–6, 88–9
    transition from foster care 86–8
Adult Attachment Interview (AAI) 117
Ainsworth, Mary
    and attachment theory 41–2
"angels in the nursery" 173, 174
Angie and Charlie
    hope of 184
    resilience of 182–3
    tenacity of 183–4
Anna and Kendra
    and change 179, 180
    empathy for self 192–3
    reflective functioning 167–73
anxious-avoidant attachment 42
Ashley
    adoptive experience 82–4, 88–9
    arrival at Children's Ark 74–5
    brain development 79
    reaction to parental neglect 74–8
    relationship building 157–8
attachment theory
    with at-risk families 173–7
    anxious-avoidant attachment 42
    child-parent psychotherapy 173–4
    development of 40
    disorganized/disorientated
        attachment 42–3, 59–62
    experiments in 41–2
    from birth 41
    effects on development 41, 43–4,
        78–82

    in foster care 142–5
    and intergenerational transmission of
        caregiving 116–20, 173
    patterns of 41–3
    and Rickie 44–5
    secure attachment 42
    and The Strange Situation Procedure
        41–3, 67

Barbara
    in Circle of Security 67–8, 69
    own childhood issues 63–5
Becoming Attached (Karen) 119–20
behavior as need (Circle of Security
      principle)
    and Rachel 50–1
"being with" (Circle of Security
      principle)
    and Rachel 53–5
Bowlby, John
    and attachment theory 40, 41
Boy Who Was Raised as a Dog, The (Perry
      and Szalavitz) 44
brain development
    and Ashley 79
    in babies 79–81
    effect of trauma on 78–82
    "mirror" neurons 80
    neural networks 80–2
    social brain 79
Bruce
    experiences as child 151

Carla
  and change 179–80, 161
  and child protection system 206–10
  empathy for others 191–2
  experiences as child 149–51
  relationship building 154, 155–6
Carrie and Sean
  and change 188–9
  and child-centred environment/
    intervention 132–4
Cassidy, Jude 48–9
change
  Angie and Charlie 182–4
  capacity for relationships 181
  Carrie 188–9
  Desirae 195–6, 197–8
  empathy 190–3, 200–1
  fear of 122–3
  Heidi 187–8
  hope 181
  Isaac 196–7
  research on 197–201
  resilience 178–80, 198–9
  and "The Shift" 185
  success of 193–7, 201
  surrender 185
  Tamera 186–7
  tenacity 180–1, 199–200
  understanding 189–90
child-centred environment/intervention
  Carrie and Sean 132–4
  Connor 137–8
  creating 130–2
  finishing 134–5
  starting 137-8
  Tamera and Daisy 147–8
  Tony 139–41
child-parent psychotherapy 173–4
child protection system
  need for change in 206–11, 215–20
Children's Ark
  as "angels in the nursery" 174
  assumptions at 146–7
  building community in 216–18
  and Circle of Security 65, 72
  evidence-based practice 158–65
  opening of 40
  reflective functioning in 165–73
  relationship building in 152–8

tackling fear of change 122–3
Ted at 123–5
children's experiences
  considering 127–9, 147–8
  validating 129–30
  when adults 148–51
children's needs
  and cost of separation 211–14
  primacy of 202–4
Children's Psychotherapy Project 217–18
Circle of Security (COS)
  behavior as need principle 50–1
  "being with" principle 53–5
  and Children's Ark 65, 72, 175–6
  cues and miscues principle 51–3
  description of 65–6
  "I am here, you are worth it" principle
    48–50
  limited 68
  and needs of child 66–8
  and parents 66–9
  repair principle 55–7
  state of mind principle 57–8
commitment
  of foster carers 143–4
compassion
  for parents 112–13
Connor
  starts child-centred intervention 137–8
considering children's experiences 127–9,
  147–8
Cooper, Glen 48
Craig, Hilary and Tim
  and intergenerational transmission of
    caregiving 135–7
cues and miscues (Circle of Security
    principle)
  and Nathan 67–8
  and Rachel 51–3

Desirae
  caring, long-term relationships
    111–12
  compassion for 113
  empathy for children 190–1
  long-term change 114
  emotions of 110–11
  and intergenerational transmission of
    caregiving 119, 120

policy implications for 114–16
relationship building 154
return of children to 106–110
successful change 195–6, 197–8
disorganized/disorientated attachment 42–3
conditions for 60
effects of 60–1, 74–8
and foster care 61–2
and intergenerational transmission of caregiving 116–20
origins of 59–60
and Rachel 62
and Rickie 44–5

empathy
as prerequisite for change 190–3, 200–1
for self 192–3
for others 191–2
for children 190–1
evidence-based practice
at Children's Ark 158–65

fear of change
at Children's Ark 122–3
finishing interventions 134–5
foster care/carers
and attachment theory 142–5
commitment of 143–4
creating secure and stable placements 214–16
and disorganized/disorientated attachment 61–2
multiple placements 72
reimagining 142–5, 210–11
relationship with parents 34–7
separation costs 211–14
and special needs 102–5
support for 144–5, 205–6
timing of 144
training for 215
transition to adoption 86–8
transitions to 69–73

"ghosts in the nursery" 116–17, 173

Hannah
adoptive experience 82–3, 84–6, 88–9
arrival at Children's Ark 74
reaction to parental neglect 74–8
Heidi
and change 187–8
Hoffman, Kent 48
hope
as prerequisite for change 181, 200

"I am here, you are worth it" (Circle of Security principle)
and Rachel 48–50
intergenerational transmission of caregiving 63–5
"angels in the nursery" 173
and attachment theory 116–20, 173
and Craig, Hilary and Tim 135–7
"ghosts in the nursery" 116–17, 173
and Kraig 141–2
Isaac
change 196–7
foster placement for 214

Jonathan, Heidi and Rose
evidence-based practice at Children's Ark 159–65

Karen
relationship building 153–4
Kraig
intergenerational transmission of caregiving 141–2

Limited Circle of Security 68
Lucy
anger 95–6
developing relationship with carer 97–9
future of 99–102
hypervigilance of 94–5
special needs of 90–3, 102, 104–5

Main, Mary 42, 59
mental health
and transitions to foster care 72

"mirror" neurons 80
multiple placements
    and mental health of children 72

Nathan
    childhood issues of mother 63–5
    in Circle of Security 67–8, 69
    transition to foster care 69–73
neural networks 80–2

Ordinary Magic; Resilience in Development
    (Masten) 198–9

parents
    caring, long–term relationships
        111–12
    as children 148–51
    and Circle of Security 66–9
    compassion for 112–13
    and Desirae 106–110
    emotions in safe parenting 110–11
    long-term change 114
    intergenerational transmission of
        caregiving 63–5, 116–20
    ongoing support for 204–5
    relationship with child 63–5
    relationship with foster carers 34–7
    return of child to 36–8, 106–110
patterns of attachment 41–3
Powell, Bert 48
Powell, Sandra 51
predictability
    importance of 49–50

Rachel
    anger 46–7
    behavior as need (Circle of Security
        principle) 50–1
    "being with" (Circle of Security
        principle) 53–5
    cues and miscues (Circle of Security
        principle) 51–3
    and disorganized/disorientated
        attachment 62
    "I am here, you are worth it" (Circle
        of Security principle) 48–50

need for predictability 49–50
repair (Circle of Security principle)
    55–7
resistance to relationships 47–8
state of mind (Circle of Security
    principle) 57–8
reflective functioning
    Anna and Kendra 167–73
    in Children's Ark 165–73
    description of 176–7
Reforming Child Protection (Gilbert,
    Parton and Skivenes) 218–19
reimagining foster care 142–5
relationship building
    Ashley 157–8
    Carla 154, 155–6
    and change 181
    and child protection services 219–20
    Karen 153–4
    personalization 152–4
    time for 154–6
    truth-telling 156–8
repair (Circle of Security principle)
    and Rachel 55–7
resilience
    as prerequisite for change 178–80,
        198–9
Rickie
    after return to parents 36–8
    as "problem" 38–9
    relationships between foster carers
        and parents 34–7

secure attachment 42
separation costs 211–14
"shark music" 116, 175
"Shift, The" 185
social brain 79
social services
    system shortcomings 39–40
Solomon, Judith 42
special needs
    and foster care 102–5
    of Lucy 90–3, 102, 104–5
Special Place, A (Vansant) 220–1
state of mind (Circle of Security
    principle)
    and Rachel 57–8

Strange Situation Procedure, The
  and Circle of Security 67
  and attachment theory 41–3
support
  for foster carers 144–5, 205–6
  for parents 204–5
surrender
  as prerequisite for change 185
Susan
  experiences as child 151

Tamera and Daisy
  and change 186–7
  and child–centred intervention 147–8
Ted
  changes at Children's Ark 123–5
tenacity
  as prerequisite for change 180–1,
    199–200
Time to Care: Redesigning Child Care to
    Promote Education, Support Families,
    and Build Communities (Lombardi)
    216–17

To the End of June: The Intimate Life of
    American Foster Care (Beam) 210
Tony
  child-centred environment 139–41
transitions to adoption
  from foster care 86–8
transitions to foster care
  and mental health of children 72
  and multiple placements 72
  Nathan 69–73
trauma
  effects on developing brain 78–82
truth-telling 156–8

understanding change 189–90

validating children's experiences 129–30

AUTHOR INDEX

Adelson, E. 117
Ainsworth, M. 41–2

Beam, C. 210
Berg, E. 90
Bernard, K. 142
Bowlby, J. 40, 43, 87
Boyle, G. 194
Brach, T. 31, 111
Brooks, D. 158

Cassidy, J. 48
Chodron, P. 189, 190
Colin, V. 40
Cozolino, L. 79, 127

Day, A. 217
Dozier, M. 142, 143–4, 215
Duckworth, A. 199–200

Eagle, R.S. 213
Edwards, F. 218
Ellermann, C. 72
Epstein, M. 185
Every Child, Inc. 103

Ferguson, H. 215–16
Fisher, P.A. 215
Fonagy, P. 176
Fraiberg, S. 116–17, 173–4

George, C. 60
Gilbert, N. 218–19
Gilligan, R. 213

Hartzell, M. 80
Heineman, T.V. 217
Hesse, E. 43
Hindle, D. 86
Hoffman, K. 57

Karen, R. 119–20
Kelly, K. 217
Kemp, S.P. 216

Larrieu, J.A. 215
Lieberman, A.F. 173, 174
Lombardi, J. 216–17
Lonne, B. 210, 212, 216, 218
Lyons-Ruth, K. 118

Macgill, S. 218
Maier, S.F. 200
Main, M. 43, 117, 118
Masten, A.S. 198
McNaught, K. 217
Munro, E. 210–11, 216

Parton, N. 219
Perry, B. 44, 78–9, 80–1, 82, 198
Pollard, R. 78–9
Powell, B. 59, 66, 69, 116, 175, 177, 215, 219

Richo, D. 146
Rosenau, N. 103–4, 105
Russell, J. 218

Seligman,M. 200
Shapiro, V. 117
Shauffer, C. 142
Shulman, G. 86
Siegel, D. 80, 122, 165
Skivenes, M. 219
Slade, A. 59, 175
Smyke, A.T. 215
Solomon, J. 60
Spielman, E. 118, 119
Spratt, T. 211, 219
Sroufe, L.A. 121, 201

Stotland, J. 217
Szalavitz, M. 44, 80–1

United Cerebral Palsy and Children's
    Rights 102, 103, 104

Vasant, T. 220–1

Waldfogel, J. 210, 211

Yalom, I. 179

Zeanah, C. 66, 142, 143, 145, 215